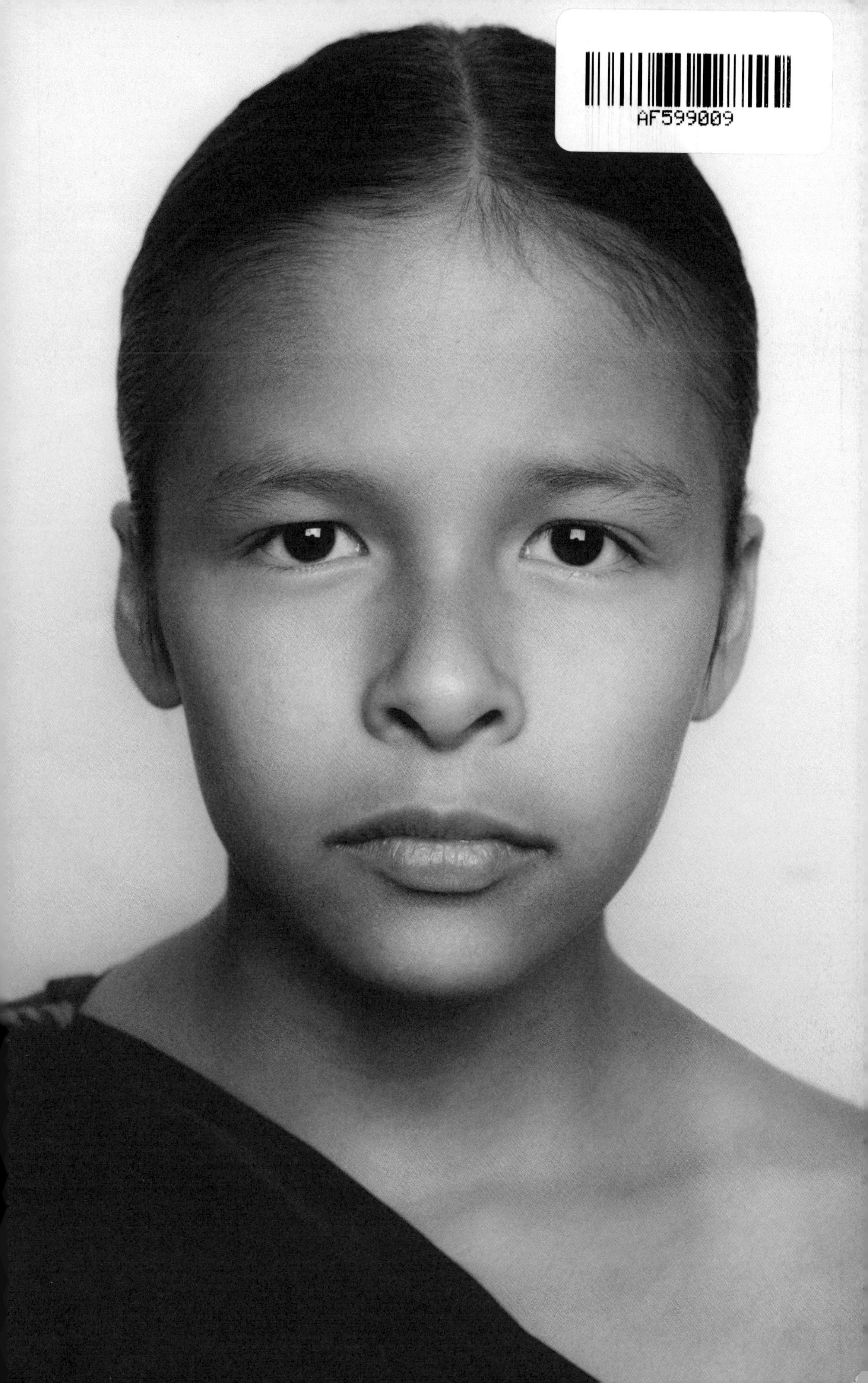

Edited by
Siera Hyte
Juan Lucero
Jill Ahlberg Yohe
with Megan Carey

Colby College Museum of Art, Waterville, Maine
DelMonico Books • D.A.P., New York

Painted Our Bodies

Pueblo Perspectives on the
American Southwest

Hearts and Village

Land Acknowledgment

The Colby College Museum of Art acknowledges that we are situated in the homeland of the Wabanaki people. We express our respect to the Indigenous communities who have lived on these ancestral lands since time immemorial, and to the future generations. With this acknowledgment, we recognize the legacies of settler colonialism and we signal an ongoing commitment to building relationships with the Wabanaki.

All That They Carry

Kimberly Suina Melwani
and Joseph H. Suina

In Pueblo culture, pottery making and the pottery itself are embedded with intergenerational teachings—lessons about community togetherness, the interconnectedness that exists between all beings in the universe (including those considered inanimate by other cultures), the importance of approaching a craft or any pursuit with a good heart, and the understanding that intergenerational ties transcend time and space. The outside world has long recognized pottery for its aesthetic qualities but has understood far less about the vital role these clay creations play in connecting us with our ancestors. They hold value beyond their utility or their beauty. They are animate, living records of our Pueblo history and culture.

In this essay, we look at the ongoing importance of pottery in the Pueblo world by focusing on one potter and her pottery: Honneyatz of the Fox clan, who also went by the name Stephanita Arquero Herrera (1889–1961). As the grandson (Joseph) and great-granddaughter (Kimberly) of this potter, we aim to move past one-dimensional understandings applied to Indigenous makers and portray them as more than creators of beautiful "objects." Honneyatz was also a bearer of traditional knowledge, a caretaker of family and community, and a small-business owner who actively engaged with the outside market as the economy shifted from barter to cash beginning in the late nineteenth century and escalating in the 1950s. Further, we aim to shed light on the role that material culture plays in allowing contemporary Pueblo people to engage with ancestors regardless of time and space, and how museums and other institutions, where many "clay kin" are kept, stir up complex feelings for members of descendant communities. Lastly, we hope to convey that despite massive shifts in Native language fluency resulting from colonialism, the philosophy at the heart of Pueblo culture continues to shape how we move through the world today.

Our grandmothers engaged in exchange with the outside, attempting to cultivate economic opportunities on terms that respected Pueblo cultural norms. They thoughtfully crafted "grandmother pots" and figurative pottery for outsiders as Pueblo culture became the driving force behind New Mexico's growing tourist economy beginning in the late nineteenth century. Whether constructed for use in Pueblo communities, or specifically for tourists and collectors, these pots carry the history of our people, including colonial encounters. Pueblo culture was faced with a curious dichotomy during the late nineteenth and early to mid-twentieth centuries: while the US government attempted to suppress our culture and assimilate us into mainstream society, anthropologists, artists, tourists, and collectors sought to own pieces of our culture, in an expression of valuing something that they perceived would soon be gone.

Our grandmothers displayed unwavering dedication to keeping traditions such as pottery alive despite the immense cultural changes happening around them, which included outright attacks by the federal government through laws restricting our traditional ceremonies and dances, efforts to assimilate Pueblo children into mainstream society through boarding schools and day schools, white encroachment on Native lands, and attempts to terminate tribes and relocate tribal members to distant cities. Throughout all of this, our grandmothers audaciously cared for our families by making pottery, which in turn continued to reinforce our worldview. As Pueblo people, we have always doubled down on our culture despite being presented with many reasons to give up. Our grandmothers' voices never wavered, as exemplified through the continuation of pottery production, and through their examples, they teach us that neither should ours. It is with this understanding that we own our narrative and our identity as a distinct culture with an existing philosophy on how to live in this world.

Pueblo culture continues to put the good of the group ahead of the individual, realizing that our strength lies in the collective. So, this is not the story of individuals; rather it is an attempt, through the exploration of individual experiences, to make sense of how colonialism has impacted our community. In what follows, we engage in a literal and figurative dialogical dance, with the understanding that this multivocal approach is consistent with the Pueblo belief that we are each part of a whole. Every family in our village, and in each of the Pueblos, has similar stories of grandmothers who lived multifaceted lives. It is through remembering them that we honor them and what they hold. As a community we continue to draw strength from accounts of these women. Their pottery is a material embodiment of our collective resilience.

Our grandmothers intended for some of their pots to travel outside of our communities with the understanding that they would be appreciated for their beauty. But beauty is not only about giving pleasure to the senses and the mind. From the Pueblo perspective, beauty is closely related to the concept of harmony. Living in harmony extends to relationships, and their grounding in mutual respect. Therefore, it is incumbent on those who steward pottery to respect the rich world in which these pots originate—a place where we talk and sing to clay. To give them a good home means recognizing all that they carry. They are not only material representations of beauty, but also testaments to matriarchal strength, an unwavering commitment to community, and symbols of our survivance in the face of cultural genocide. Like clay ambassadors, these grandmother pots continue to encourage intercultural connections and remind us of our shared humanity.

Kimberly Suina Melwani: As a community curator participating in the object selection process for an exhibition at the Museum of Indian Arts and Culture in Santa Fe, a museum focusing on the history and culture of Indigenous people of the Southwest, my first experience entering its collection storage area was profound. Among the hundreds of historic and contemporary pottery pieces that ran up and down rows and rows of shelves were some created by Ku-ghe-teh/Cochiti women, including those made by my great-grandmother, a prolific potter in the early to mid-twentieth century. I lived alongside one of her large pots, which "watched over us," sitting in various parts of our house; the dough bowl was moved to different rooms whenever our space needed freshening up.

Joseph H. Suina: My grandmother and I lived in a one-room house in the inner circle of homes on the plaza. She was also a senior member of an important traditional society. I was the chosen one among her more than three dozen grandchildren, perhaps because I was the firstborn in my family and lived a short walk from her home. I was there to "take care of her" from age five to nine, but I am sure it was the other way around. She was the potter in the Pueblo, well known for her dough-mixing bowls and extra-large storage pots that kept bread and tortillas fresh for days on end.

KSM: Seeing what I believed to be one of my great-grandmother's pots in the museum basement brought about emotions not unlike what other Pueblo people have described when seeing historic pottery. My brother, a potter, contacted me after his own emotional experience. We entered a fast and furious round of texting the day he had viewed some of great-grandmother's pots in storage at another museum. In this exchange, we mirrored each other's observations, revealing our shared outlook on the world. Like mine, his meeting with a grandmother pot was akin to a reunion with a long-lost family member. The pots offered us both a tangible through line to our great-grandmother, whom we had never met. Like portals connecting across time, these pots also reminded us that we exist only in relation to those who came before us.

JHS: My grandmother was totally immersed in our Keres language. She was born into it, and she became an elder in it and a carrier of our culture. To her it was

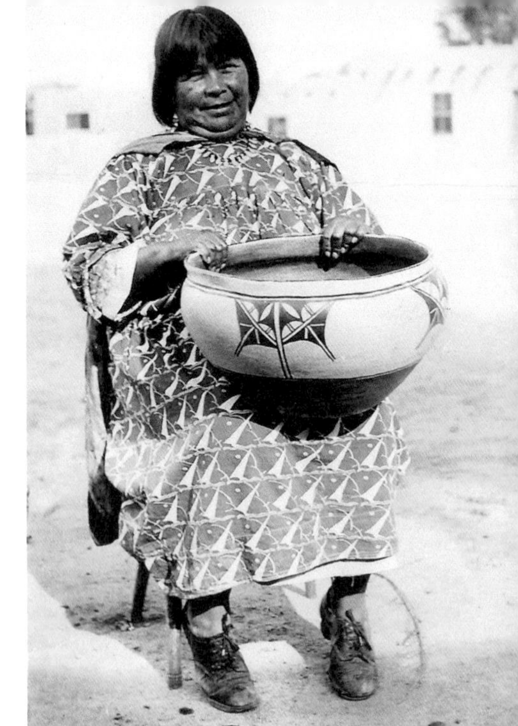

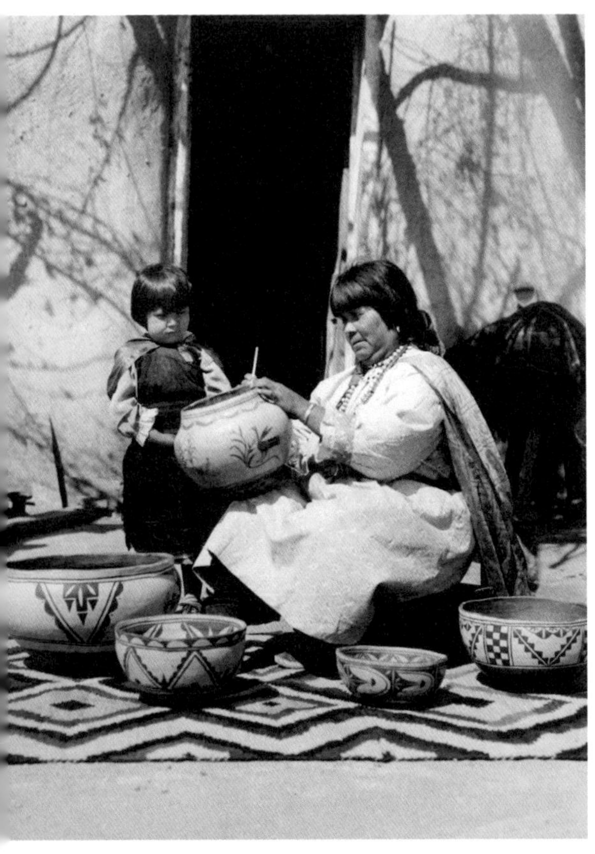

Top: Estephanita Arquero Herrera holding one of her large pots sought by tourists and villagers alike, Cochiti Pueblo, c. 1950

Bottom: Estephanita Arquero Herrera and grandchild, Cochiti Pueblo, 1936

like the air she breathed, second nature and comfortable in her prayers, songs, stories, and conversations with other villagers. Spanish was for her a trade language, learned in her youth, and she knew just enough to carry on chitchat with neighboring Hispanics. English was a newcomer, a total stranger she was forced to meet in the marketplace, where white traders and tourists reigned. Once, after making a pottery sale in a curio shop in Santa Fe, she took me to You and I, a restaurant south of the Santa Fe Plaza frequented by Hispanos, Natives, and Anglos for its tasty Southwestern food. When asked by the hairy-armed white proprietor in English for our order, grandmother responded, "Mexicans." He busted out laughing, hollering to his cook in the back, "Hey, the Indians are ordering Mexicans!" Lots of fun for them, but not for my grandmother and me. She took my hand and we walked out silently, not having eaten, not fully understanding why we were the butt of the joke. She never said a word about the incident, and I knew enough not to ask.

KSM: During my own reunion, I wondered if this pot recognized me too as her great-grandchild, if she knew me as the baby of her baby—the grandson she lovingly cared for, the grandson whom she fed with the money generated from maybe being sold to outsiders, to wind up on a shelf away from home. Although unsigned, two possible makers of the large pot were speculated. Whether or not the pot was unquestionably marked by my great-grandmother's hands, I would like to think that I could recognize her. I introduced myself in the best way I knew how, telling her that I was happy to meet her. I hold enough Keres to form only self-conscious words and clumsy, simple sentences, including one drilled into me as a child: "My Indian name is…, my clan is…." These words I shyly and awkwardly muttered in childhood, and still do now, even if they only shape my inner dialogue or are whispered so low that only the spirits can hear me. I usually follow up in English with, "Please excuse me, I am trying my best." My generation has experienced a devastating learning gap in Keres fluency, a language that for eons passed seamlessly from one generation to the next—until mine. In these moments, I remind myself of what I do carry. I carry the knowing that these exchanges mean something, and that even though I lack total language comprehension, I can try my best to act in a respectful way. I was grateful to be led through this experience by a Pueblo colleague, to whom I looked for cues on how to carry myself in this unusual setting. Like me, she has had to piece together her own approach when interacting with Pueblo patrimony in the museum where she works.

JHS: Grandmother stressed the importance of greeting people whenever and wherever I happened to meet them. The younger one must not pass without "showing his or her face" in recognition of the elder. "Aho-weh, papah?" (Are you coming, grandmother?), "Ahay-teh' muh mu?" (Are you there, grandfather?). These words are more than casual courtesy. They are a way of honoring those who love and care for us and who hold the knowledge of being a good Pueblo citizen. If not adhered to, the elder would ask sharply, "Can you speak?" and remind you on the spot what you seem to be ignorant about. If this got back to your parents, you got another scolding and maybe even a whipping, as no parent wants to feel faulty for improper upbringing of a child.

KSM: Because it was a first-time meeting, it felt like it should have some degree of fanfare. I wanted to holler, "Hey, this is my great-grandma, isn't she a beauty!" But those feelings quickly dissipated when I realized that what I experienced was real, intimate, and no amount of selfie taking, or internet chatter making—which mainstream influences at times compel me to do—could convey the significance of that moment, and in fact would be disrespectful to great-grandmother and that occasion. It may be because these pots carry many things. They carry intentions, they carry prayers, they carry songs, they carry stories, they carry worries, they carry hope, they carry tears, they carry laughter, they carry observations, they carry diligence, they carry creativity, they carry brilliance, they carry all those things that great-grandmother put into them, and you can feel it, and it is powerful. It is powerful because her actions were not simply performative; she crafted layers of meaning into her pottery.

JHS: Her favorite spot in the home for shaping, sanding, polishing, applying slip, and painting was just under the window where the natural daylight was best. She liked to sing when she was touching clay, as if singing into vision what she had in her mind. She would say in our language: being happy at what one is passionate about brings forth the gift of creativity with ease.

KSM: Like other Cochiti pottery of the time, great-grandmother's designs include stylized clouds, birds, flowers, and other significant Pueblo motifs; a discerning use of black-, rust-, and cream-colored paints; and an affinity for balance. She painstakingly applied sheen to her pots with a smooth rock which itself had been worn by water. The final look would be marked by the interaction of heat and environmental conditions on the day that she undertook an outdoor firing. All this knowledge she acquired through trial and error and by watching other potters in our community.

JHS: Grandmother was always engaged in pottery production in some way or another. If she was not working with clay directly, we would be out picking *wahcah* (Rocky Mountain bee plant), which she would boil into a cake for later use. If not the *wahcah*, we were out looking for cow dung for firing, or going for clay and that special sand she mixed in with it. She always approached any gathering of material with a prayerful request and a cornmeal offering to the creator. After gathering materials, which were never more than she needed, she gave thanks to the source for what she took, voicing her gratitude just enough for me to hear and learn about our relationship with all things—yes, even cow dung.

Grandmother taught me that all things are connected and that each has its unique purpose for existence. All living things, plants, and animals as well as inanimate objects have their realm of existence, and when we take one, we create disturbance in how it was meant to be. Each item that goes into the creation of pottery must be treated with the same dignity and respect lest we forget and become indifferent to the many resources we have been blessed with on this Earth.

KSM: Stories of grandmothers making daylong treks on foot from our village to the surrounding hills hauling heavy sacks of earthen clays and tempers leave current generations of Pueblo people in awe of the sacrifices they made to support our families with their pottery. From the gathering and preparation of clays, slips, tempers, pigments, tools, and fuel, traditional pottery making is a labor-intensive, highly physical undertaking. In this endeavor, Pueblo bodies commingle with the earth and are marked by its elements—backs ache from digging up and processing organic materials; fingernails become embedded with wet chunks of rust-colored clay turned to dry crumbly bits; and arms, along with everything else in the perimeter, are blanketed with a fine layer of dust kicked into the air during the tedious task of sanding. Throughout this whole process, the senses are also on high alert, as nostrils are flooded with the earthy aroma of heaps of boiling wild spinach leaves, which hours later transform into crusty patties to be later rehydrated and used as black paint. The tips of the fingers take pleasure in gliding over silky-smooth polishing stones. And the ears are on high alert, tuned in to every crackle and sputter of the fire during the nail-biting process of an outdoor firing, as the potter waits to see if their pieces make it through crack-free, prepared to accept the outcome whichever way it goes. With the absolute presence of mind, body, and spirit that pottery making requires of the maker, it is no wonder that many generations later, these pots still affect us on many levels.

JHS: I learned from grandmother that the creation of beauty is a form of human satisfaction that comes to one when all other needs in life have been sufficiently met. It is when the physical, mental, spiritual, and social needs are in order in one's life that creativity comes from the spirits in dance, art, language, and all other forms, to those with a good heart and no expectations other than to share the beauty and the profits with others. For grandmother, the creation of beauty began with the assembly of our creator's gifts: earth, plants, rocks, water, fire, air, and the ability of heart, mind, and body to transform it all into something pleasing to the senses and the soul so that beholders are led to their own higher level of appreciation and creativity.

KSM: In the decades before I was born, an outsider tried to buy the grandmother pot now sitting in our house from my maternal grandparents. This offer was turned down. It was common for white prospectors to buy family heirlooms right off the shelves of Pueblo homes, for either museums or collectors. Pueblo people sometimes rejected these economic lifelines and sometimes accepted them, grappling with the difficult decision of letting meaningful items leave our community. Our willingness to share aspects of our culture with

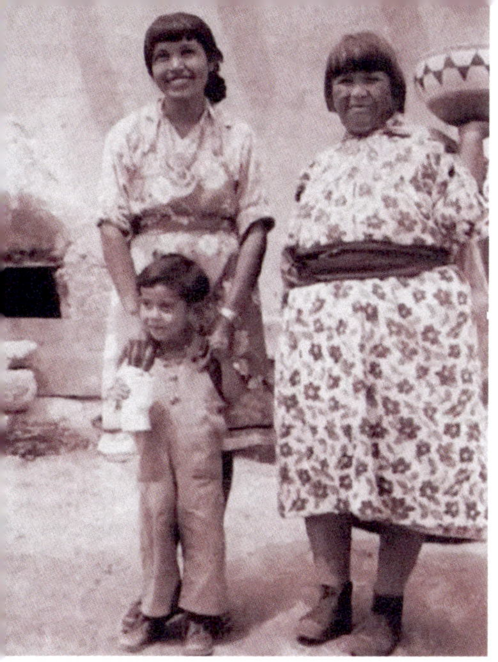

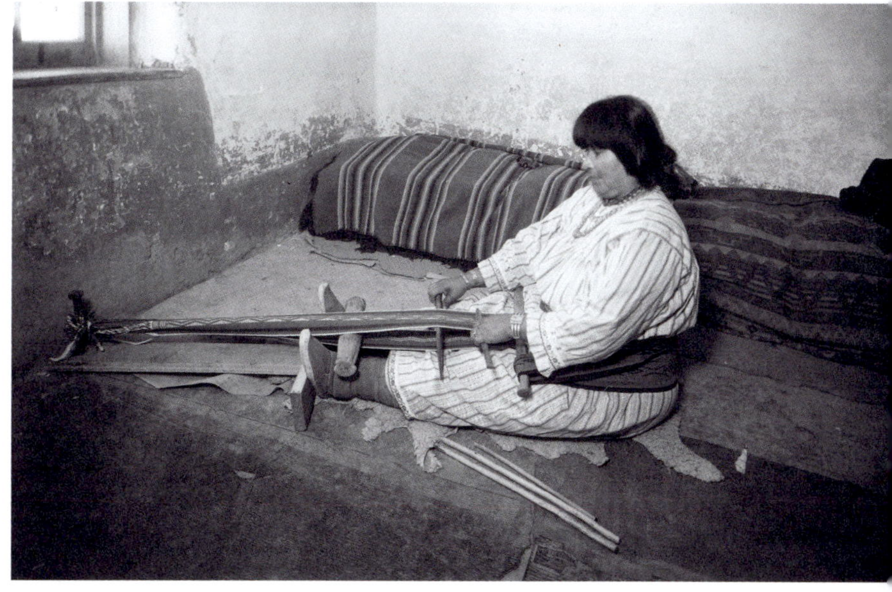

Top: Justina Herrera Suina, Estephanita Arquero Herrera, and Joseph H. Suina, Cochiti Pueblo, c. 1950

Bottom: Estephanita Arquero Herrera weaving in front of the window where she often painted pottery, Cochiti Pueblo, c. 1925–45

outsiders and our financial need were exploited in such instances. But grandmother pot remained with us, continuing to observe our community of women and girls coming together to make traditional foods and the laughter that punctuates these gatherings, continuing to hear men and boys hum traditional songs, maybe an earworm from the past or a new composition, and continuing to accept blessings brought into our home after family members had taken part in traditional dances. And we have come to know her and all that she carries.

JHS: Two Anglo ladies once came knocking, asking for Grandma Honey. One was familiar as a friend of a family in the Pueblo. The other may have been a shop proprietor, a museum curator, or a tourist interested in seeing Honneyatz's pottery and meeting her in person. The two had a running conversation in English as they examined each piece from every angle and ran their fingers gently over it. Neither grandmother nor I understood their words, but we could see from their body language that they greatly admired her work. The stranger kept using a word that had a nice, heartfelt ring to it: "Exquisite, exquisite." She kept repeating it, at times almost in a whisper, as if worshiping a deity. That day grandmother sold some "potteries," including some that she had had no intention of selling. The power of the almighty dollar was too much to overcome even in the sanctuary of our home. I had heard about others in the village selling family heirlooms simply because they needed to make ends meet, or they were seduced by the heavy admiration.

KSM: I left the museum that day warmed by the experience but also carrying a heaviness, thinking about grandmother pot sitting on a shelf, in a room that stays at exactly the right temperature, with carefully considered lighting, no sunshine, no dust blown in from the plaza, no pests to bother her—of the insect ilk, or the grandchild ilk—seemingly alone. But no, she is not fully alone. She sits with all the other grandmother pots, and all that they carry.

Afterword

Although the grandmother pot in our house has cracks throughout her body, showing wear and tear from her days of cradling dough, she served our community well. Made from earth and crafted by human hands, ideally, she will eventually go back to the earth or be incorporated into the next generation of pottery when found as a sherd, inspiring a future potter with her painted-on designs, or acting as the temper that binds clay together. In some villages, old pottery sherds are ground up and mixed into raw clay, making explicit the cycles of regeneration that bind ancestors and descendants. We can only hope that what made our grandmothers strong has likewise been sprinkled into our DNA.

Kimberly Suina Melwani (Cochiti Pueblo) is a freelance researcher and writer.

Dr. Joseph H. Suina (Cochiti Pueblo) is a professor emeritus at the College of Education at the University of New Mexico. He is a former governor of Cochiti Pueblo, serves on the tribal council, and has devoted much of his career to developing training programs for educators of Native American students. Suina served on the advisory council for *Painted: Our Bodies, Hearts, and Village*.

The Beauty of Confusion

Nora Naranjo Morse

In broken English, the old man remembered his
youth at Taos Pueblo:

We lived in a bubble of community and family.
No one spoke English.
We lived by the seasons.
At night we heard animal stories.
We drank water from the creek.
It was a happy life.

Illustrators
photographers
painters
visionaries—

creative pioneers who left war and disease
dared expansive
harsh terrain
in exploration
of endless vistas
where people lived by the seasons,

seeking refuge with other pioneers.
Masters in search of their muse.

With camera
paint
and skill as large and deep as the land,
cultural hunters staged
romantic impressions
with clay reds
and autumn yellows,
conjuring the myth
with
feathered headdress
ceremonial vessels
and Pueblo people modeled in stoic pose
peering into an uncertain future.

Distant worlds meeting
below Taos Mountain.
Change in culture
a canvas away.

The gallery is a respectful quiet.

My sister and I stand in front of a painted evening scene
of Taos Pueblo
men on horseback returning from the mountains
women in brightly colored shawls
bending over adobe ovens
baking bread.

I confess in a whisper

I'm torn
Yes
I have respect for these creative geniuses

Nodding to the painting.

Yes
Generations of Pueblo people will know their ancestors
because of these paintings.

Yes
These visionaries were Indian advocates.

Yes
I know.

But
nagging
confused
remembrances
are waiting to be heard.

I tell my story.

I was eight years old
sitting at the base of Taos Mountain.
A tourist visiting Indians
put religious literature in my hand and
instructed me to smile.
The picture was published in a missionary quarterly.
I was paid fifty cents.

I can still hear the coins dropping into my open hand.

My sister nods.
She's been there too.

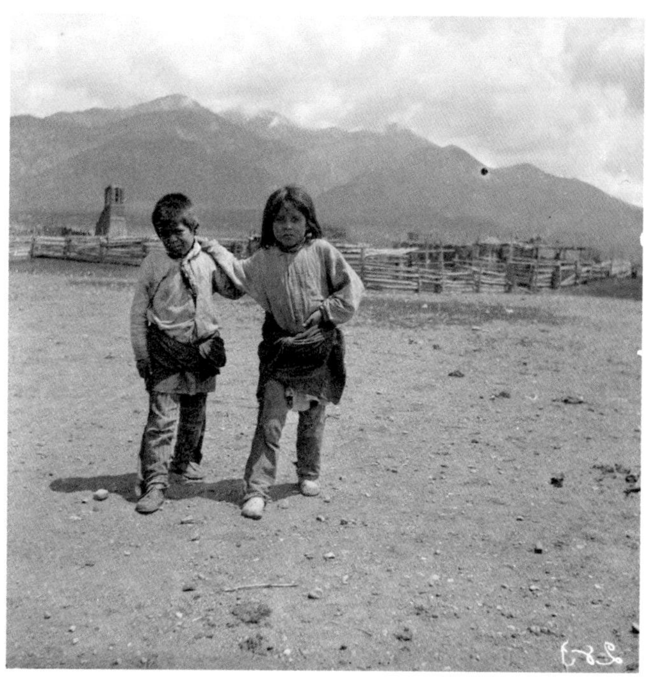

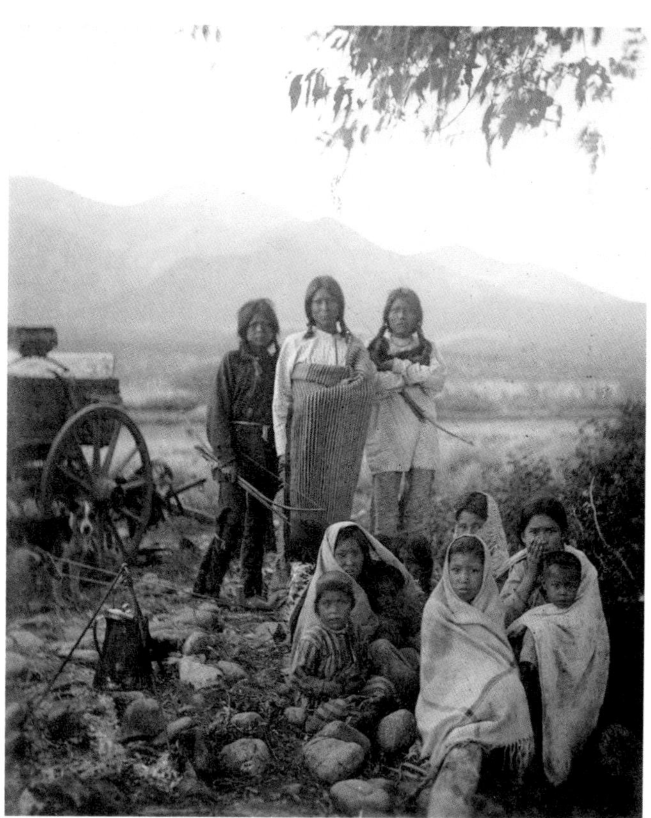

Top: A foot race, two unidentified boys, Taos Pueblo, c. 1900

Bottom: Group of children, Taos Pueblo, c. 1892–1905

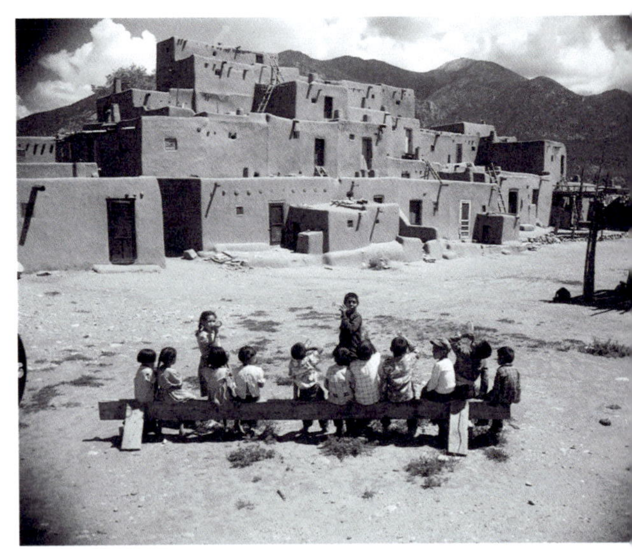

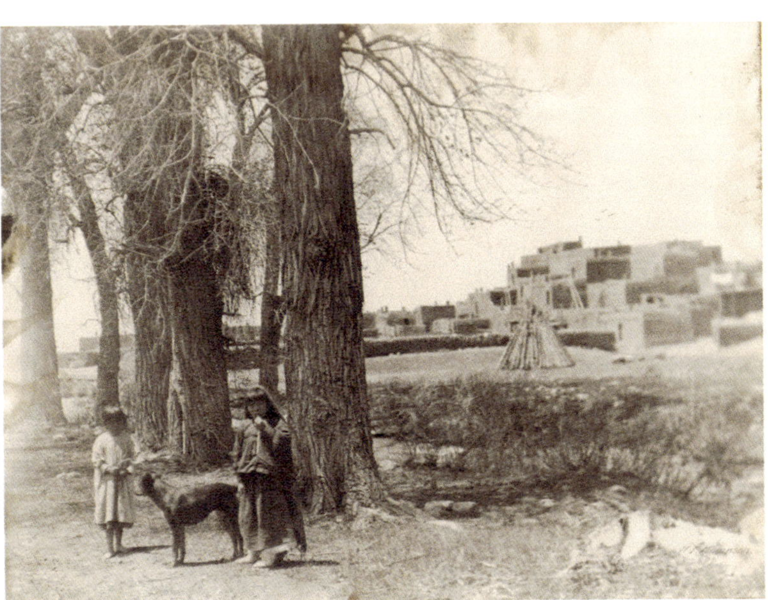

Top: Children at Taos Pueblo, c. 1950

Bottom: Taos Pueblo, 1909

Captured impressions of culture
defined how we were seen by the world.
A dying breed on canvas
railroad calendars
and religious literature.
Painting
how Pueblo people saw themselves
how Pueblo people see themselves.

Navigating identity staged by others
is tricky business.
Was then.
Still is.

Black and white
does not exist here.
Instead it's colored
dense with
history
culture
mythology.
Even fifty cents.
Seismic shifts all around.

Breaking through the gallery's respectful quiet
pursing her lips toward the painting of Taos Pueblo
my sister responds
Dang
Pueblo women don't bake bread at night.
What's up with that?

Nora Naranjo Morse (Tewa/Kha'P'o Owinge) is an artist, filmmaker, and poet. She is the author of the poetry collection *Mud Woman: Poems from the Clay* (1992), which combines poems with photographs of her clay figures, and the children's book *A First Clay Gathering* (1993).

Curators
Siera Hyte
Juan Lucero
Jill Ahlberg Yohe

Advisory Council
Ron Martinez Looking Elk
Patricia Michaels
Theresa Secord
Sarah Sockbeson
Joseph H. Suina

Additional Contributors
Dominic Bellido '24
Mary Bevilacqua '23
Shánd́íín Brown
Caroline Jean Fernald
Beth Finch
J. R. Henneman
Miz Insigne '26
Daniel Juzych '26
Alexis Kinney '22
Davison Koenig
Kimberly Suina Melwani
Ramey Mize
Nora Naranjo Morse
Jami Powell
Gilbert Suazo
Rina Swentzell
Brian Vallo
Ashton Wesner
Maya Wong '25

Lunder Institute Research Fellows
Caroline Fernald
Elizabeth "Betsy" S. Hawley
Jessica L. Horton
Hadley Jensen
Juan Lucero
Patricia Norby
Jill Ahlberg Yohe

Artists
Margeaux Abeyta
Mozart Gabriel Abeyta
Tony Abeyta
Oscar E. Berninghaus
Ernest L. Blumenschein
Gerald Cassidy
Pop Chalee
Berdina Charley
E. Irving Couse
William Herbert Dunton
Nicolai Fechin
Jody Naranjo Folwell
Susan Folwell
Jason Garcia
Theresa Neptune Gardner
Jessa Rae Growing Thunder
Marsden Hartley
Ernest Martin Hennings
Seferina Herrera
Victor Higgins
Ahkima Honyumptewa
Clara Neptune Keezer
Albert Looking Elk
John Marin
Patricia Michaels
Robert Mirabal
Thomas Moran
Dan Namingha
Michael Namingha
Madeline Naranjo
Virgil Ortiz
Molly Neptune Parker
Bert Geer Phillips
Juan Pino
William Robinson Leigh
Cara Romero
Diego Romero
Ken Romero
John Yellowbird Samora
Mary Sanipass
Joseph Henry Sharp
Sarah Sockbeson
Roxanne Swentzell
Awa Tsireh
Walter Ufer

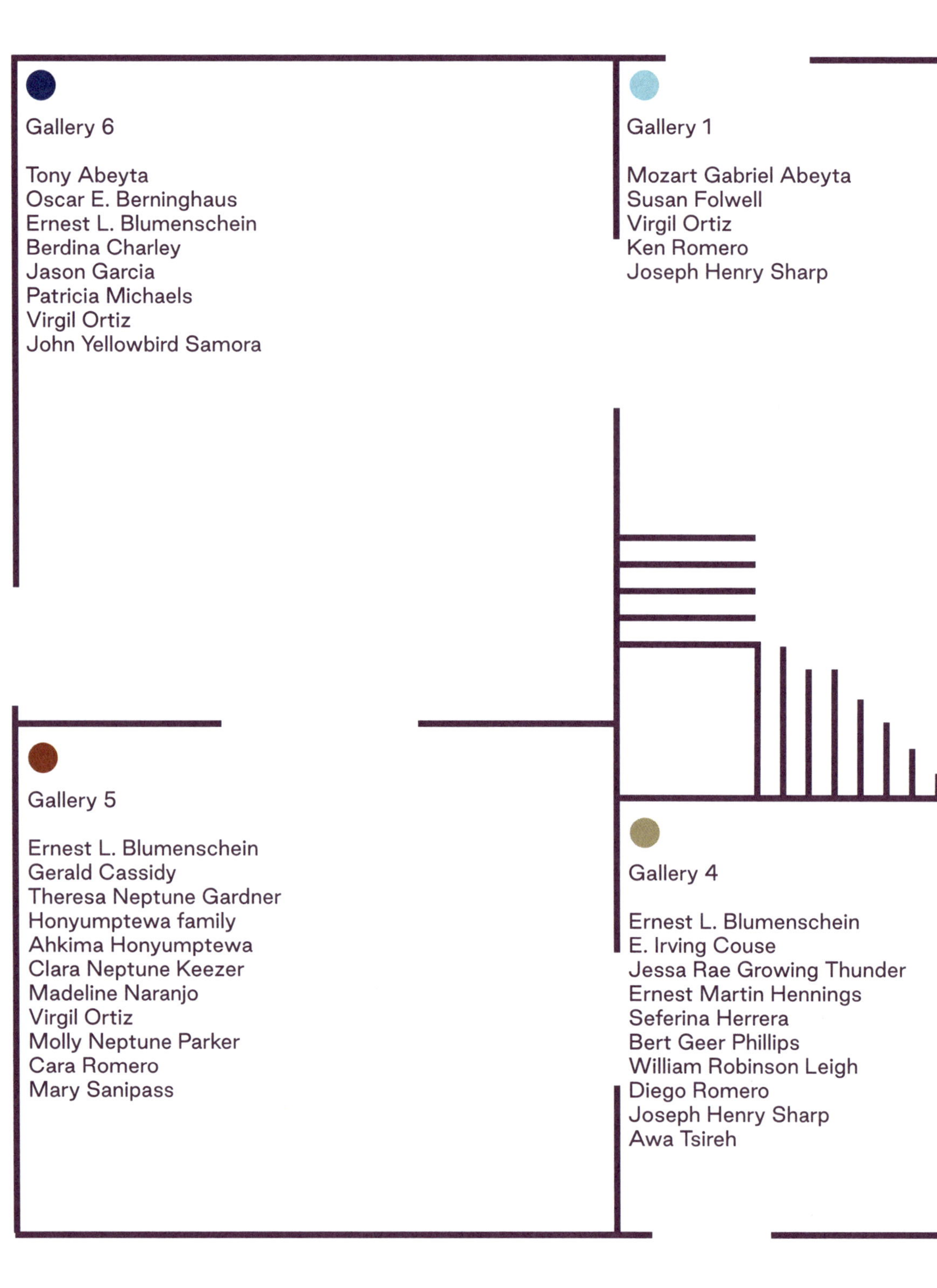
Gallery 6
Tony Abeyta
Oscar E. Berninghaus
Ernest L. Blumenschein
Berdina Charley
Jason Garcia
Patricia Michaels
Virgil Ortiz
John Yellowbird Samora
Gallery 1
Mozart Gabriel Abeyta
Susan Folwell
Virgil Ortiz
Ken Romero
Joseph Henry Sharp
Gallery 5
Ernest L. Blumenschein
Gerald Cassidy
Theresa Neptune Gardner
Honyumptewa family
Ahkima Honyumptewa
Clara Neptune Keezer
Madeline Naranjo
Virgil Ortiz
Molly Neptune Parker
Cara Romero
Mary Sanipass
Gallery 4
Ernest L. Blumenschein
E. Irving Couse
Jessa Rae Growing Thunder
Ernest Martin Hennings
Seferina Herrera
Bert Geer Phillips
William Robinson Leigh
Diego Romero
Joseph Henry Sharp
Awa Tsireh

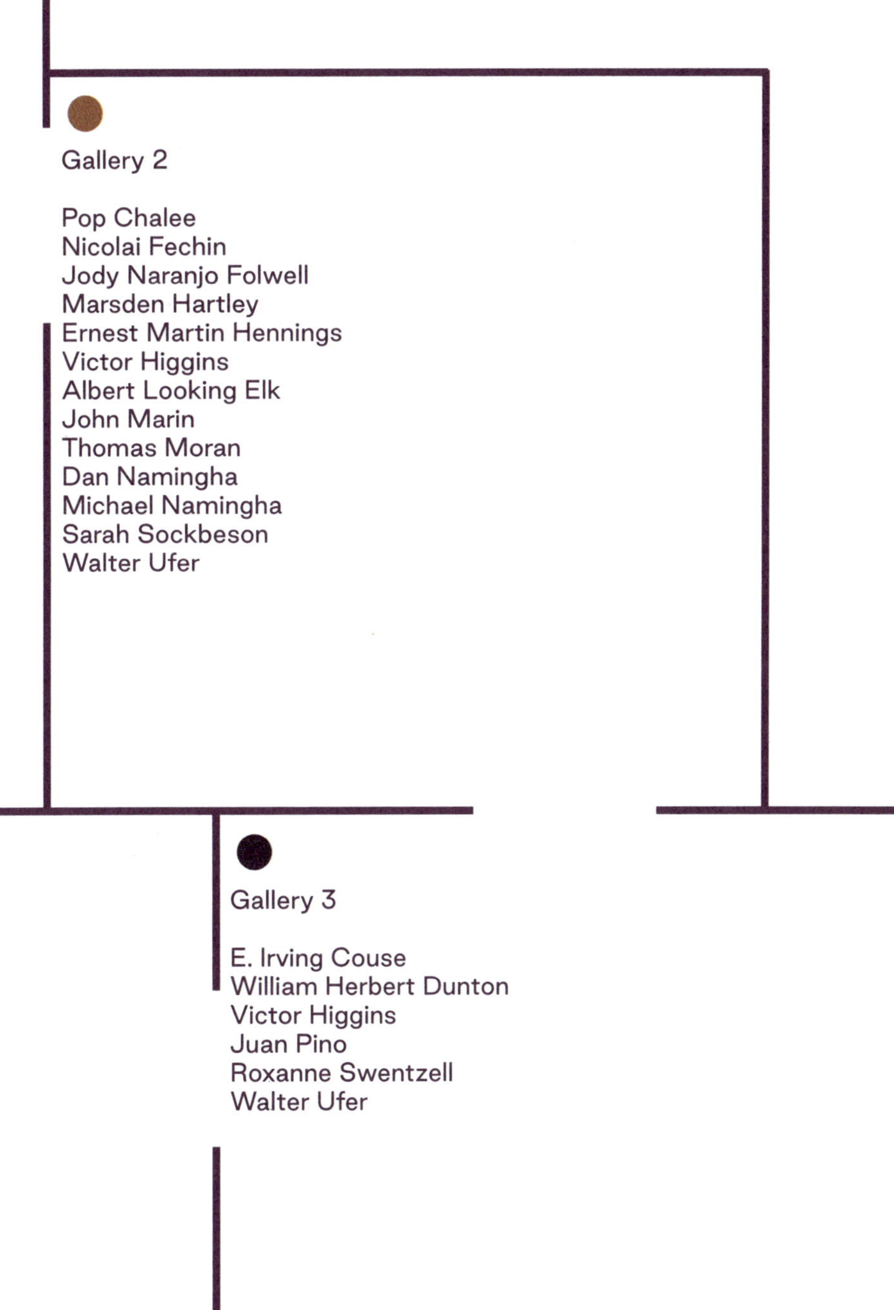

Throughout galleries: Robert Mirabal (Taos Pueblo), *The Society*, 2023. Musical composition

Curatorial Statement

Siera Hyte, Juan Lucero, and Jill Ahlberg Yohe

In organizing *Painted: Our Bodies, Hearts, and Village*, we—the exhibition's co-curators, Siera Hyte (Cherokee Nation), Juan Lucero (Isleta Pueblo), and Jill Ahlberg Yohe—worked together, in consultation with an advisory board of Pueblo and Wabanaki leaders and a host of contemporary Pueblo and other Native artists and community members, to tell a story about Pueblo art, land, and people. Readers of this publication will see the result of these collaborations in the many voices, primarily from Pueblo contributors, reflected across the project. Thousands of miles away from Pueblo homelands, on the territory of the Wabanaki Confederacy, this exhibition and its accompanying catalogue offer a shift in the curation of American art—a shift that is both generous and softly, intentionally radical.

But the seemingly radical methodology we used is really not radical at all. Our process follows standards that have been established in most Native communities for centuries: seek counsel from knowledge sharers, listen, and proceed through consensus. Our work with our advisory board was grounded in learning through listening, and our aim was to follow the gifts given to us. We thank our advisory council, Dr. Joseph H. Suina (Cochiti Pueblo), Theresa Secord (Penobscot), Patricia Michaels (Taos Pueblo), Ron Martinez Looking Elk (Isleta Pueblo/Taos Pueblo), and Sarah Sockbeson (Penobscot), for illuminating our path forward by sharing with us their expertise, feedback, and stories. Their contributions to this project have been invaluable.

Perhaps the most radical act we chose in creating the exhibition was to center Pueblo perspectives in *all* aspects of the show—curation, design, and voices—to reframe Taos Society of Artists (TSA) paintings. By flipping this script to enwrap these works made by European-trained,

White, male artists in Pueblo ideologies and aesthetics, we see *all* the art in the exhibition differently, and in fact the TSA paintings become richer and more moving through this approach. The methodology allowed us to honor the full complexity of the people and relationships represented within the exhibition by providing multilayered social, political, and historic context for experiencing the art on view and understanding the time period in which the TSA was active.

The TSA was founded in the early twentieth century in Taos, New Mexico, a place where Anglo-American artists sought to create a distinctly American genre of painting to rival that of Europe. Taos people and places—a thriving community with vast blue skies and towering mountains—became the source for building this artistic canon. While aesthetically beautiful and captivating, these works were also built upon and fostered an ideology of memorializing cultures that the group's members believed would become lost to history—a prevailing idea of the era. In the late nineteenth and early twentieth centuries, Native people were considered a vanishing race.[1] The majority of White people believed there was no hope for Native people to survive many decades more—a belief that grew out of federally sponsored tactics to eradicate Native peoples and cultures.

Historically, American museums and other spaces of learning have both displaced *and* idealized Native identity in their presentations and interpretations of Native cultures. These frameworks have bolstered a general perception among non-Native museum visitors that Native communities should be understood in the past tense, reaffirming the perception of vanishment. Because of this, many Native museumgoers have been forced to view themselves in exhibitions developed from White perspectives, rather than through lived experience or collaborative scholarship. We believe that the standard for American art institutions should be not just to include, but to *foreground*, Native perspectives in presentations of both art by Native artists and art by non-Native artists that purports to depict Native peoples, places, and cultures. It is still commonplace across museums to encounter stories about Native people that were created without consultation or permission from Native partners. The Colby Museum's prior installation of TSA works, which displayed historic paintings featuring Pueblo sitters without the interpretation or expertise of Pueblo people, was typical in this respect.

In order to understand how this dynamic developed, it is important to acknowledge how Native art first came to be collected institutionally in US (and European) museums. As the sole

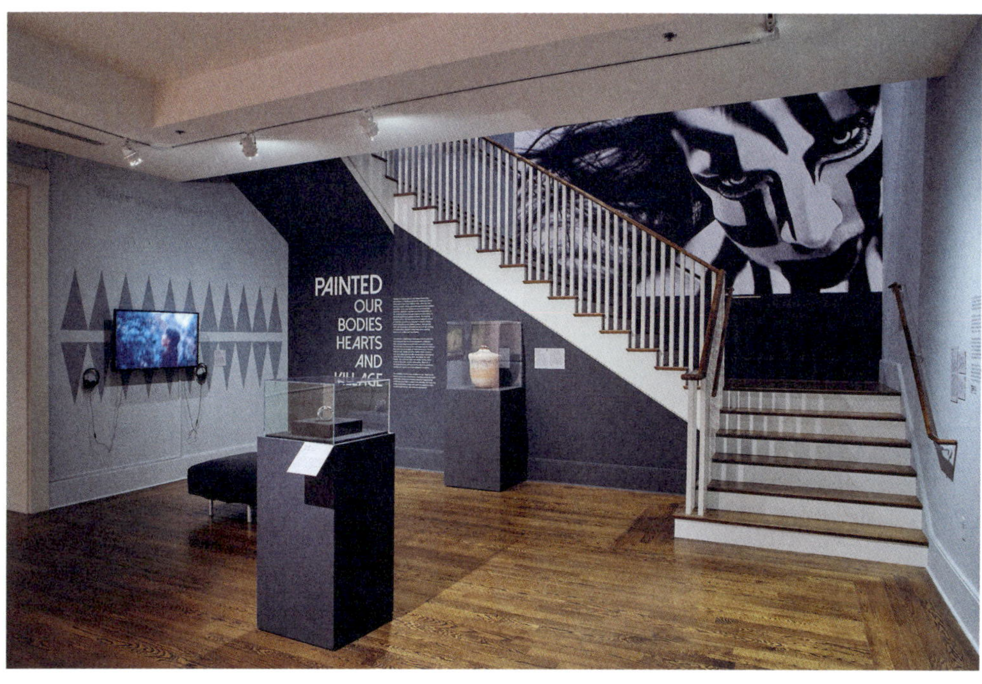

Installation view, *Painted: Our Bodies, Hearts, and Village*, Colby College Museum of Art, Waterville, Maine, 2023

Pueblo curator of the show, Juan Lucero shares insights:

> There was a collection boom in the early 1900s happening in the Southwest, with much of the focus on excavating Pueblo ancestors. This was happening at the same time that our relatives were being shipped to boarding schools and forced into assimilation. Our identities—across tribal nations—were actively being terminated by the US government. In fact, we weren't legally allowed to celebrate our religion until 1978. Our histories cannot even be shared in a factual manner through school systems to this day. Which makes me wonder why it would be acceptable for a White artist to paint us when we weren't until recently allowed to celebrate our own identities. White artists use the excuse that they are honoring our people by painting us or replicating our art. The most frustrating aspect of this is that White artists, scholars, and curators know they'll be heard because of their skin color, which brings instant validation in the art and museum worlds. To me it boils down to capitalism and White supremacy, and the inability of European descendants to acknowledge their ancestral pasts and what was done to our people. Without acknowledgment of the treatment of our ancestors, American museums will remain stagnant. This exhibition aims to begin reconciliation efforts from an institutional level.

The cycle is continued by the refusal of US museums and academic institutions to tell historic truths, including acknowledging the ways in which their organizations persist in benefiting from the theft of Native lands, culture, and belongings. Repair and restorative justice for Native communities cannot be complete without dismantling the historic foundations of museum practice. As we establish our place in institutions as Native professionals and artists, we can begin to decolonize US museum practice and find new ways to protect our art and communities.

It is quite rare to see museums exhibiting Native art and non-Native art in earnest dialogue, using multiple layers and voices in the visualization and interpretation. Rarely if ever is the art of the Southwest, including works by White artists, curated through Pueblo perspectives. If it is, it may be limited and small, perhaps in a label text or through educational programming. We wanted to do something entirely different. We wanted all aspects of this project—design, co-curation, the list of works, interpretive framing, educational resources—to center Pueblo and Wabanaki people, philosophies, histories, art, and understandings. In order to create a show of this kind, the Colby Museum recognized the need to balance its spectacular holdings of TSA paintings with full representations of Pueblo art histories. Contemporary Native art establishes presence and a counterpoint to the TSA paintings, creating space for living, practicing Pueblo artists to depict their ideas of identity, portraying themselves and their communities as they want to be seen and heard. Again, Juan Lucero:

> It is important to note that Indigenous art practices are not necessarily separated by linear era, so, whether one is looking at older or current works, Pueblo practice is always recognized as contemporary. This in turn allows the conversation between TSA and

Pueblo art and identity to remain relevant throughout the show. The energy created in the gallery through exhibition design and stories shared is immense. This is the same feeling you experience when visiting the Southwest. "Alive" is the only way I can describe it, and I think that is the most appropriate word for the Pueblo perspective in this exhibition. These strategies make Pueblo perspective a multidimensional pedagogy.

This exhibition was initially conceived as a reinstallation of the museum's galleries devoted to the art of the Southwest. For the occasion, the Colby Museum made a pivotal commitment to growing its holdings by contemporary Native artists, acquiring work by Berdina Charley (Diné), Jody Naranjo Folwell (Santa Clara Pueblo/Tewa), Susan Folwell (Santa Clara Pueblo), Jason Garcia (Santa Clara Pueblo), Jessa Rae Growing Thunder (Sisituwan/Wahpetuwan/Hohe), Dan Namingha (Hopi/Tewa), Michael Namingha (Hopi/Ohkay Owingeh), Madeline Naranjo (Santa Clara Pueblo), Virgil Ortiz (Cochiti Pueblo), Cara Romero (Chemehuevi), Diego Romero (Cochiti Pueblo), Ken Romero (Taos Pueblo/Laguna Pueblo), Sarah Sockbeson (Penobscot), and Roxanne Swentzell (Santa Clara Pueblo) in the lead-up to the exhibition. Beyond these acquisitions, key loans of works by Pop Chalee (Taos Pueblo), Seferina Herrera (Cochiti Pueblo), Ahkima Honyumptewa (Hopi), Juan Pino (Tesuque Pueblo), and Awa Tsireh (San Ildefonso Pueblo) allowed us to include additional narratives. We engaged artists, advisory council members, and other scholars to author in-gallery texts for the majority of the works in the show, and their generous texts represent a significant new contribution to the field, allowing visitors to engage with the art differently by learning directly from many Native perspectives.

We also brought audiovisual interpretive elements into the galleries by commissioning original responses from Robert Mirabal (Taos Pueblo), Mozart Gabriel Abeyta (Taos Pueblo/Diné), and Margeaux Abeyta (Taos Pueblo/Diné), who respectively contributed a soundscape, a film, and a series of illustrations and prose for visitors to experience. Through these stunning contributions, the exhibition's interpretation extended beyond text alone to engage viewers in a multisensory way. Perhaps the most innovative intervention in the exhibition came from the renowned multidisciplinary artist Virgil Ortiz (Cochiti Pueblo), who worked with us as the exhibition designer. Ortiz's *Translator*, an image of the eponymous figure from his series *Revolt 1680/2180*, greeted visitors from the gallery stairwell, and his *Rez Spine* designs on the various gallery walls offered a welcoming iconography to draw viewers into the show. Ortiz's design was a powerful tool in utilizing space to establish identity and narrative, giving the impression that the exhibition was itself housed in a Pueblo pottery vessel. Ortiz set the stage for all of the work in the reinstallation to look more alive, and ensured that art by both Native and non-Native artists was enveloped within Pueblo visual languages. Within Ortiz's vessel, the TSA paintings were enmeshed and reconstituted into a narrative that centered Taos Pueblo in the past, present, and future. Juan Lucero notes:

> Virgil Ortiz mentioned that while walking through the exhibition, he forgot that some of what he is looking at is non-Native art. This is one of the more powerful statements I heard about this show. As a Pueblo person who grew up among New Mexico

museums, whether devoted to history or art, I found myself lost in dialogues written by non-Native academics, which had very ethnographic viewpoints. It is interesting that these roles were potentially reversed in this show, with White viewers being lost in Pueblo dialogue. To me, this exhibition helped establish Pueblo presence and perspective in the US museum field. Here we control and share our own narrative and art.

Ortiz's designs breathed life into the historic works of art, generously holding and connecting these works of Pueblo and non-Pueblo art, encouraging dialogue. While serious discussions—of exploitation, power, the White gaze, and privilege—were indeed a part of the exhibition, Ortiz set the tone for these conversations to occur through his lifelong commitment to Pueblo artistic visions, based on reminding us all of the sovereignty and history of Pueblo people. These principles and values include learning our shared histories and truths through acts of generosity, respect, and care.

The survival of Native people has depended on our ability to pass down knowledge within our own communities, despite the attempted eradication of our cultures by the federal government. We have held the responsibility for caring for our histories and ways of being since time immemorial. Native-led curatorial practice breaks the pattern of institutional exclusion of Native voices by respecting that Native people can, and do, tell their own stories. The future of US museums and curation does not reside in exhibiting historic paintings by White male artists through univocal curatorial decisions and voices. The future of museums and curation lies in situating historical works that depict Native people and Native lands—where we all reside in America—in dialogue with Native art (historical and contemporary), worldviews, aesthetic canons, and curatorial practices. The future is in leading curatorial practices with Native understandings, relationships, and acquisitions of contemporary Native art to tell a better and more truthful story of American art history.

Note

1 See Sarah Fling, "The Myth of the Vanishing Indian," Art in the White House Collection website, https://www.whitehousehistory.org/the-myth-of-the-vanishing-indian.

Siera Hyte (Cherokee Nation) is an artist, a curator, and the inaugural Schiller Family Curator of Indigenous American Art at the Virginia Museum of Fine Arts. She was Manager of Programs and Fellowships at the Lunder Institute for American Art and Assistant Curator of Modern and Contemporary Art at the Colby Museum.

Juan Lucero (Isleta Pueblo), originally from New Mexico and now in the Twin Cities, is a dedicated father to two children and husband to a Dakota *winyan*. A member of the Southern Tiwa tribe, Isleta Pueblo, he is an independent curator and advocate for Native art and artists. Lucero was the Mdewakanton Native Fellow at the Minneapolis Institute of Art, curating the exhibition *Parska/Shada* and co-curating the Native American galleries. He was a 2021–22 Lunder Institute Research Fellow and developed a Pueblo artist-in-residence program at the Weisman Art Museum. Currently, he is Program Manager for Indigenous Initiatives and Partnerships at the Terra Foundation for American Art.

Jill Ahlberg Yohe, PhD, is the Curator of Modern and Contemporary Art at Cafesjian Art Trust Museum (The CAT) in the Twin Cities. Ahlberg Yohe has curated and co-curated many major exhibitions, most notably the 2019 landmark show *Hearts of Our People: Native Women Artists* alongside Teri Greeves (Kiowa) and twenty-one exhibition advisory board members. She has written extensively, published widely, and co-edited four exhibition catalogues. Ahlberg Yohe is committed to championing curatorial and museum practices that benefit the communities she serves. Ahlberg Yohe was a 2021–22 Lunder Institute Research Fellow.

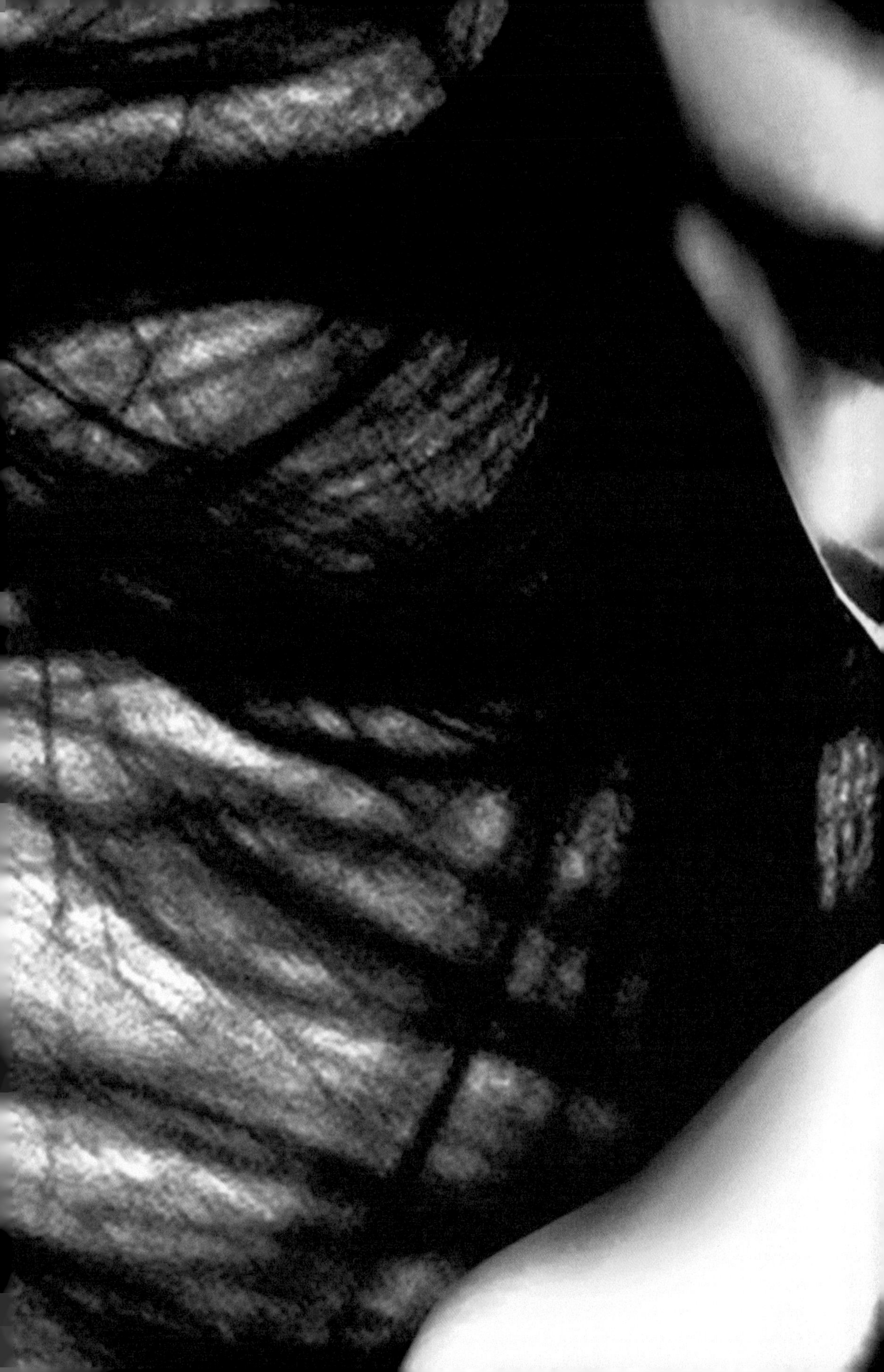

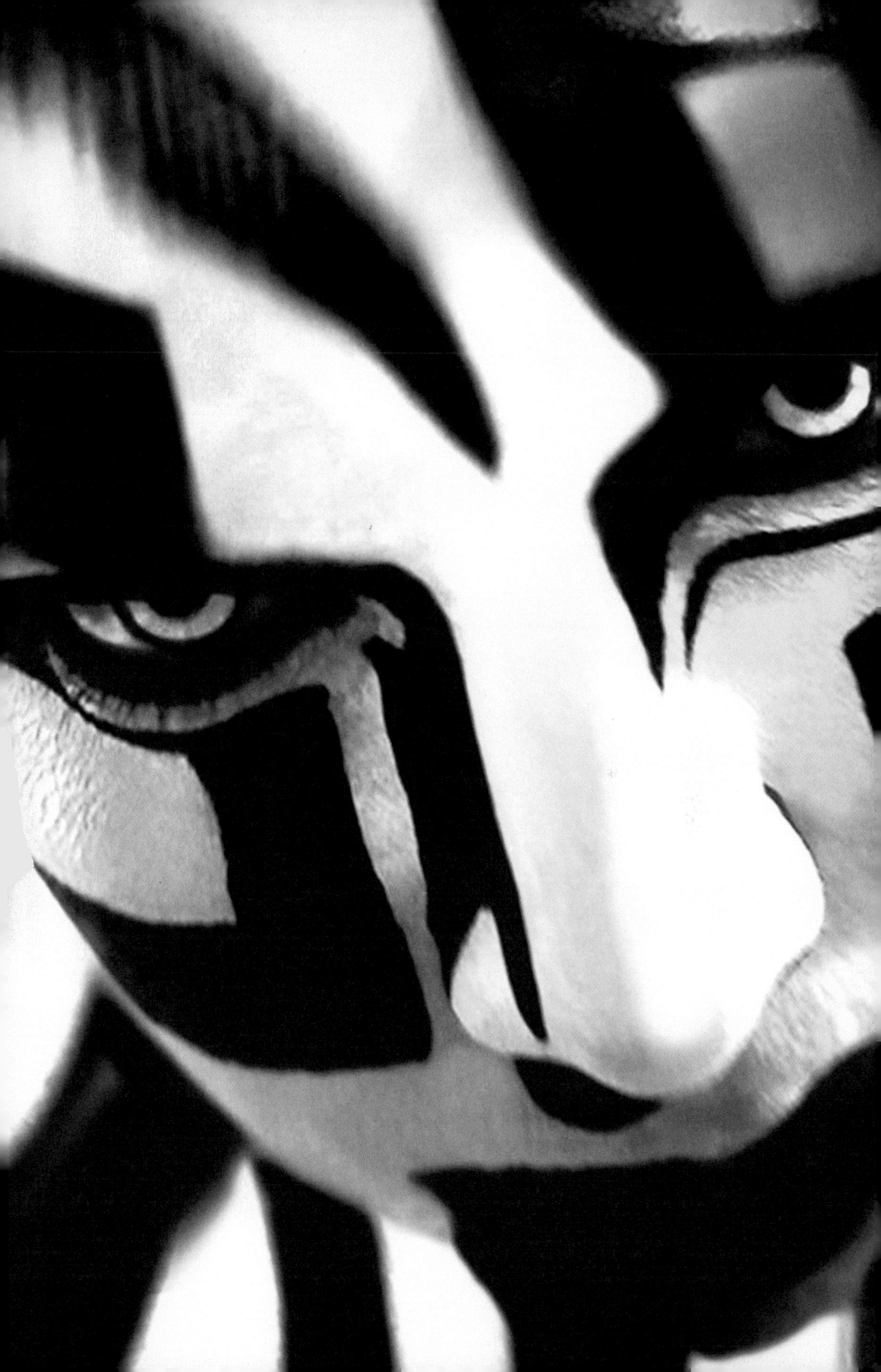

Gallery 1

Mozart Gabriel Abeyta
Susan Folwell
Virgil Ortiz
Ken Romero
Joseph Henry Sharp

Previous spread:
Virgil Ortiz (Cochiti Pueblo), *Translator 2180*, 2012, from the series *Revolt 1680/2180*

Joseph Henry Sharp
American, 1859–1953
The Sunlight of Taos—A Conversation among Friends, after 1893
Oil on canvas. 17 ½ × 26 in. (44.5 × 66 cm)
The Lunder Collection, 2013.263

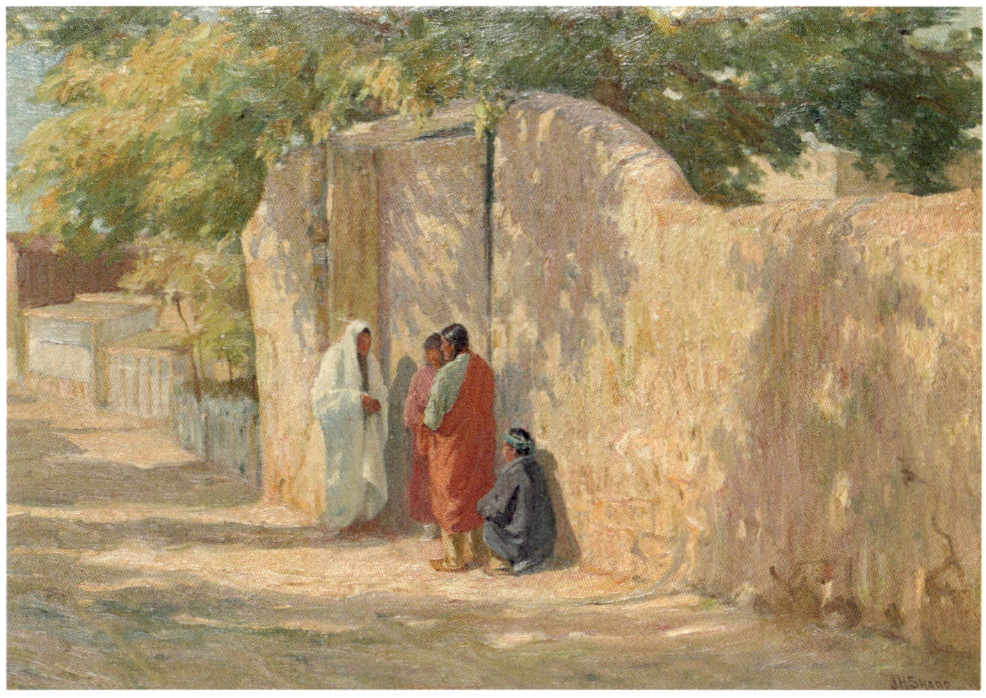

When visiting a Pueblo community in the present, you are greeted with signs declaring that all photography, sketching, and recording are prohibited throughout the reservation. As you near the entrance to the main village, you'll see more and more signs strictly prohibiting photography, sketching, or recording. In some instances, there is a statement that violators will be prosecuted and banned. These notices aren't without reason; many visitors in the past have violated the trusting and welcoming nature of Pueblo communities.

In viewing this painting, imagine yourself approaching the men and being greeted with a smile, a handshake, and a warm welcome as you pass through the gate. As you enter the village, you are guided to a home and sit at a table to share a meal with community members. Afterward, you are invited to extend your stay and exchange life experiences. When you leave, you find yourself covered in the warm blanket of a culture and people older than colonization.

Sadly, the days of warm welcomes and open hearts are in the past. Colonialism, capitalism, and unequal privilege have made many Pueblo communities wary of visitors and their intentions. Feast-day celebrations remain the only time warm welcomes are extended without hesitation, but without proper human etiquette, even those invitations may cease.

—Juan Lucero

Ken Romero
Taos Pueblo/Laguna Pueblo, born 1956
Drums, Song, and Dance, c. 2015
Sterling silver, natural stones
6 ½ (inside dia.) × 2 in. wide (16.5 × 5.1 cm)
Museum purchase from the William A. Oates Jr. '65 Endowed Fund for the Museum and the A. A. D'Amico Art Fund, 2024.008

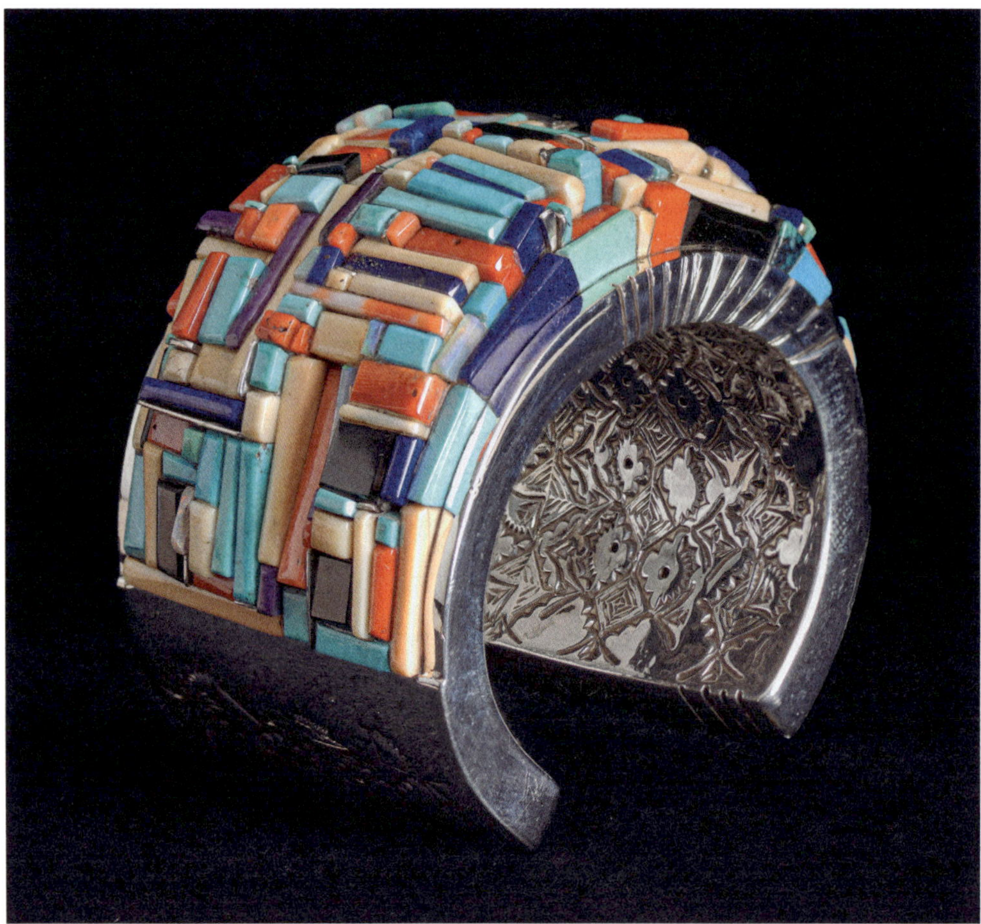

A colorful day at the Pueblo of Laguna. It's September 19, time to celebrate our annual Fiesta Day. The village is full of Laguna tribal members, family, friends, and visitors from all over. My house smells of red chili stew cooking. "Come inside, everyone, and eat." The Corn Dancers dance in the plaza all day. They are in step with the drums, and they all look colorful in their traditional mantas and traditional dress. The day is full of Drums, Song, and Dance.

—Ken Romero

Mozart Gabriel Abeyta
Taos Pueblo/Diné, born 1990
Through Eyes That Capture Us, 2023
Video, color, sound, 12:34 min.
Courtesy the artist

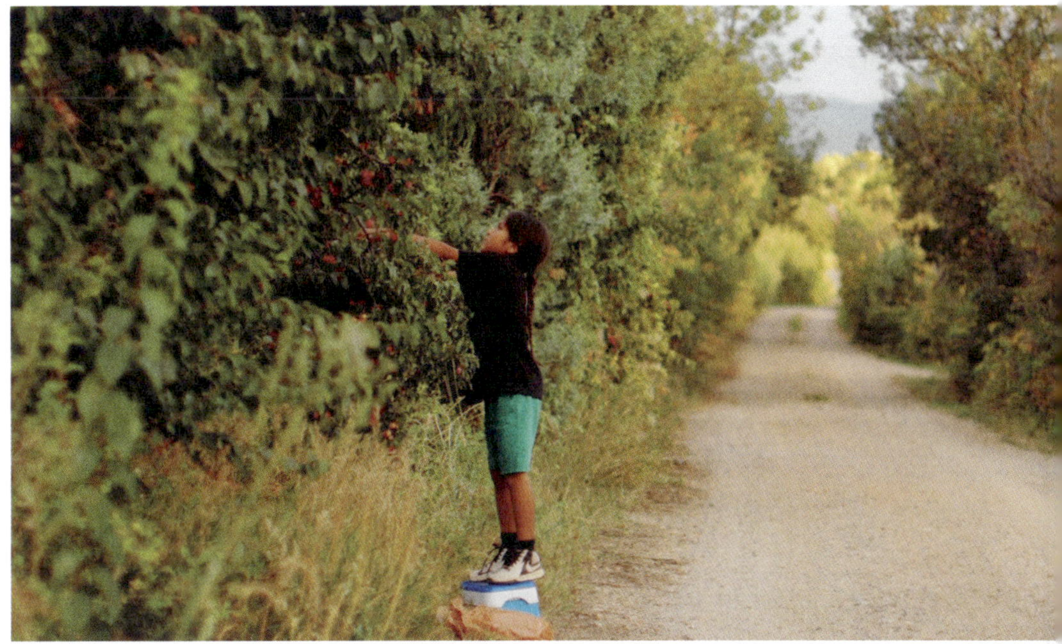

Specially commissioned for this presentation, *Through Eyes That Capture Us* features commentary from Taos Pueblo community members Gilbert Suazo, Robert Mirabal, and Jonathan Warm Day, whose grandparents posed for the TSA. They discuss aspects of social, cultural, and political life in Taos Pueblo when the TSA was active. Filmmaker Mozart Gabriel Abeyta intersperses their stories with scenes of Taos Pueblo in the present.

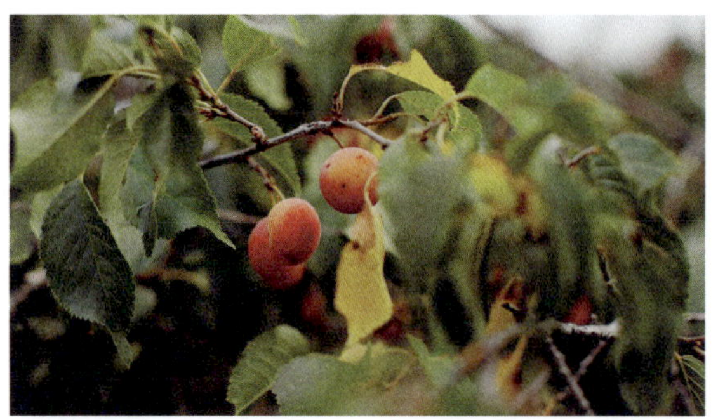

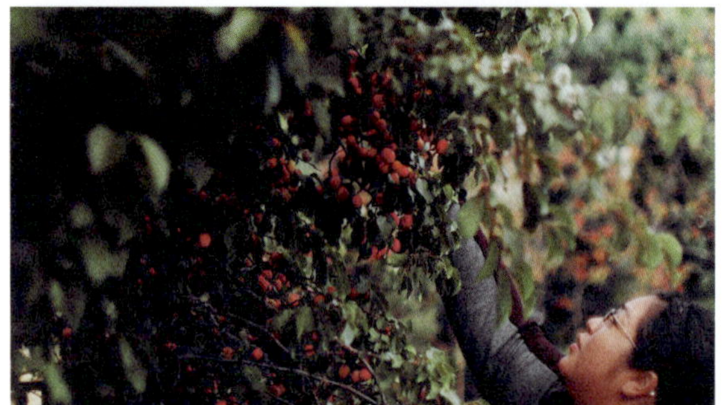

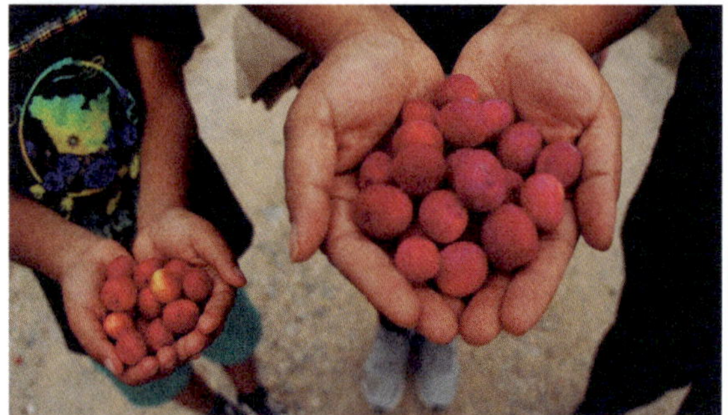

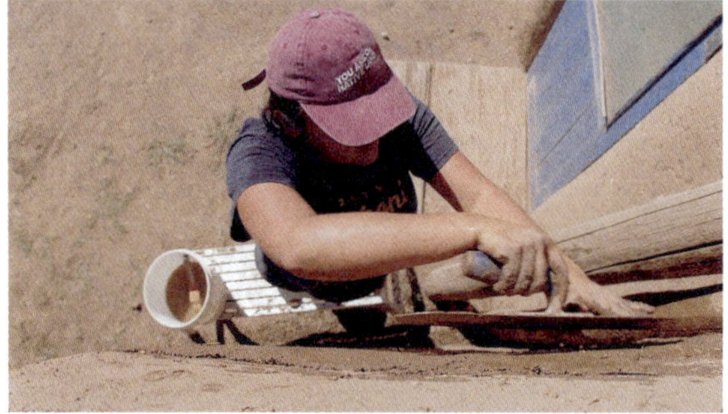

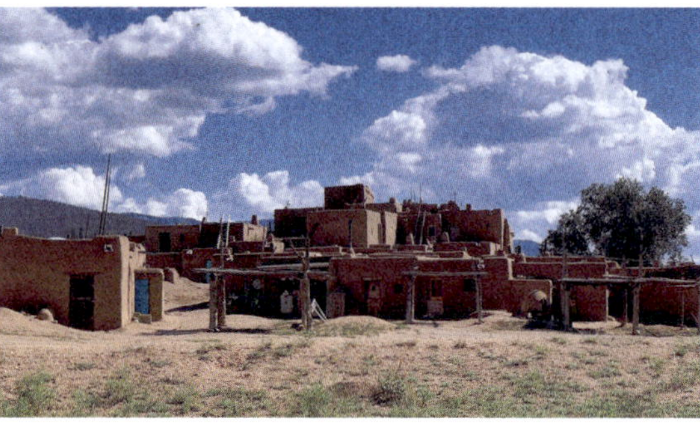

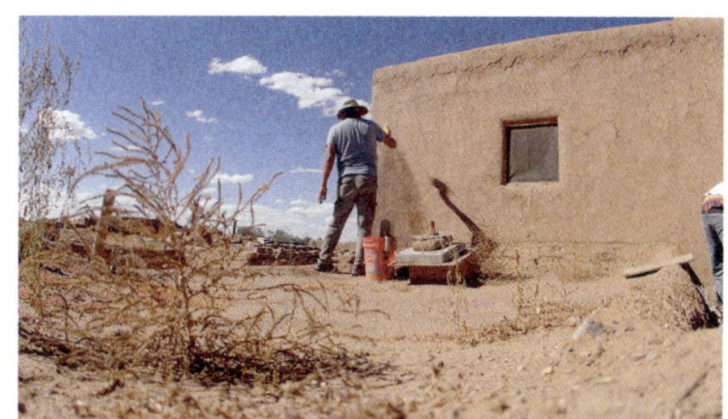

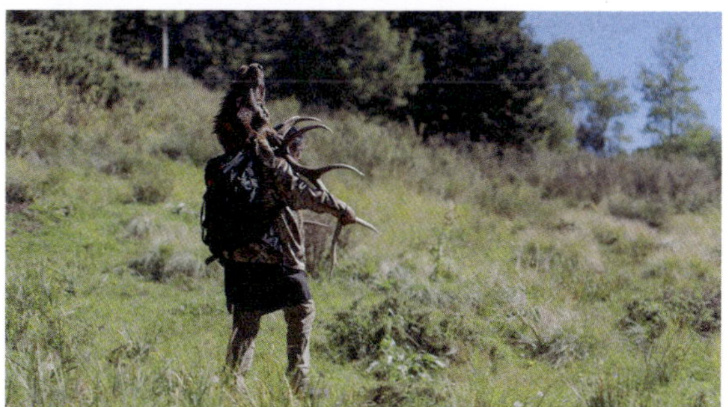

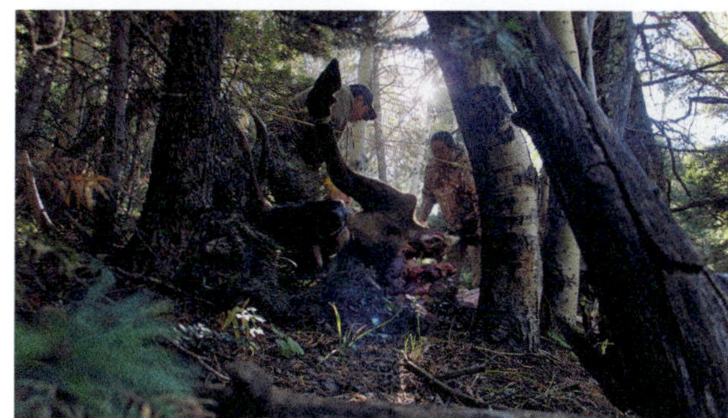

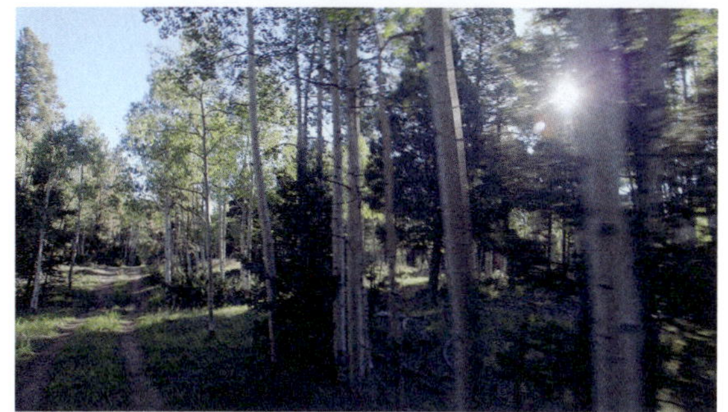

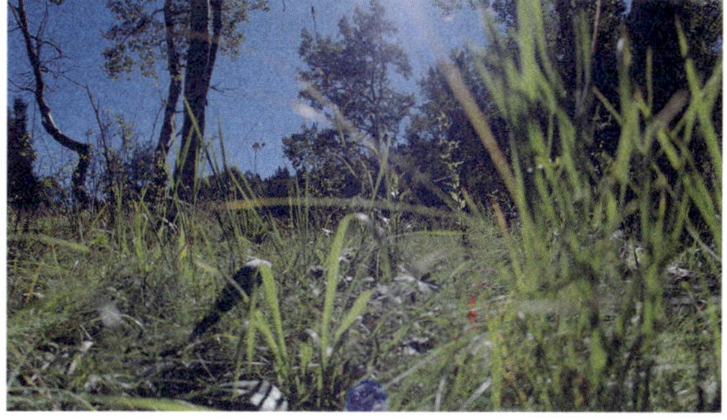

Susan Folwell
Santa Clara Pueblo, born 1970
The Gathering, 2023
Watercolor, ink, and acrylic on micaceous clay, found tin, Zuni panther fetish
21 × 19 × 19 in. (53.3 × 48.3 × 48.3 cm)
Museum purchase from the Jere Abbott Acquisitions Fund, 2023.013

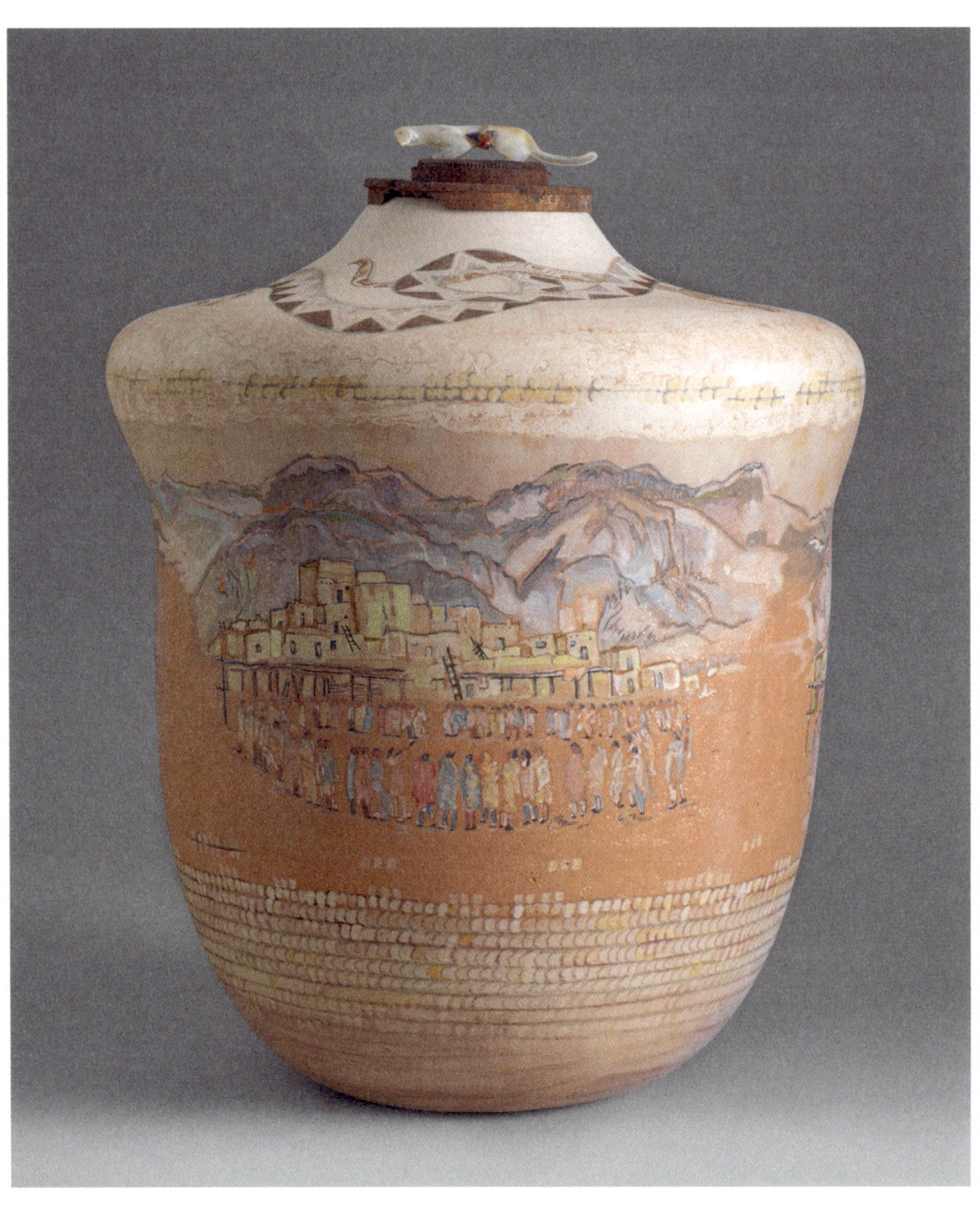

Susan Folwell

From the artist's talk at the Painted *symposium, November 2023*

I am from Santa Clara Pueblo, New Mexico, and I come from a long line of potters. At the moment, in just my family alone, there's four generations of active potters. So it's an art form that's alive and well, and it's not going away anytime soon. I still dig my own clay; I hand coil in the traditional method; I do kiln firing. And from there, I do a lot of social commentary with my work regarding things that I see and questions I have, for instance: How does the Native world interact with the contemporary world?

My preparation for this particular exhibition started a few years back when my husband and I moved to Taos, and he began working with the history of the Taos Society of Artists. I also started to explore their work and revisit looking at Native America through an Anglo lens. The piece I chose to use as a springboard for my contribution to this show, an Oscar E. Berninghaus painting, is not actually a part of this exhibition, but it *is* part of the Lunder Collection, and I love it because I live in Taos and this view of the mountains is one of the views from my own home. So it feels very personal to me. I've been getting so much nourishment from living in Taos, being back in New Mexico. All of my family is still in the state. So I chose this piece as a spiritual thought for myself.

I had a grand idea of it being spiritual, anyway. The original title Berninghaus gave his painting was *Inspection of Firearms*, and it depicts Taos Pueblo men gathered in the middle of the Pueblo, shooting their firearms. Because I felt that the original painting was very male-centric, I decided that my pot was going to be rusty, with handles and leather straps attached. Also in the original painting, there's a lot of snow on the ground. When I finished this piece, it was spring in Taos, so I incorporated that idea—the snow is melting and spring is coming along. The wildflowers are out, the air is turning warm. The door to my studio is open, and the green in the mountains is emerging. It's a little more romantic, as opposed to rustic, and very earthy.

Interestingly enough, when I started building this piece, I was having several dreams. My dreams are very vivid to me, and sometimes I write them down. At this moment I kept having recurring dreams about snakes and cats—mountain lions, bobcats, leopards—and I thought that was fascinating. Originally what I wanted to do, and which was part of the sketches I submitted to Colby, was a basket design honoring the Wabanaki artists who were participating. But in the end I decided to put the panther and the snakes together. The bottom pattern is a combination of snake scale and corn. You can look at it any way you want—it's either a basket, snake scale, or corn, or all three. I chose to incorporate that on the top of the pot as well—you can see some of that pattern starting to happen, the snake scale, the corn, the snakes, and the panther.

I bought the Zuni fetish that serves as a handle pull in Arizona, probably in my early twenties. I've had it and held on to it that long, and it's always been among the things I treasure. It was with my cornmeal to pray, and with some other pieces my mother has given me, and the elk teeth my grandmother gave me. It felt very appropriate to add it to this piece. How I was going to do that was another story. I like to scavenge—my husband and I look for found objects in the mountains where we live, and we find a lot of rusted metal pieces. So, amazingly, the neck that I made for the pot actually fit a rusted piece found outside, near my home.

It felt so serendipitous in how it all came together. The pot is a combination of red and white micaceous clay local to Taos Pueblo and Taos Pueblo potters—something I've never done before, but that I will do again. It is so large, it's incredibly heavy, and was even heavier when the clay was still wet. Just a large, cumbersome piece. I affectionately called it "the beast." I'd be like, okay, it's coming off the table; now it's coming onto my lap; now I'm slowly turning it as I'm working on it. It was so big, I'd thought I had enough clay, but I ran out. You can see where I started coiling from the bottom with the golden-red clay, and then it stops right about here. Then I realized I had just about enough golden clay left in storage to finish, so I mixed the two types, the two colors, and it made this very interesting swirl. Like those swirly kits from the 1970s. I just love it, it was such a neat transition, particularly through the sky and then getting real solidity to the snakes in the sky, the snakes and the panther.

You have to compromise with clay. You can sketch as much as you want, you can make plans, you can intend a size, you can intend a shape, but the clay will say what it wants to say. At some point you have to negotiate regarding what the two of you want to say together. And once that happened with this piece, it moved along quickly. It was a lot of space to design, but it was done within a two-week period, moving along constantly. So in that regard as well, this pot is so special to me. It came from a place of the unconscious, and I feel intensely connected to the final outcome.

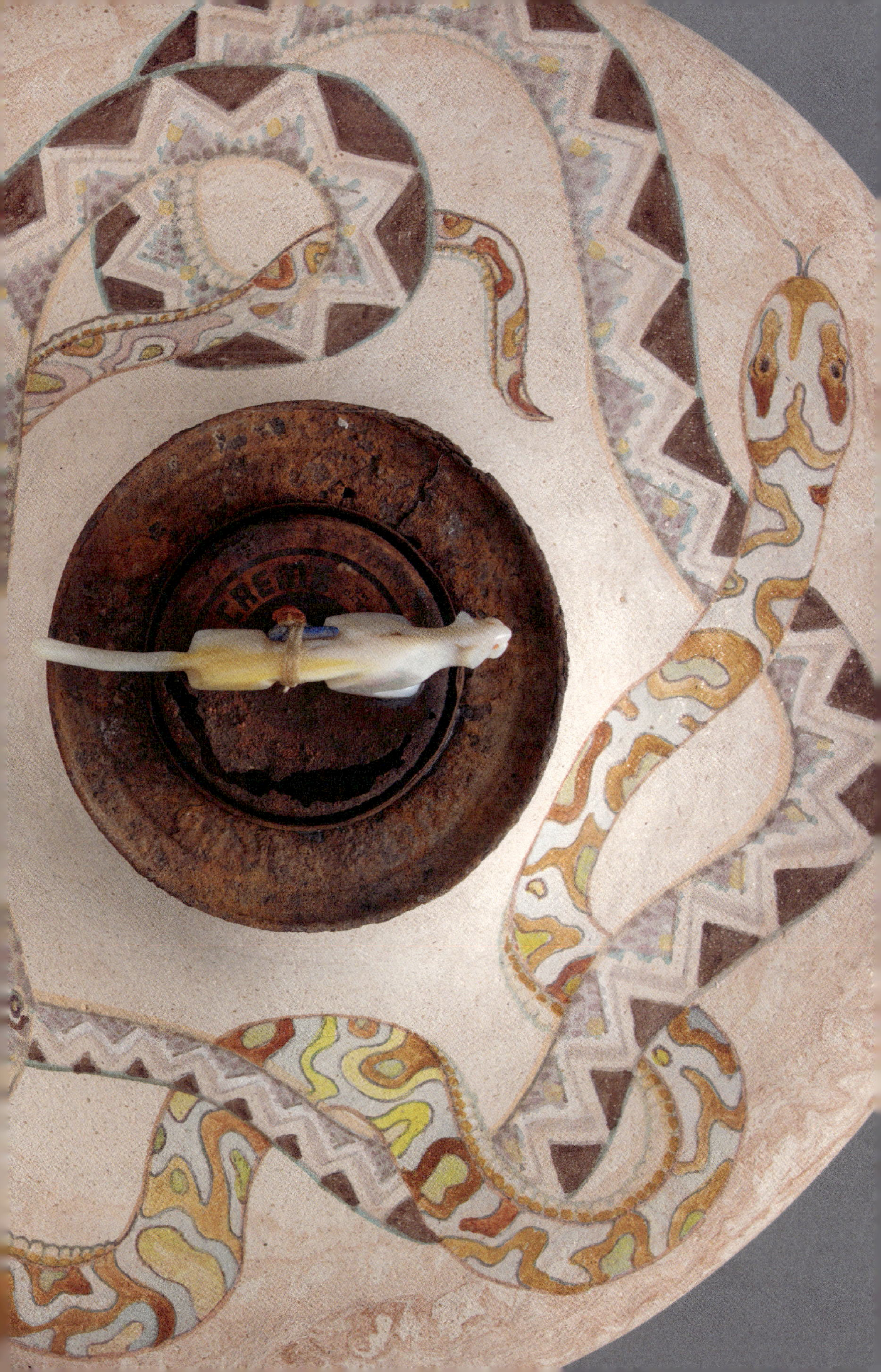

Virgil Ortiz and Dominic Bellido in Conversation

Dominic Bellido '24, writer-in-residence for the Colby College Museum of Art magazine, the Lantern, *spoke with Virgil Ortiz (Cochiti Pueblo), artist and* Painted *exhibition designer, in April 2023 via Zoom.*

Dominic Bellido: Your Zoom virtual background is very cool. I definitely want to know more about the pieces in it.

Virgil Ortiz: It's a mockup for a show I'm doing in Denver at the History Colorado Center, *Virgil Ortiz: Revolt 1680/2180: Runners + Gliders*. These photographs will be about nine feet tall. They feature some of my new characters called the Runners and the Gliders.

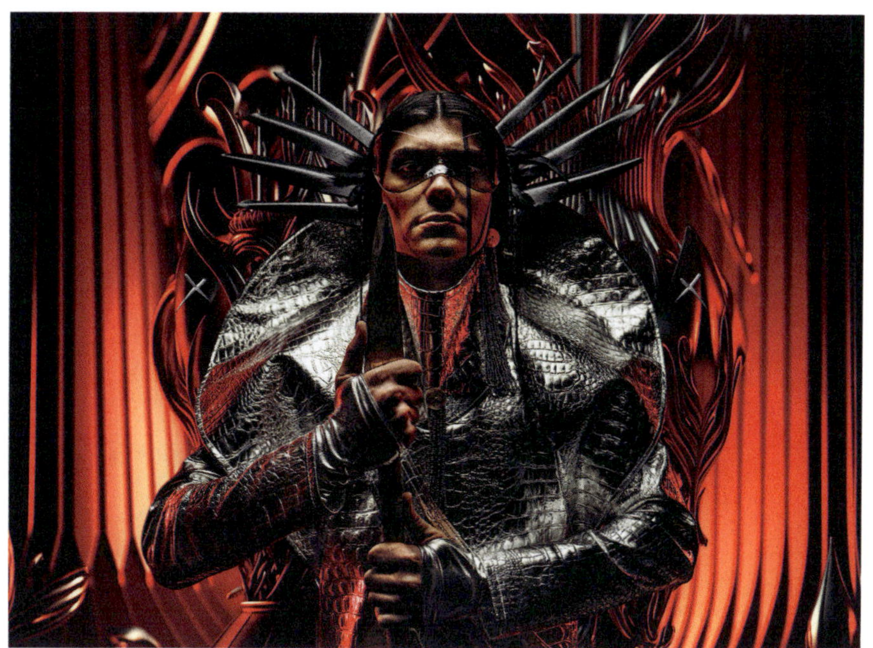

Virgil Ortiz, rendering for History Colorado Center, Denver, c. 2023

DB: This is a nice segue because I'm really interested in the lore of your project *Revolt 1680/2180*. The first thing that leaps out at me when I walk into the *Painted* galleries is the figure on the wallpaper staring out from the stairwell. Could you describe the character and the associated context, the lore?

VO: That character is called the Translator. They're kind of like the Yoda character in *Star Wars*. Because my storyline of

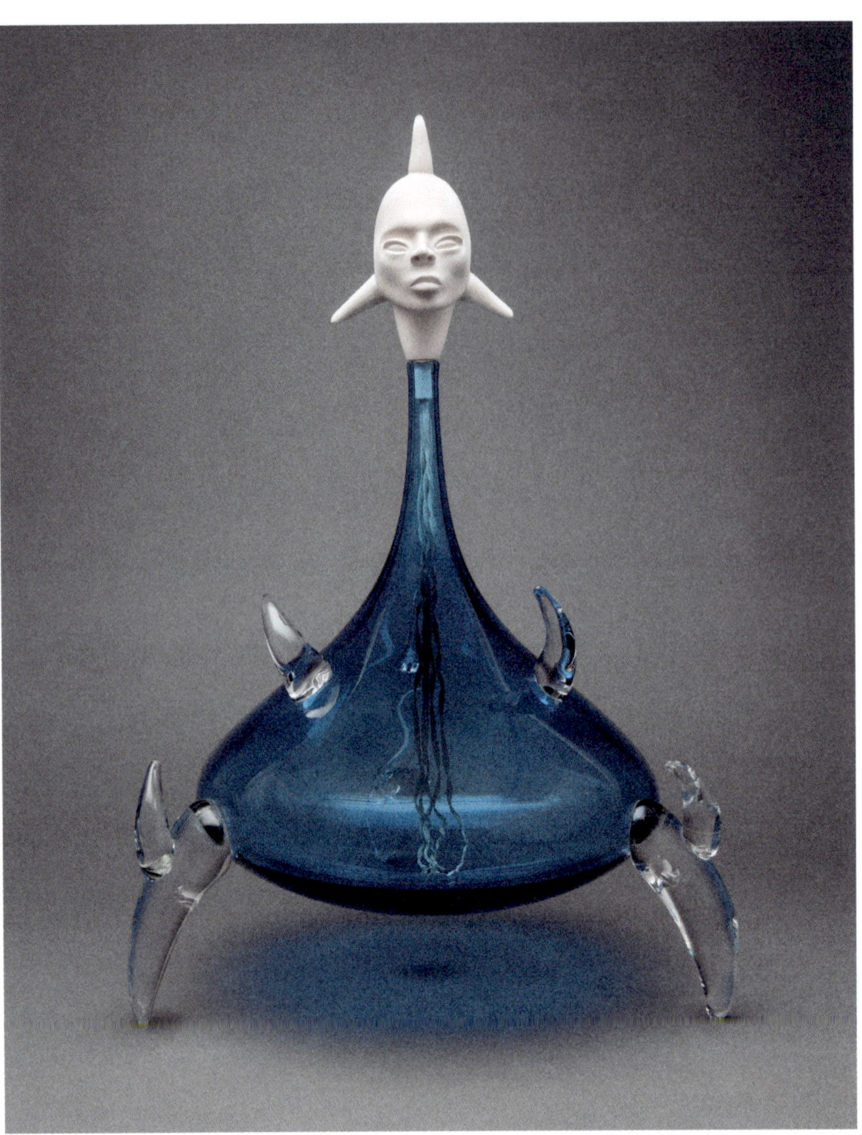

Virgil Ortiz, *Translator 2180*, 2015, from the series *Revolt 1680/2180*. Glass, high-fire clay finial, underglazes, acrylic paint. 27 × 18 × 18 in. (68.6 × 45.7 × 45.7 cm). Lowe Art Museum, Miami, Florida

the Pueblo Revolt happens simultaneously in 2180 and 1680, I had to find a main character who could connect those two dimensions, like through wormholes. The Translator helps Tahu, Po'Pay, and other figures in the storyline translate everything from the different times.

DB: One of the few glass sculptures you've made, the blue glass with the white head, also looks like a Translator figure. Is that the same character, or maybe a kind of companion character?

VO: It's the same character, and it's unisex, androgynous. Depending on who you are or how you view the Translator, it could be a male or a female. It's everything to everyone.

DB: Right, because the Translator needs to be the position that connects every point in your storyline of an Indigenous futuristic outlook on Pueblo society. How do you conceive of your art practice, which encompasses everything from pottery to fashion, as contributing to your overarching remit of recording Pueblo culture?

VO: I should say, I never went to school for any of the art mediums I practice in. All the different types of work I learned either at "YouTube university" or just through trial and error. I try to learn as much as possible because I know I'm going to use it all eventually, whether Photoshop or photography or videography or fashion. I couldn't afford the fashions I saw in magazines when I was a kid, so I figured, okay, I'll just make them myself. I dove in and started sewing. You can't go to Party City or the Halloween store and buy these costumes because they're my original characters. I made the Recon Watchmen characters—the most high-tech costumes so far—with friends. We make plaster casts of their faces and then take it to the level of—do you know what *Face Off* is? The TV show?

DB: Yes, I love it.

VO: We're taking it to that level—making plaster molds of the faces, then sculpting on top of the plaster with Monster Clay, which is an oil-based clay that doesn't dry out. After that, we make another silicone mold of the sculpted face and pour in resin to make really perfect-fitting masks. Utilizing all of these techniques helps me tell the story. And it saves me a ton of money to learn as much as I can and do things myself. Over the years, as I hired graphic designers to do ads and other collateral, I would sit next to them and pay attention, and that's how I learned to use Photoshop and other programs. Now I can do all my own ads. I know how to create print-ready material—banners, anything. I tell the students I work with to learn as much as they can. Just try things and learn through trial and error. You can't be lazy. And don't be afraid of failing, because failures are our best teachers. The more you fail, the quicker you learn.

DB: Like the Yoda quote, "Do...there is no 'try.'" What are some of the bigger challenges when you move from ceramics, like the Cochiti Pueblo pottery, to fashion, or wallpaper design, or room design?

VO: I'm constantly working, and so the works inevitably influence each other. If I'm in the midst of a fashion project, in my head I'm picturing the person I'm making it for. Then I'm imagining how their makeup would look, their hairdos. When I'm sewing, I think, "How cool. I could do this...." Then I jump to clay, and make a physical piece of it. Then I create that piece in armor, or foam. I can always drop what I'm doing and jump to some other medium.

DB: The flexibility across mediums that you're describing feels very in the mode of the Translator.

VO: I'm super ADD, so I'm always thinking of everything at once. But it's therapeutic to be able to jump back and forth like that. Art is therapy, and it saved my life.

DB: In walking through the Colby Museum exhibition, viewers are constantly encountering your wall designs—the organic and geometric motifs—which also show up in a lot of your other work. Could you walk me through the design process, and explain why you landed on those motifs specifically?

VO: The curatorial team and I wanted to try to make the exhibition design feel almost like a Pueblo home or a piece of Pueblo pottery. To get that aesthetic and feel, I realized that we could make a background for the paintings, a kind of watermark. It's not overpowering, but it's there. All those designs are taken from Cochiti Pueblo pottery, and they're signature design elements I use in my fashion work and my personal work. Their use as backgrounds ties everything together, I think, while adding another element for people to look at. The stair-like design represents mountains and also the Kiva steps to our roundhouses, our ceremonial houses. The stairs, the stepladder, are a portal to our next life. So it is all prayer as well.

And the wall designs are connected to the large wallpaper featuring the Pueblo women who are the Blind Archers. The backstory of the Blind Archers is that they were all blinded as kids, yet became ace archers. It's their superpower. A lot of my work is about women's empowerment. Once there was a big forest fire in Cochiti Canyon, and I went up there to scout a location to shoot my sisters and my nieces as these characters. When I arrived at that place, all scarred from the forest fire, I got closer to the burned trees and could see little green buds coming out. That spoke to me of rebirth and regeneration, and the strength of the Earth in healing itself.

The wildflower design, the swirly one, is in that same room. My idea was for it to be somewhat unexpected, but the Earth creates it and it is there, like the buds.

DB: In Peruvian iconography we have what's called a *chakana*, which is three steps, mirrored on either side and representing three planes of existence: the underworld, the middle world, and the higher world. I like art that includes geometric designs, since it encourages looking at it from the other side or underneath or the reverse. That's what I find fascinating about the pieces in your *Velocity* series or your Monos figures—how looking at a different side will reveal a different side of the character, and also different movement. With the Monos figurines, do you begin with a very specific idea for the lines and the designs, or is it more improvised as you go along?

VO: Sometimes I can control what I want to design, but a lot of the time it's all improvised. Especially on a Monos figure, since I'm dressing it as well. I used to try to sketch out the clay pieces beforehand, but the clay itself always dictates—you have to collaborate with the clay mother.

DB: How does working in traditional practices like pottery shape your relationship to the environment and the materials you source?

VO: My family on my mother's side are all potters. So I grew up collecting all sorts of natural ingredients needed to make pottery. We were taught to gather clay at the clay vein where our people have been sourcing it for who knows how long. But before we dig or break into her, into clay mother, we have to feed the area and ask for permission. We introduce ourselves, we state our purpose, and we ask for guidance to make sure that pottery making will never die out. It's a prayer and it's very respectful.

DB: That's beautiful. My mom knits and sews. She learned a lot of it from her sisters and her mother. I definitely understand that there is not just an aesthetic need to create these pieces, but also a cultural remit to preserve the practice.

Let's talk about other exhibitions you've helped design, such as your *Sirens, Passkeys and Portals* room at Meow Wolf in Santa Fe last year. How have you needed to rethink the traditional space of the museum, in which things are in glass cases or displayed in a certain way, to show your pieces or other artists' pieces?

VO: Working with Meow Wolf definitely challenged my aesthetic in terms of how I wanted to display things. I knew thousands of people would be coming to Meow Wolf, taking selfies, maybe touching the pieces. So I had to think about all that foot traffic and the need to use 409 to spray down and wipe things clean, instead of it all being behind glass. So I leaned into making it interactive. For all my future museum and gallery exhibitions, I want things to be interactive. I'm very interested in augmented reality, for instance.

Like my Zoom background, the one for the History Colorado Center in Denver: the photographs will be nine feet tall, and beautiful by themselves already, but then you'll also be able to pull out your smartphone and look at them through augmented reality, and all the images will come alive. Colby and History Colorado both took a chance on me to push my design and my aesthetic, and I give them a lot of props for that.

DB: What you say about interactivity, and virtual reality as well, seems to me a necessary step forward for traditional museum spaces, not only for cleaning purposes but also for accommodating people with different needs.

VO: Or if they want to appeal to a younger demographic who wouldn't already be museumgoers. Plus, augmented reality or interactive works within a cool exhibition can stimulate learning. People might see my work and think, "What? I never knew about the Pueblo Revolt." And then to envelop them with wallpaper or with AR, and maybe show fashion as well, it stimulates everybody's senses and all of a sudden they're getting a history lesson without realizing it. That's my goal—to make it as easy as possible to learn, not by reading a lot of text but by feeling it.

DB: People love *Star Wars* because they can imagine themselves in that world with the characters. I wonder, if I apply that same model to the *Revolt 1680/2180* storyline, how would I perceive that world? What would be my role in it? If I were a Blind Archer, how would my perception change? I think these are questions that the exhibition brings out.

Omtua, your sculpture included in *Painted* (pp. 176–77), just blows me away. I'm sure a lot of people have told you they've never seen anything like it before.

VO: That piece was made when COVID-19 first hit. I was teaching at Arizona State University. Nobody knew what was going on, of course, so they told me, "You could go back to New Mexico and still get paid for this teaching job." But together with the students that we were in a bubble with, we decided to go up to Reitz Ranch, which is just north of ASU. There were only three people at that iconic ceramics place. When I was making *Omtua*, I was thinking about all the real-life Pueblo Revolt runners who were tortured, whipped, and hung in Santa Fe Plaza. So that piece incorporates the designs, but also the whip markings on his back, his scars. If you look at it closely, your eye immediately recognizes the whipping marks, but I also designed it to be beautiful in a way. It's such a sad story. Omtua and Catua were twin runners, and the first ones to give their lives to the cause. So to me Omtua is one of the real heroes of the story, along with Po'Pay, who led the Pueblo Revolt.

DB: The lashing marks also remind me of the wildflower designs. The same body, the beauty, the pain.

VO: And if you look at it straight on, it looks like the figure is tied with his arms up, but it also evokes the Christian cross. It has a lot of meanings.

DB: A lot of your pieces combine natural curves, or more organic shapes, with rigid geometries so it seems as if the natural and the unnatural are coming together.

VO: A lot of it comes out of physically dealing with the wet clay. If the work is leaning forward, I figure, I have to add something in the back for structural reasons. But then also, I'm not a realist. Even if I'm sculpting a human body, it doesn't have to have the correct proportions. And I love that. Those points in *Omtua* make the figure look intimidating already, but then they also represent a cross. That's what the people feared a long time ago, because Christianity, the church, was what caused so much bloodshed and genocide. My hope is that the viewer's brain can intuit the story naturally.

DB: Now that I look some more, the three points—two at the bottom, one at the top—are like a triangle, a shape that pops up a lot in your art.

VO: There are certain messages or icons that resonate with anyone. Circles, crosses. And then the human body—as you just noted, you see the sorrow, you see the pain, but then you also see something beautiful. I'm trying to elicit everybody's different types of reactions or emotions.

DB: One of the things I admire most about your practice, and your family members' practices, is that it's often a study in how to use minimal shapes, minimal lines or structures, but still tell a complete story. Like the Storyteller figures that your mother and your grandmother created. I'm so in love with the simple cross, the hash marks, or the sash. It's just two lines or a little knot, but I understand immediately.

VO: It's so cool to see the older pieces. For a long time we never had access to them because they were in museums or Ivy League college collections and whatnot. It was insane to finally see historic pieces made in the 1800s for the first time and study them and try to revive them, to revive their meanings. The older I get and the more I do, I can dissect it

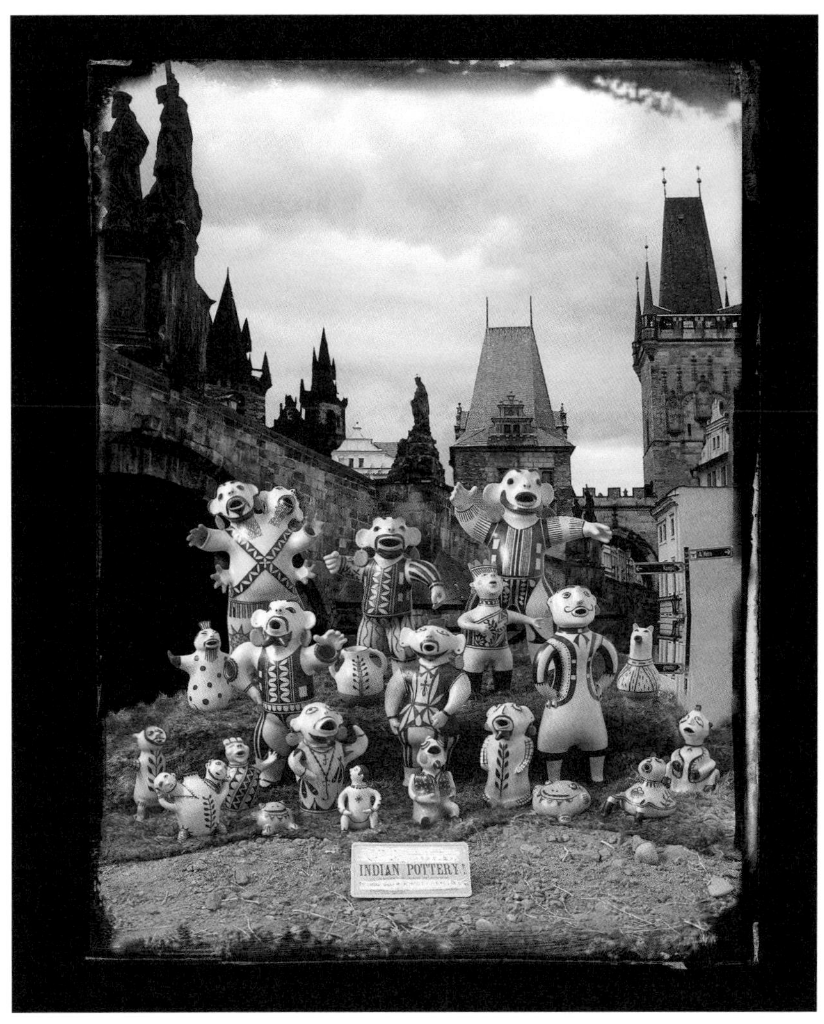

Virgil Ortiz, *Vertigo: A Spin on Tradition—Reviving the Past*, 2011. Ortiz invited four generations of potters from his family to re-create each ceramic figure pictured in an 1880 photograph by Ben Wittick.

myself now, try to stimulate emotions and meanings in the viewer. Now it's purposeful, but at first I didn't even know what was happening. I was being guided. Like a conduit, right? I'm not the first. I won't be the last, hopefully.

DB: In recent years there has been a lot of controversy surrounding horrifying things in museum collections that were once regarded as "anthropological," like the human hair samples at Harvard's Peabody Museum. Do you see museums or universities as having a responsibility to the Indigenous art—or even body parts—tucked away in their collection storage?

VO: When I am invited to work with an institution such as a museum, I do ask if I can see the vault. And I do often say, "Hmm, this is iffy. You should think about doing NAGPRA."[1] Most of them don't even know what's sacred and that they shouldn't have it until someone from that tribe goes and sees it and identifies it. Overall I find it impressive that they're allowing us to do that. Eventually everybody will learn.

DB: I'm a real sci-fi nerd, and so I wanted to ask you: If you could time-travel anywhere, where would you go first?

VO: I would go back to visit my ancestors. I'm so amazed by these pieces from the 1800s—how massive and cool they are. Those people were masters with clay, despite having no running water, no plumbing, no electricity. I would love to go back to that time and see how they did it and learn from them, so I could bring back that knowledge to where I'm at now.

But then also I would visit the future, because I would love to see that it's all still alive. And that we're not repeating our history, the atrocities that happened. I'd like to know that my work will outlive me, and see that it made an impact with all people. Because that's my whole thing: educating globally about the Pueblo Revolt through art. I would want to see that it worked.

DB: You come from the Cochiti Pueblo tradition, but have there been other artists from other traditions, either in the US Southwest or elsewhere, who have shaped the way you think about your art?

VO: In fashion, I love Rick Owens and Alexander McQueen. Very gothic, very old-school. I'm a goth at heart. And then growing up, I had the best professors, which were my mom and my grandmother. And then there are up-and-comers like Jared Tso, a fourth-generation Diné potter. To watch him revive his family style of making pottery is so impressive. I'm happy to know him and call him a friend and help push his practice and get him out there, too. It is awesome to see him thriving, working with traditional methods and materials in his people's way.

DB: If you help build this community, then you have not just yourself to bounce ideas off of.

VO: Absolutely.

DB: How do you see your art practice developing in the future?

VO: As fast as it's moving, through AR and everything, there's no stopping. And as I move along, I try to learn as much as I can with all different mediums. There's so much to learn, and that excites me to try a lot of new sculptures, like outdoor sculpture. I'd love to learn more about welding and steel, and make really big, landmark-size sculptures. There's so much to do and so little time.

Note

1 The 1990 Native American Graves Protection and Repatriation Act requires museums and federal agencies to return Native American cultural items and ancestral remains to tribal communities.

Gallery 2

Pop Chalee
Nicolai Fechin
Jody Naranjo Folwell
Marsden Hartley
Ernest Martin Hennings
Victor Higgins
Albert Looking Elk
John Marin
Thomas Moran
Dan Namingha
Michael Namingha
Sarah Sockbeson
Walter Ufer

"The story of my people and the story of this place are one single story."

In 1906, just a few years before the founding of the Taos Society of Artists, the US government seized forty-eight thousand acres of Taos Pueblo land, including Blue Lake, a sacred site for Taos Pueblo. Almost all of the historical paintings in this exhibition were made in the years immediately following the theft of Blue Lake, and each of the Pueblo models featured in the TSA's paintings would have been directly affected by the federal dispossession of their homelands. The TSA painters visually implied a strong connection between their sitters and the outdoor environment, consistently depicting the two in relation. What their renderings did not directly reflect was the Taos Pueblo community's contemporaneous experience of being forcibly separated from their rightful territories.

Blue Lake and the surrounding area were legally returned to Taos Pueblo in 1970, after a decades-long effort by tribal members. Toward the end of their struggle to regain legal stewardship of Blue Lake, Taos Pueblo circulated a public statement: "We have lived upon this land from days beyond history's records, far past any living memory, deep into the time of legend. The story of my people and the story of this place are one single story. No man can think of us without also thinking of this place. We are always joined together."

Though this exhibition took place far from Pueblo territories, many of its featured artworks allow us to clearly visualize what was at stake in Taos Pueblo's battle for sovereignty and to honor the profound, enduring connections between Pueblo peoples and their homelands. Blue Lake is one of many instances of land-based injustice committed by the US government in violation of tribal sovereignty. Despite this, Native communities continue to be on the front lines of efforts to safeguard our environment from threats brought about by climate change and extractive industries.

On This Land

The Colby College Museum of Art occupies Wabanaki territory, which encompasses what are now known as Maine and Maritime Canada. Wabanaki communities have lived on and cared for these lands since time immemorial. Over the past century, Wabanaki sustainable land practices and stewardship have been instrumental in reviving fish populations, improving water quality, and restoring forest ecosystems in this region. Wabanaki activists and artists are also leading contemporary efforts to protect the brown ash tree. Currently under threat due to the emerald ash borer, an invasive beetle species, brown ash is central to Wabanaki identity and the continuation of traditional Wabanaki basketry. By pushing for a robust, collaborative response to the ash borer, Wabanaki advocates are protecting this vital cultural resource and ensuring its survival for generations to come. Though this exhibition primarily focused on bringing Pueblo perspectives into dialogue with the Taos Society of Artists and its legacy, Wabanaki and other Native voices were also included throughout. Through this process, the curatorial team—in consultation with the exhibition's advisory council—sought to create an intertribal dialogue that respected and acknowledged that the exhibition took place on Wabanaki territory.

—Siera Hyte

Jody Naranjo Folwell
Santa Clara Pueblo/Tewa, born 1942
Ghost Hunters, c. 2015
Redware, paint
16 × 6 ½ × 6 ½ in. (40.6 × 16.5 × 16.5 cm)
Museum purchase from the Jere Abbott Acquisitions Fund, 2022.063

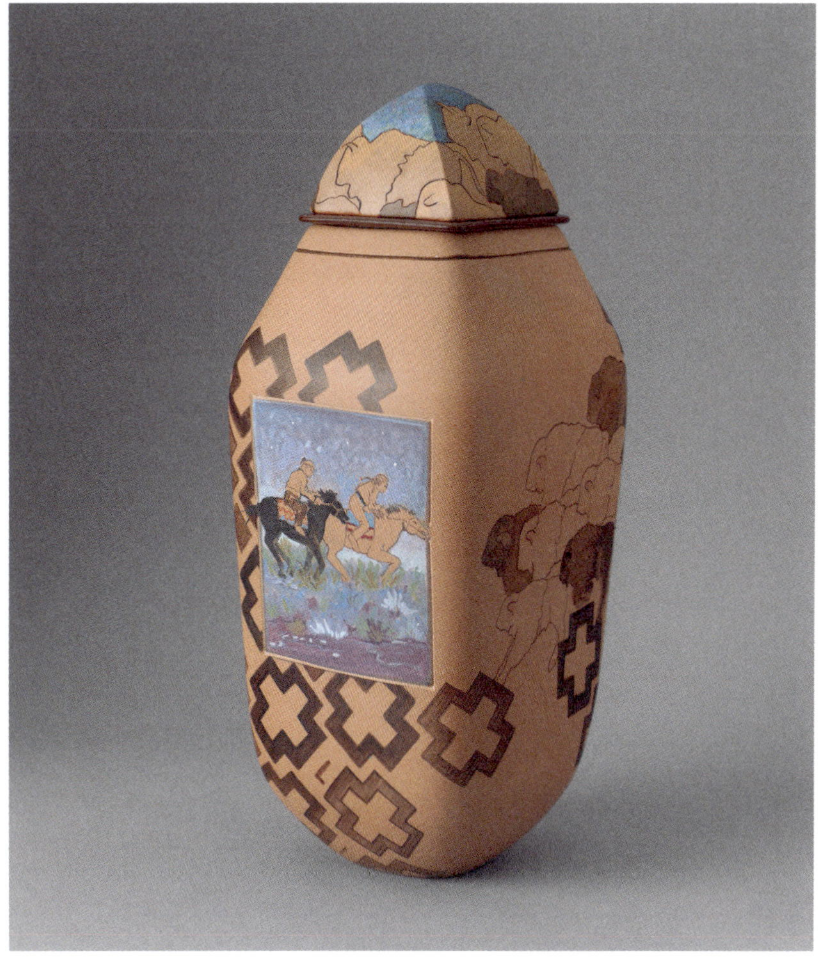

I created this work to honor the relatives up north and the buffalo. When I learned about the government's campaign to annihilate the buffalo from the Earth, I felt very angry and sad. It starved my people, Indian people. This is a tribute to those people and the buffalo. These riders are hunting ghosts now.

—Jody Naranjo Folwell

Walter Ufer
American, 1876–1936
In His Garden, 1922
Oil on canvas
30 ½ × 30 ½ in. (77.5 × 77.5 cm)
The Lunder Collection, 285.2008

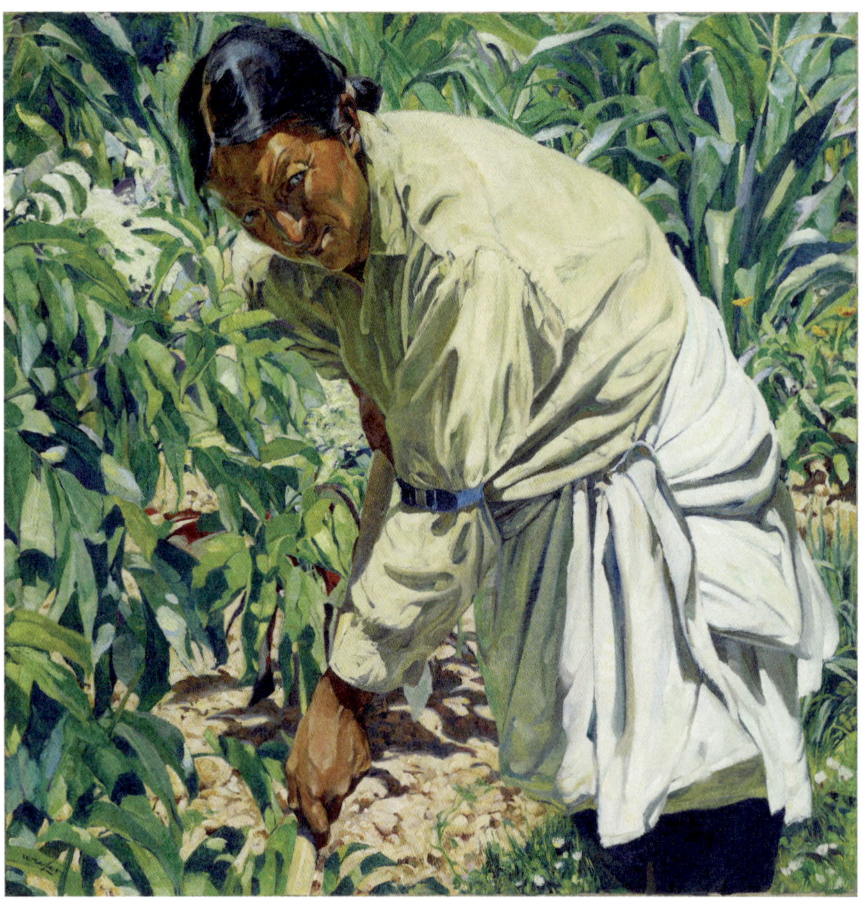

Corn is part of Pueblo family dynamics and gives our people the foundation to function as a cohesive community. Like each stalk and kernel, each community member works in tandem to support the entirety of the village. We care for our fields in the same manner that we care for our children, ensuring that they grow with the support, patience, and nourishment needed to thrive in life. Living in the desert, watching our fields grow, we learn to live our lives without excess or taking more than we need. The work put into tending fields brings longevity and a true appreciation for abundant harvests and community blessings.

—Juan Lucero

Thomas Moran
American, 1837–1926
Acoma, 1902
Oil on canvas
20 × 30 in. (50.8 × 76.2 cm)
The Lunder Collection, 2013.211

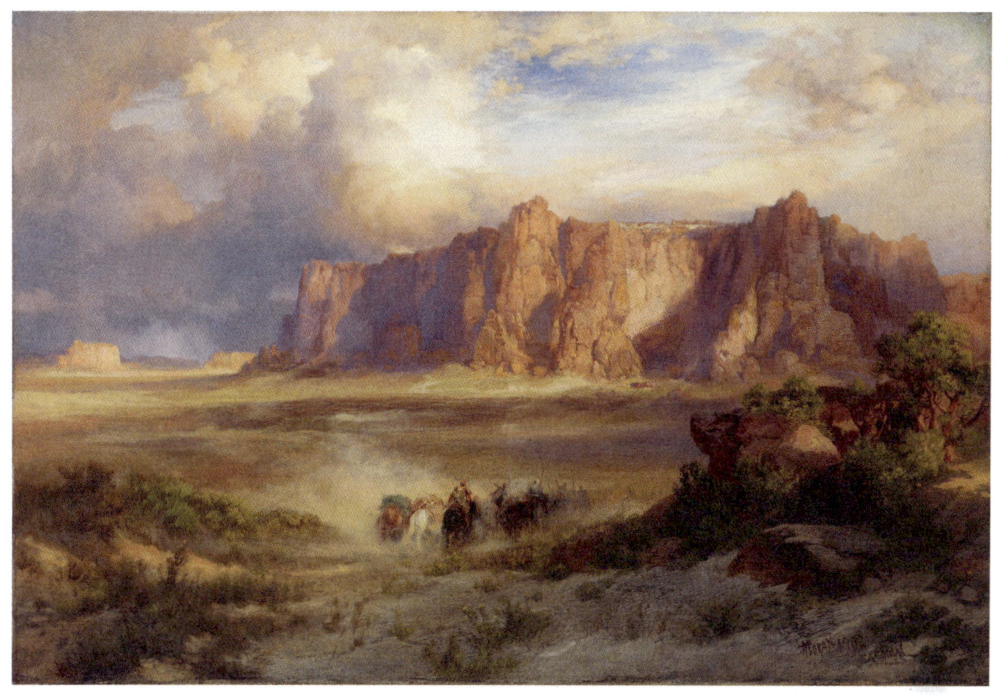

Sponsored by the Santa Fe Railway, Thomas Moran made numerous trips to the Southwest during the early 1900s. The resulting paintings have much in common with the earlier compositions of Yellowstone, Green River, and the Grand Canyon that made him famous. For example, ancient geographies and dramatic skies often dwarf human activity and human habitation. Notice how Acoma Pueblo peeks over the edge of rugged cliffs, and swirling dust partially obscures the small group of horseback riders. Moran meditates here on the overwhelming scale and beauty of a landscape that was new to Euro-Americans but deeply familiar to the Indigenous caretakers who had inhabited it for thousands of years.

—J. R. Henneman, director and curator of the Petrie Institute of Western American Art, Denver Art Museum

Michael Namingha
Hopi/Ohkay Owingeh, born 1977
Altered Landscape 15, 2022
Chromogenic print on shaped acrylic mount
25 × 50 × 1 in. (63.5 × 127 × 2.5 cm)
Museum purchase from the Jere Abbott
Acquisitions Fund, 2022.065

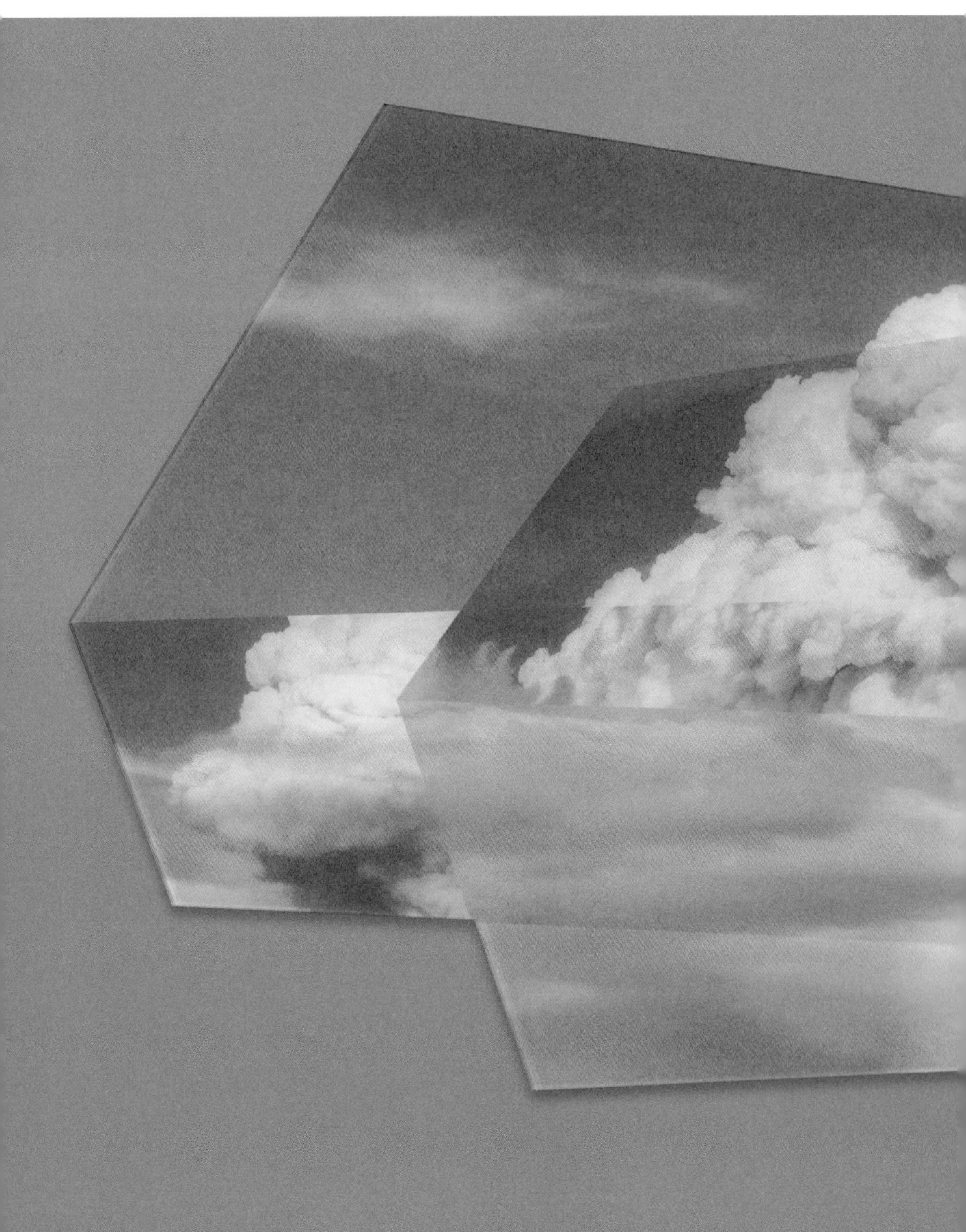

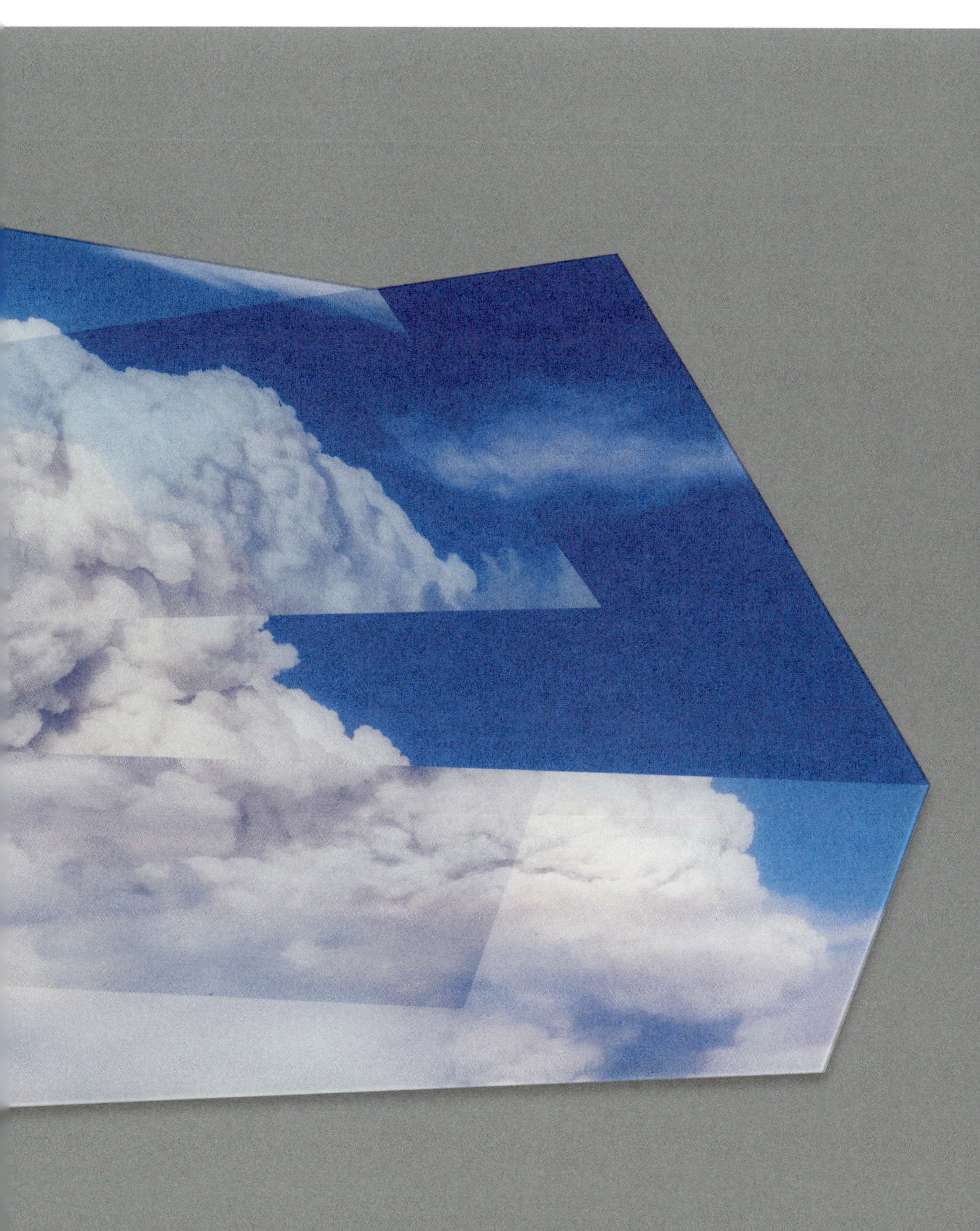

Michael Namingha
From the artist's talk at the Painted *symposium, November 2023*

I was born and raised in Santa Fe, New Mexico. My father is from the Hopi tribe in Arizona, and my mother is from Ohkay Owingeh Pueblo, about thirty miles north of Santa Fe. I grew up at Ohkay Owingeh until I was in the third grade. My father, who is an artist as well, is also included in this exhibition. His name is Dan Namingha, and he has been painting professionally since 1970. My brother, Arlo Namingha, became an artist, too—he's a sculptor. My great-great-great-grandmother was a Hopi potter by the name of Nampeyo. I come from a long line of Hopi pottery makers. And I have had grandfathers who were weavers because among the Hopi, it's the men who do the weaving. I had grandfathers who were also kachina doll carvers. When my brother was younger, he carved kachina dolls before he embarked on his career as a professional artist.

I attended Parsons School of Design in New York. I did not study fine art, but rather strategic design and management. Tom Ford became the head designer at Gucci in the 1990s, and he also is from Santa Fe, so I thought, oh, maybe I want to be the next Tom Ford! Design Strategy and Management is a unique program at Parsons in that it focuses on the marketing side of the fashion industry. While I was there, I was able to work on a project for Hermès doing product development for their home collection. I thought, wow, this is great! I can do this for the rest of my life. And then 9/11 happened. I had a very distorted perception of what was going on—seeing the city and our lives change literally overnight. It brought things into a different perspective for me. I realized: I don't think this is the path I want to take.

Coming from a long line of artists, it seemed natural to fall into that role. But what kind of artist did I want to become? I didn't want to paint, I didn't want to sculpt. But I remembered as a young boy using one of my dad's cameras. For my sixteenth birthday, he had gotten me my own camera and said, "My camera's very nice, so here's your own. Go and experiment." He was so helpful in that he always encouraged my brother and me to try new things and never be afraid of what someone might tell you is wrong. There was no right or wrong in what we created as kids.

It took me a while to figure out what type of photography I wanted to do, and what I wanted to say with my work. But early on, I knew it had to do with social commentary of some type. And I knew I was frustrated with photography being confined to a square or a rectangle. I started to look at artists like Ellsworth Kelly and Ronald Davis, who painted on shaped canvases to create a sense of illusion.

Another formative influence on the theatricality of my work was my membership in the Young Associate group at the Metropolitan Opera in New York, when I was a student and in the years following (I currently live back in Santa Fe, but a lot of my work's production still happens in New York). As a Young Associate, you get cheap tickets, but you're all over the theater, never in the same place. I started to observe how set designers skew sets to trick the eye. Then I started to think about how I could take an analogous approach to photographs.

One day I was photographing a landscape about thirty miles south of Santa Fe, in a place called the Galisteo Basin. I was chasing a storm, I was chasing a sunset, I was chasing after something I thought was going to be this beautiful, picturesque scene. I got out there, I got the photograph, but on my way to and from that place, I saw all these signs alongside the road: "No drilling in Galisteo. No oil in Lamy." I didn't know what they meant. Back at my studio, I started to do some research on the Galisteo Basin to find out. It turned out, the village of Galisteo had been battling with oil and natural gas companies for a few decades, because underneath the basin sits a large deposit of oil. The people who live in the village had been fighting against the companies that wanted to drill, and they were successful in stopping them. Now I started to think about how some of that could inflect my work. I took my photograph of the sunset, made it black and white, and put a block of color over a portion of it to represent a piece that may not be there someday.

My work soon came to offer more commentary on what's happening environmentally. I had an exhibition in 2018 at the Georgia O'Keeffe Museum in Santa Fe where they asked me to create a body of work in response to hers. I chose a series that O'Keeffe painted in the 1930s and 1940s of what she called the Black Place. It's in the Four Corners region, not far from Chaco Canyon, and it's a very otherworldly landscape. It looks as if you are on Mars. I started to research it using Google Earth and got used to looking at an aerial perspective. When it came time to produce the work for that exhibition, I used a drone to photograph the landscape because it just seemed so much more interesting from the sky.

When I finally went out to photograph the Black Place, I discovered that the landscape is very fragile. When you step on it, you leave a mark that will be there forever. Then I discovered that oil and natural gas companies had moved in and started to build infrastructure. In 2014, NASA found that the largest methane gas cloud in North America sits over that region and Chaco Canyon. On their satellite images, the infrared photography makes the methane gas cloud show up as red, pink, and yellow. So I started to use those three colors in a lot of my work related to the Black Place.

My work included in this exhibition is from a series titled *Altered Landscapes*, which looks at how we as humans are changing the landscapes in which we live. This is a photograph of a pyro-cumulonimbus cloud that occurred in 2022. A pyro-cumulonimbus cloud is created during an immense forest fire that basically sucks up all the ash and sends it into the air in a gigantic plume. Then the cloud creates its own weather system. So you have this forest fire burning underneath and this storm being created on top of it, which then brews its own thundercloud that adds to the already-burning forest beneath. This fire was in Las Vegas, New Mexico. It ended up burning 348,000 acres, making it the largest fire in New Mexico's history. It affected a lot of rural communities. Many little Spanish villages and reservations were burned along its path.

The fires raged from April until August 2022, when they were finally contained. A cloud of this nature appeared, I believe, six times. Over that same summer, I was also looking into New Mexico's history with the atomic bomb. Our state has had a heavy relationship with nuclear power. Pyro-cumulonimbus clouds would appear over our mountain ranges—which we call the Sangre de Cristo. On one side of the mountains you would have blue sky, and then a little cloud would start to appear, and then it would build into a massive pyro-cumulonimbus cloud. Also in 2022, smoke from the immense fires in California, Arizona, and Colorado was drifting through. We'd have a massive cloud on one side and these very ominous yellow clouds on the other. Sunset brought about very scary, hazy environments. Yet in contrast to my other work, this one looks almost pretty, with the sky a bright blue and not a poisonous yellow. That's the hook: in the midst of what was happening environmentally, the clouds were still very beautiful. A movie I saw a few years ago had a line: "Sometimes awful things have their own kind of beauty."

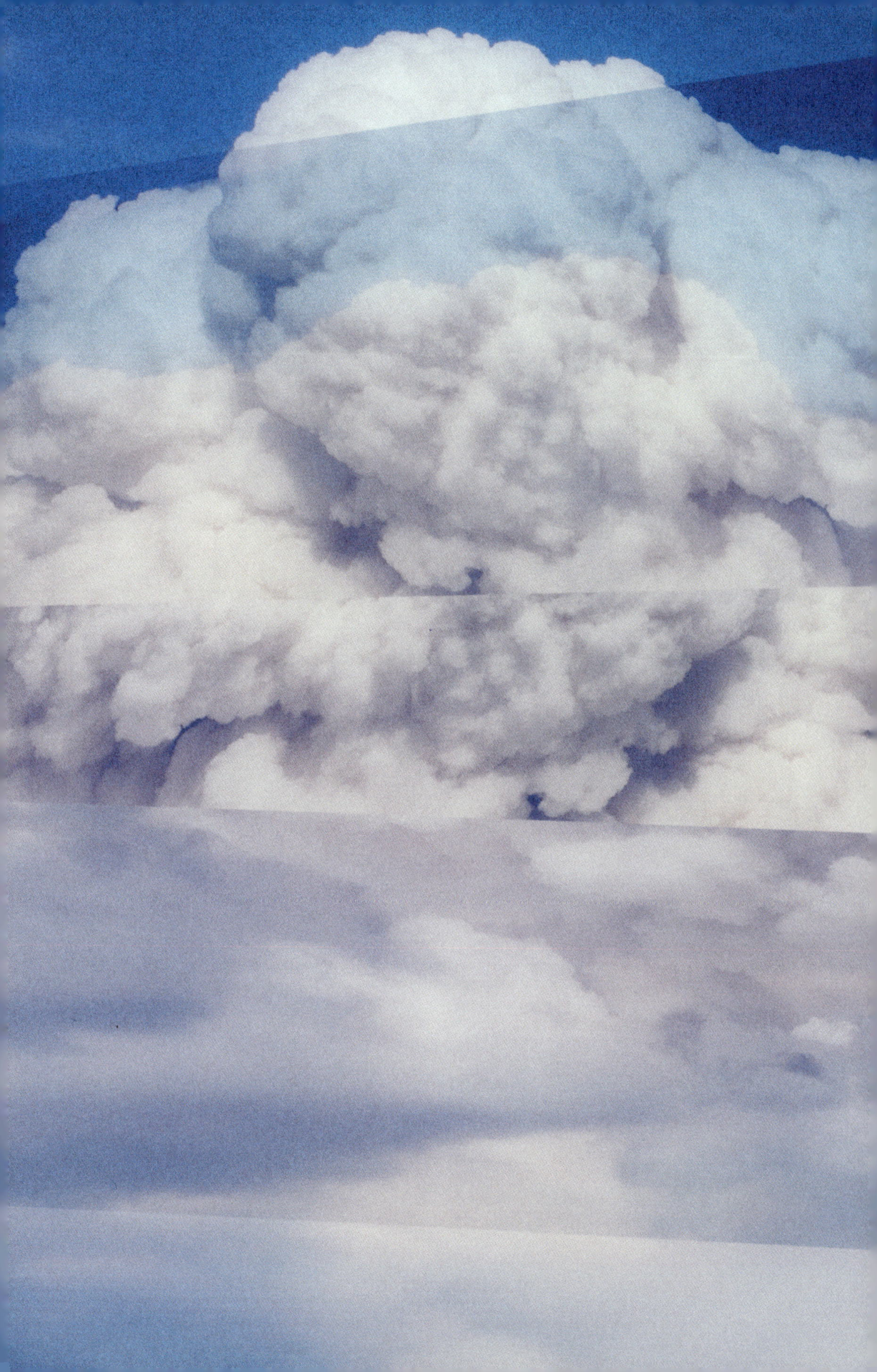

Ernest Martin Hennings
American, 1886–1956
Taos Indian on Horseback, c. 1930
Oil on canvas. 24 × 30 in. (61 × 76.2 cm)
The Lunder Collection, 2013.135

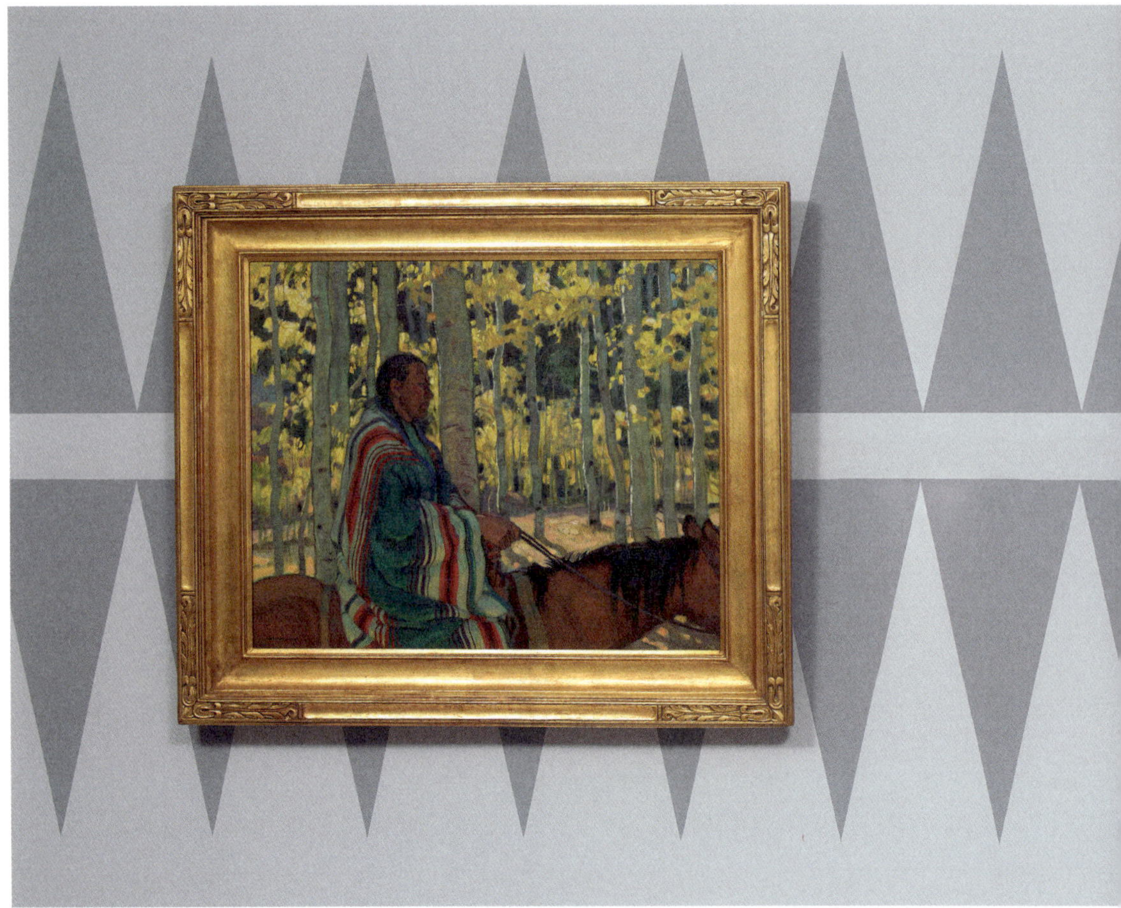

TSA painters had various personalities, sensibilities, and artistic practices that guided their interactions with Taos Pueblo people. Some artists developed enduring familial relationships with community members, while others took a more distant approach. Ernest Martin Hennings built his life and career in relation to Taos Pueblo people and recognized the importance of fostering deep friendships with the community and the individuals he depicted, and that closeness between artist and sitter is evident in his works. Hennings visited Taos in 1914, and in 1917 he moved there permanently. *Taos Indian on Horseback* represents one of Hennings's most familiar scenes: Taos Pueblo people riding horses through a light-filled aspen forest. Hennings's decision to exclude the horse's face and tail draws attention to the rider and blanket. Light pouring through yellow leaves and tall white aspens evokes serenity and pulls us into the painting as if we were likewise an essential part of the scene.

—Jill Ahlberg Yohe

Dan Namingha
Hopi/Tewa, born 1950
August Moon, 2022
Acrylic on canvas. 33 × 36 in. (83.8 × 91.4 cm)
Museum purchase from the Jere Abbott
Acquisitions Fund, 2022.064

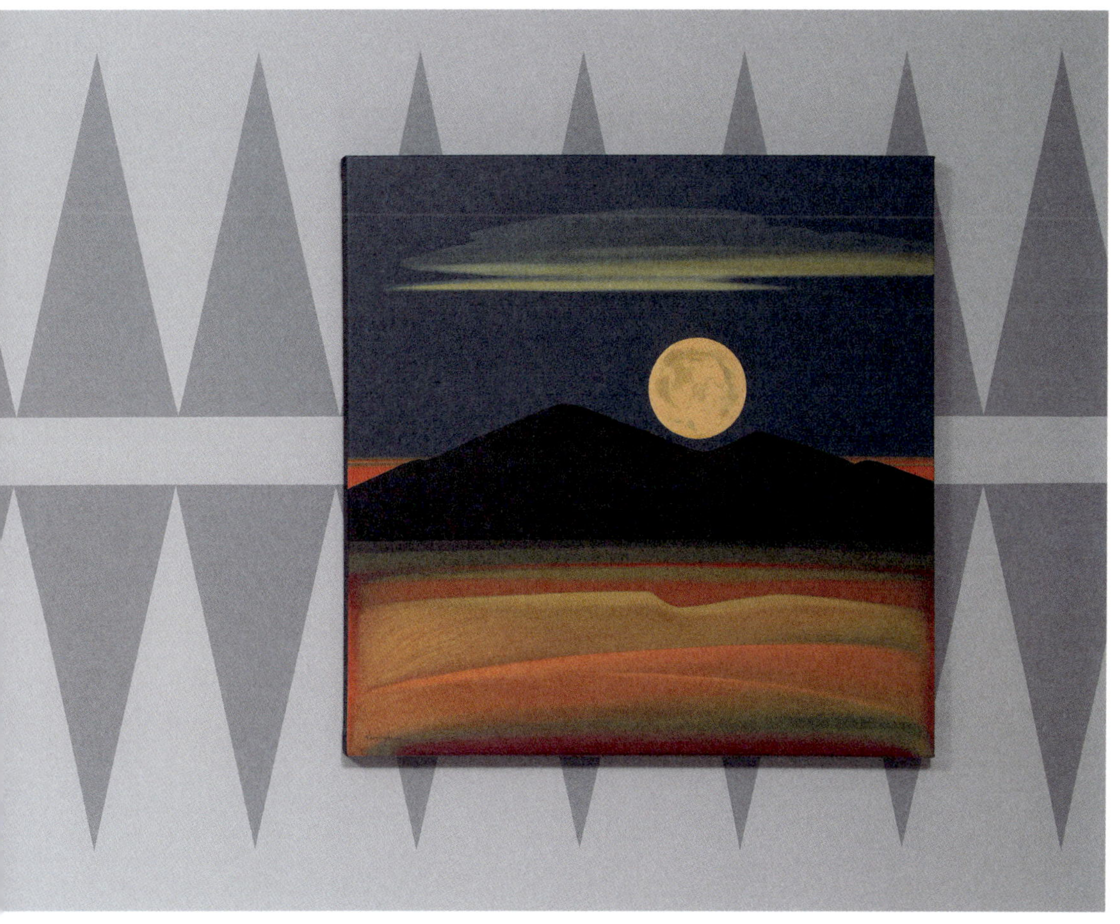

Capturing prayers for nourishment, growth, and the well-being of communities, the moon plays an integral role as the mother of our people, watching over us, sharing light, and encouraging caution as we journey through life. The full moon is our indication to create, meet, transition, and go into ceremony. She also reminds us to rest and approach dreams. Her protection as we sleep casts shadows over challenges and light over clear paths that allow our people a future. Dan Namingha is a highly celebrated and accomplished Hopi/Tewa painter and sculptor from Polacca, on the Hopi Reservation. He is the great-great grandson of the famed Hopi potter Nampeyo. His ability to create works from an authentic Indigenous perspective allows viewers to truly experience his worldview through his eyes.

—Juan Lucero

Pop Chalee
Taos Pueblo, 1906–1993
Untitled (Black Horse), n.d.
Watercolor
18 × 24 in. (45.7 × 61 cm)
Collection of Jay Fell, Colby College '66

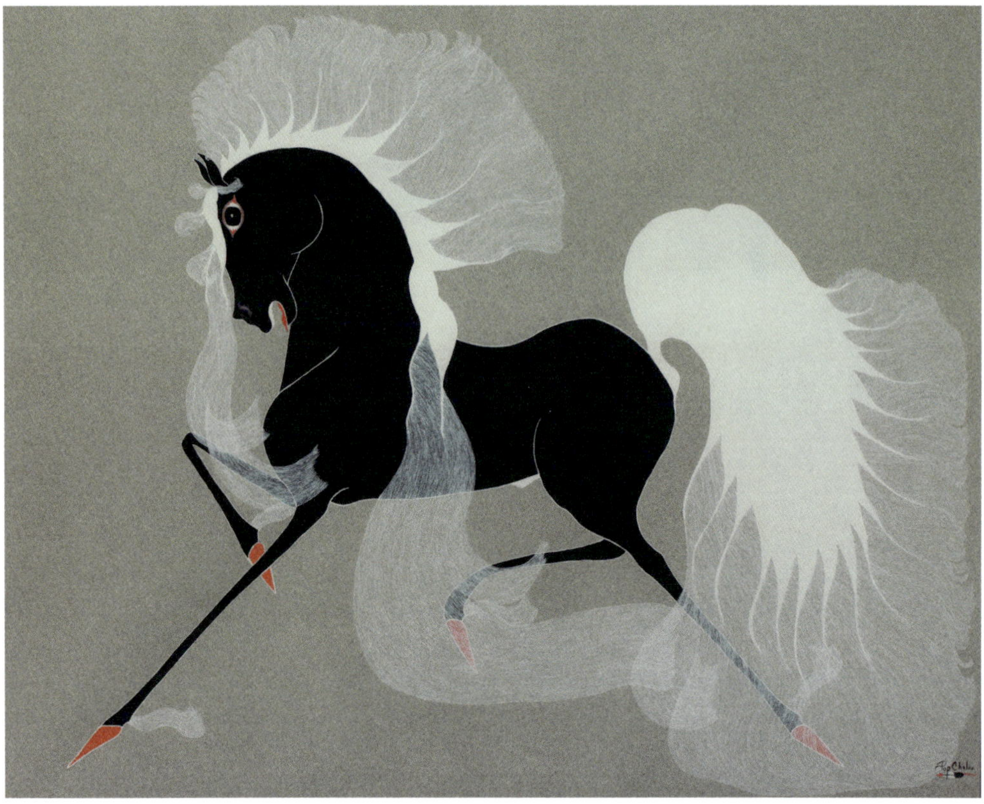

Pop Chalee made her paintings of forests and animals in a "flat-style" technique, with limited shading and dimension. Native art students were encouraged to paint flat style—a method widely promoted by Dorothy Dunn's Studio School, an offshoot of the federal government's Santa Fe Indian School—because Dunn felt it yielded more "authentic" renditions of Native American art. In the 1930s, Chalee studied with Dunn as well as with Oscar E. Berninghaus and other TSA artists. Though the students were trained to paint in this one particular fashion, each developed a distinctive artistic practice. Chalee utilized an almost otherworldly color palette, unconstrained by conventions of realism. She populated her singular world with dreamy images, often returning to the motif of psychedelic horses galloping with mythic grace.

—Siera Hyte

Right: Illustration by Margeaux Abeyta (Taos Pueblo/Diné), commissioned for *Painted*, 2023

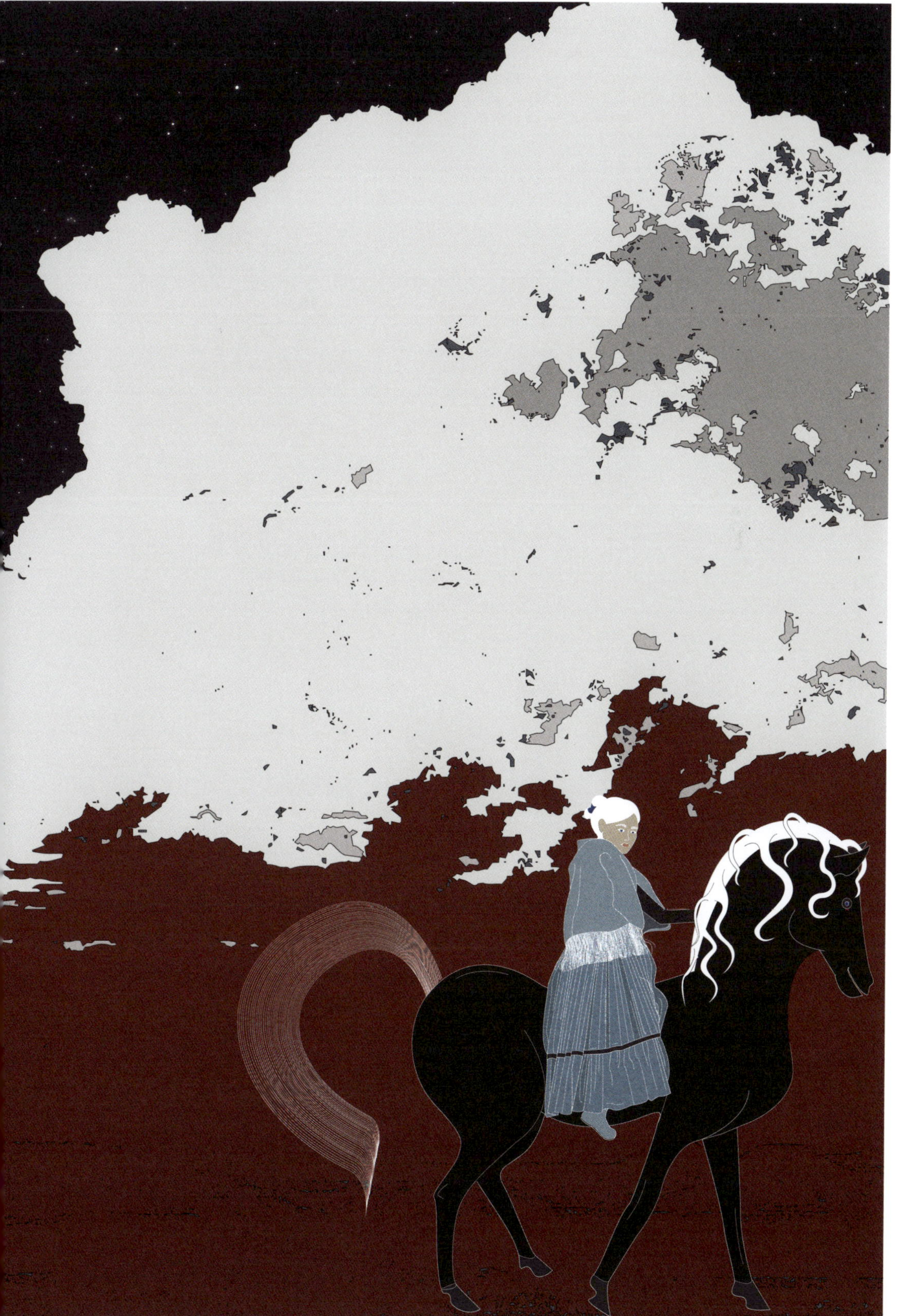

John Marin
American, 1870–1953
New Mexico Landscape, 1929
Watercolor and charcoal on paper
14 × 20 in. (35.6 × 50.8 cm)
Gift of John Marin, Jr. and Norma B. Marin, 1973.050

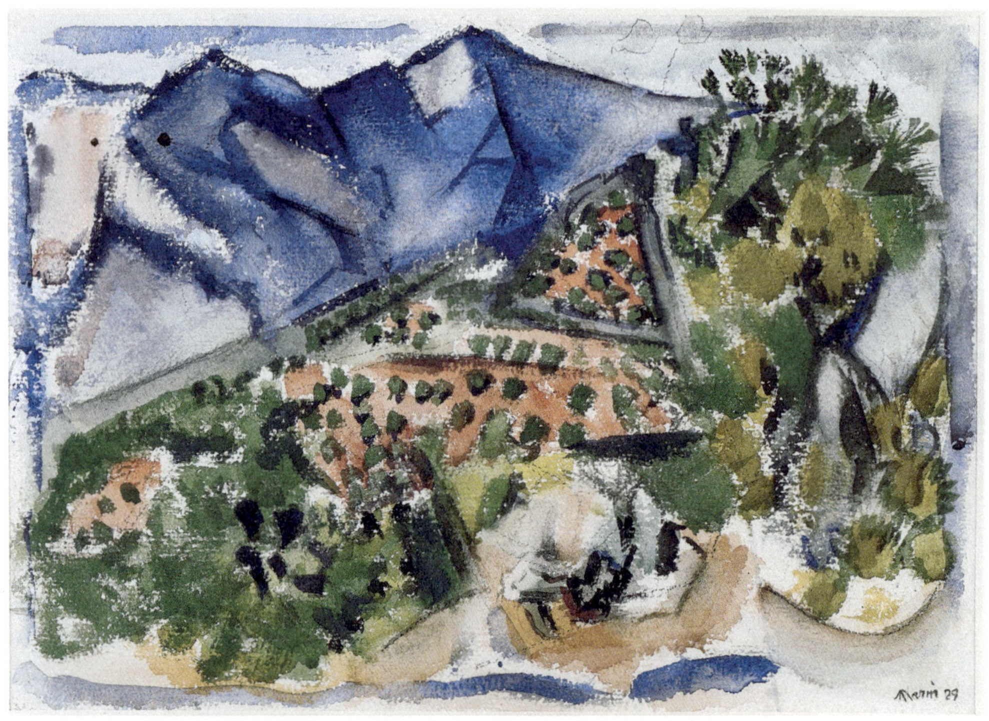

In the summers of 1929 and 1930, John Marin made almost one hundred paintings of the Southwest during extended visits to Taos. At the time, the artist primarily lived between Maine and New York City. He and other painters, among them Georgia O'Keeffe, Marsden Hartley, and Andrew Dasburg, belonged to the second generation of artists to arrive in Taos following the disbanding of the TSA in 1927. Their group shared an interest in abstraction, drawing inspiration from the stark forms of the Southwestern landscape. Many of Marin's New Mexican watercolors combine bold geometric shapes with more expressive, brushy marks. In this painting, blue mountains stretch to the top of the paper, perhaps reflecting an artistic reverence for the enormity of the Southwestern mountain ranges. Marin made this painting in 1929, just five years after the federal government granted Native people citizenship on their own lands.

—Siera Hyte

Marsden Hartley
American, 1877–1943
New Mexico Landscape, 1918
Pastel on paper
17 × 27 ½ in. (43.2 × 69.9 cm)
Bequest of Adelaide Moise, 1986.031

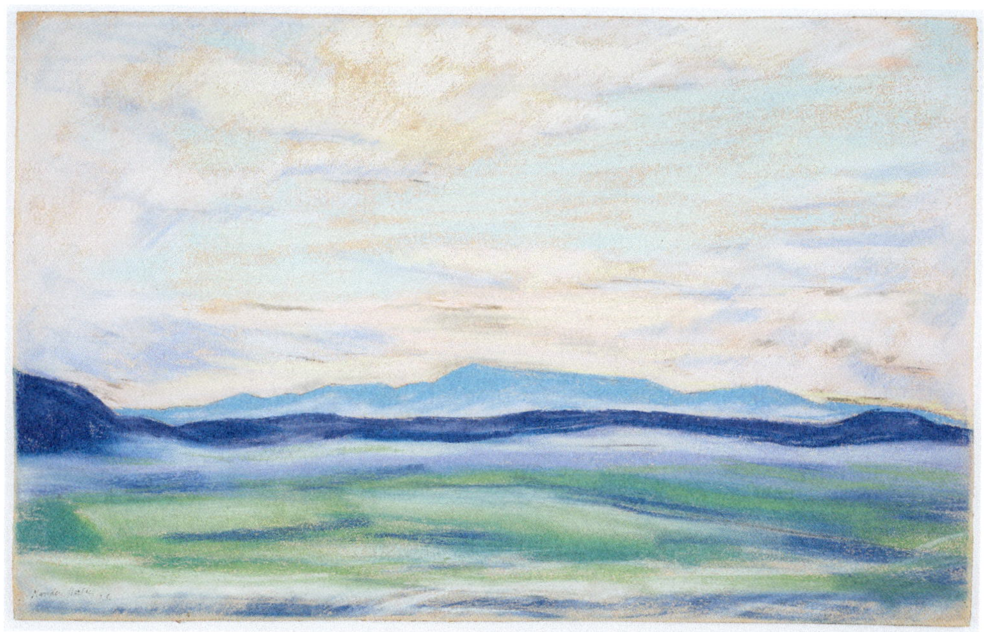

American modernist Marsden Hartley moved away from his more rugged New Mexico landscapes with this pastel. Vast, creamy, wispy skies, calm blue mountains, and soft green pastures create a serene setting. *New Mexico Landscape* likely depicts the fertile valley and mountain just northwest of the Taos Pueblo village. Northern New Mexico became a continual source of inspiration for the development of a distinctly American style of painting. Hartley made this work in 1918, a time in which Native peoples on their own lands were not considered legal citizens by the United States government.

—Jill Ahlberg Yohe

Albert Looking Elk
Taos Pueblo, 1888–1940
Untitled, c. 1925–35
Oil on board
8 ¼ × 11 in. (21 × 27.9 cm)
Collection of the Millicent Rogers
Museum, Taos, New Mexico,
Gift of Brad and Fran Taylor

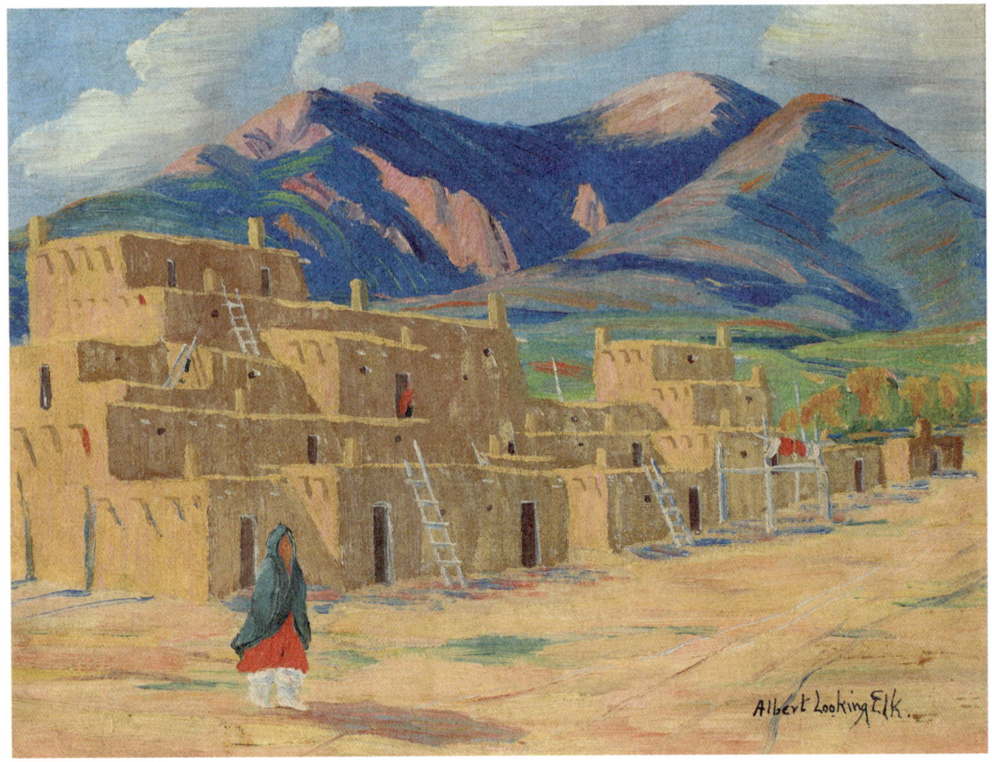

Sarah Sockbeson
Penobscot, born 1984
Untitled Basket, 2023
Aluminum house siding, found vinyl, enamel spray paint, found plastic, faux leather
12 × 12 × 12 in. (30.5 × 30.5 × 30.5 cm)
Museum purchase from the Jetté Acquisitions Fund, 2023.046

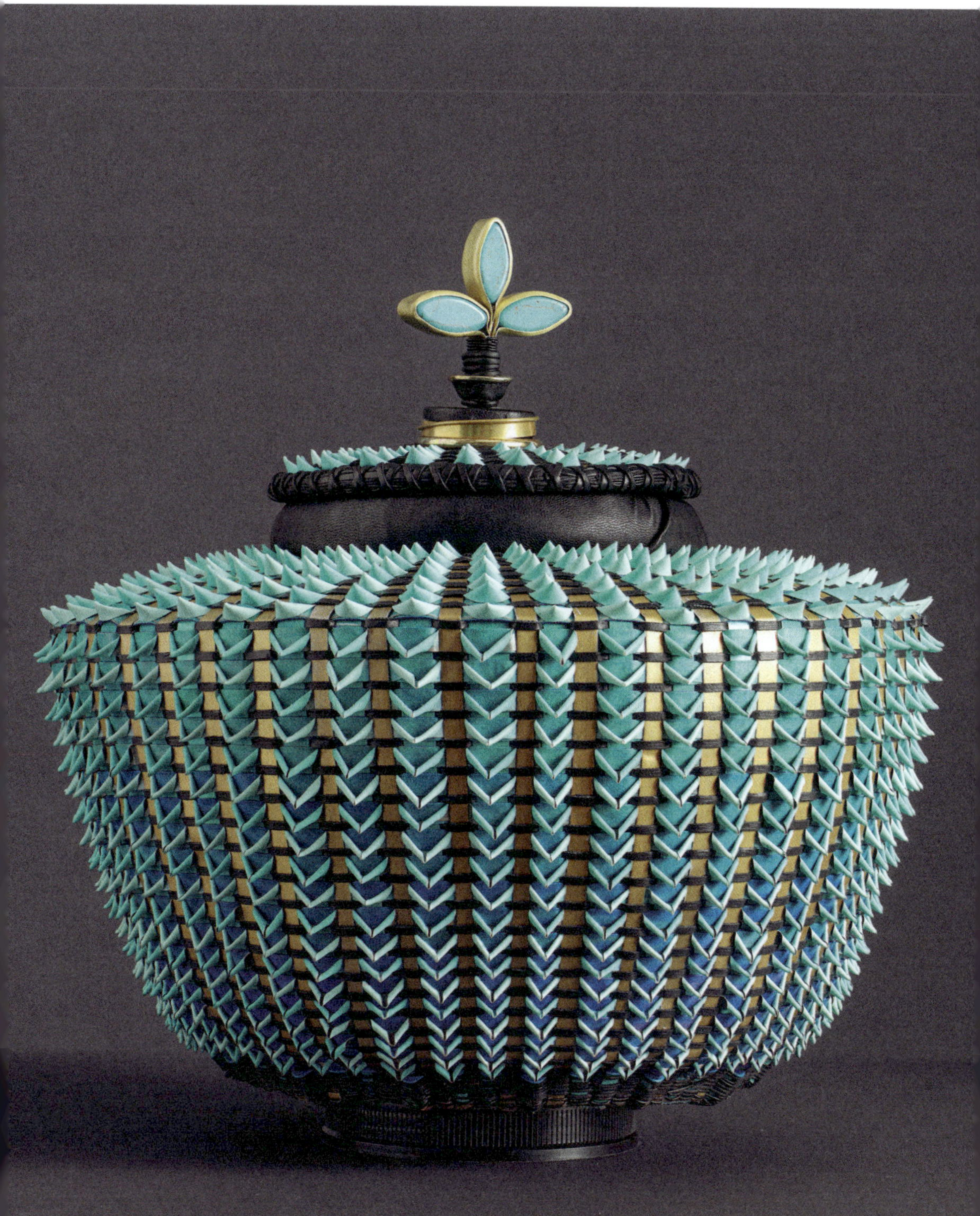

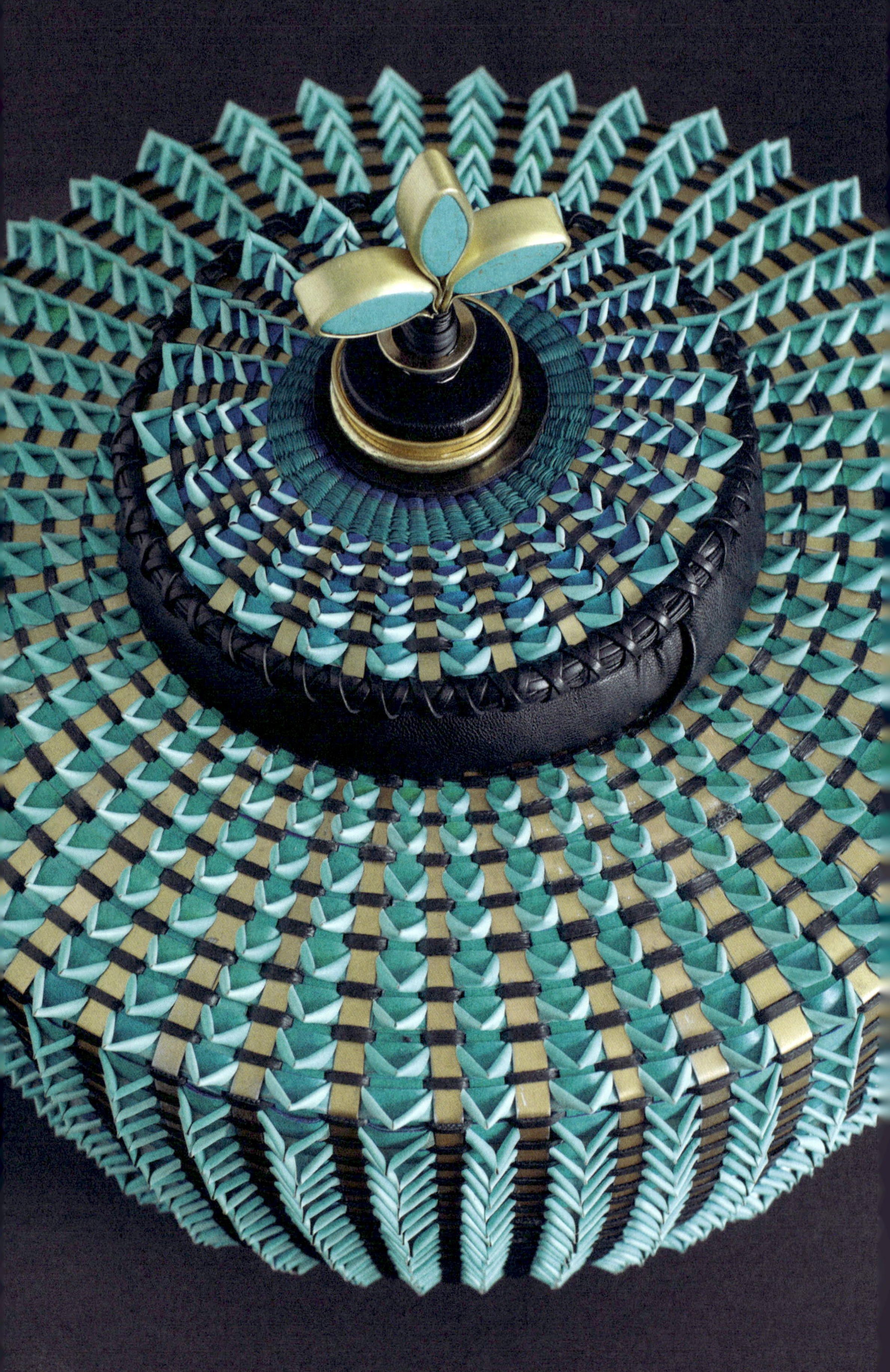

Sarah Sockbeson
From the artist's talk at the Painted *symposium, November 2023*

I made this basket specifically to be in conversation with the other pieces in this exhibition. When it comes to my inspiration and how I came to create this piece, I had two things in mind. Number one was exploring and innovating within materials that I was unfamiliar with. I had done a lot of experimenting with alternative materials in the past, and had found some that were successful and felt similar to ash. Second, I wanted to simulate the look of a traditional work, thinking that maybe people would walk past and assume that it's an actual ash and sweetgrass basket. I was thinking about that illusion.

With the design in my head, the first step was to form the skeletal structure. Traditionally we use a mold when weaving a basket. We weave around the mold and then remove it, and the basket then keeps that shape. Part of my process is also about gathering and harvesting scraps, in this case, trash—things that otherwise are destined for the landfill. When I was in that gathering process for this work, I found a hanging basket that a plant pot would sit in. I knew it would work well as a structural mold to get that initial shape.

The standards—the pieces that traditionally go up and down the basket—are the armature of the work, so they need to be firm and rigid to make a strong foundation. For this, I ended up using metal house siding. My uncle did siding for a living, and had a lot of scraps left over. I went to him and asked, "Hey, can I have some of this old material?" and he gladly let me take it off his hands. When listing my materials for the object label, I thought, "Oh, let's just say 'aluminum,' that'll be fine," but co-curator Siera Hyte told me, "No, you need to say house siding specifically!" More amazing, I guess. While spending time in the Southwest, I've worked with jewelers and other artists who use metal. In my studio I have metalworking tools, and I know how to finish and polish metal. All of the aluminum in this basket was perfectly sanded and polished as if it were a piece of jewelry, like something someone was going to wear. Every single piece was contoured to be exactly how it needed to be.

The weavers—the pieces that run horizontally around the vertical stakes—are laminated fabric. The bottom layer is a nylon type of fabric, and the top layer is a piece of silk that I painted to achieve the color I wanted. As with sewing, I laminated by using interfacing, ironing the pieces together. I did this to get the thickness I needed, because ash has layers. Interestingly, when you look into the inside of the basket, it's all purple because the bottom fabric I used is purple. It's a totally different pattern on the inside.

Concerning color, I didn't know how the basket would be displayed or what it would be in contrast with. The exhibition design was still a work in progress. I just knew that I wanted to work with blues, specifically turquoise; it's a color I enjoy. I also wanted the materials to reflect light, so I used metallic spray paint on the aluminum siding to give it a glowing quality. There's some shimmer and shine, almost an optical illusion.

I love a basket's geometric qualities—how it is a woven pattern, a repeating pattern (here the porcupine points are a traditional weave pattern). I always start with a smaller diameter at the bottom, then scale up to the large curvature in the widest part of the piece. That scaling also contributes to that geometric optical illusion that happens when you see the finished piece. A lot of people, I think, are amazed at the repetition. That comes with practice. When you do the same weave pattern over and over and over for long periods, you become more and more consistent in how you form it.

I wanted to both highlight the threat to the ash—that we might not always have access to it—but also think about the nature of invention and how Native people are always resourceful, utilizing what we have in creative ways. I have a strong sense of experimentation even though I also have, for the most part, a traditional kind of practice. I am always trying to reflect within my work, and I hope that this piece reflects my own personal experience, what's molded me as a person living in the contemporary world.

The embellishment at the top is made of stone, a faux turquoise, with brass wrapped around. I used jewelry techniques to make a bezel type of setting. For the rest of the cover and the handle, I played with different materials: there's a cap to a sports drink, different pieces of molded plastic, faux leather, really just whatever I wanted to mess around with. I approached it with the thought of how things would be if we didn't have our natural resources. I wanted it completely unnatural. I think people appreciate that the tradition has evolved over time, always changing and adapting.

In the exhibition as it finally took form, I was so surprised that so many people saw this basket as in conversation with the Southwestern pieces in the show. They said, "Wow, this goes so well with the other work! Did you plan for this to have some sort of Southwestern style?" And the answer is no. But I did research in order to be a part of the exhibition, and I certainly have visited the Southwest frequently, so I'm sure that my visits and absorbing everything there naturally came through when assembling this piece. So while a Southwestern theme wasn't something I was trying to call attention to, apparently it just came through in the work.

Nicolai Fechin
American, born Russia, 1881–1955
Old Mexican House, Taos, 1936
Oil on canvas. 20 × 32 in. (50.8 × 81.3 cm)
The Lunder Collection, 2013.123

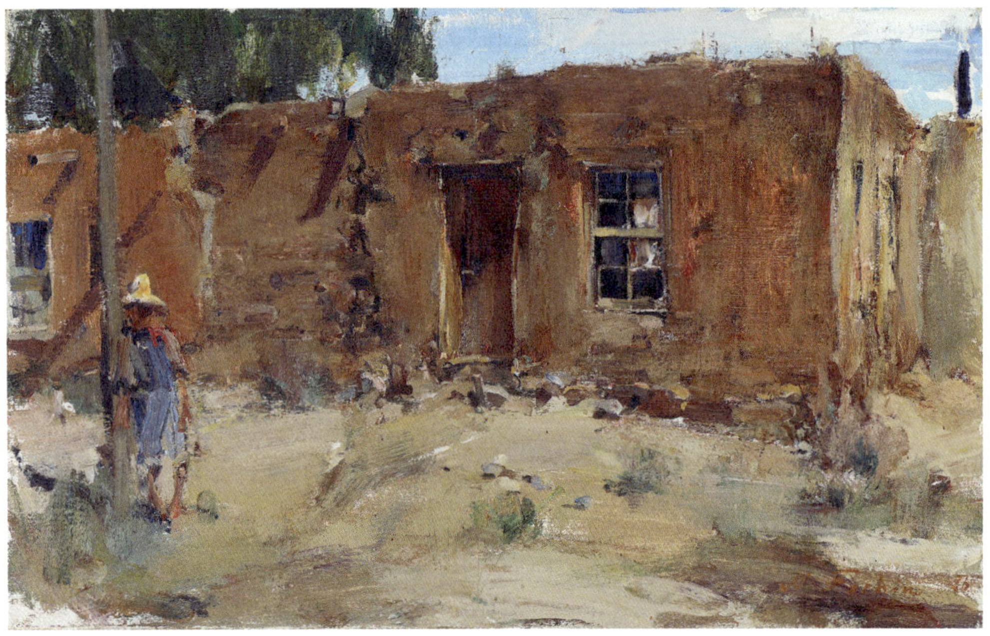

Victor Higgins
American, 1884–1949
Taos, c. 1914–15
Oil on canvas. 27 × 30 in. (68.6 × 76.2 cm)
The Lunder Collection, 2013.139

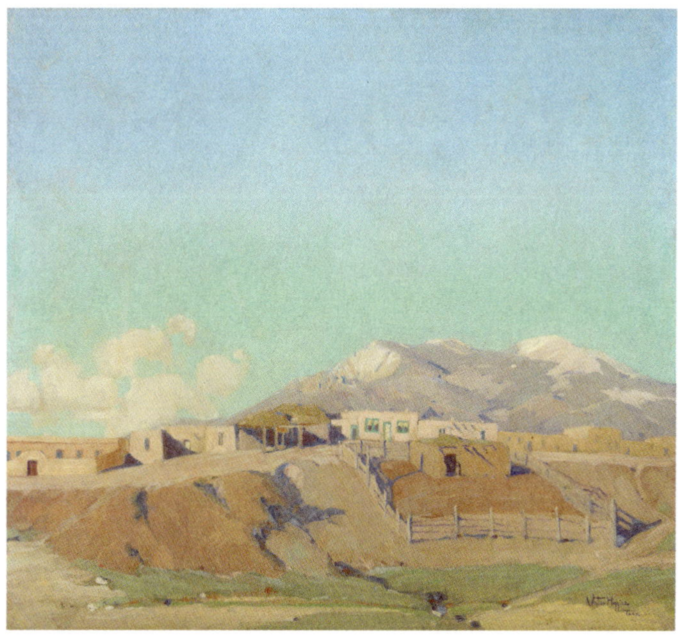

"During that period of time when that land was taken away from us, we were under the restriction of the federal government in how we would use that land. In other words, we couldn't go hunting up there any time we wanted to. So I remember during those years, when we would go hunting, we were always hiding. We were hiding because we didn't want the forest rangers or anybody to see us up there, because they would report it....The fear was always there—[that fear] of being on [our] own land and hunting on [our] own land."

This story from Gilbert Suazo, currently a Taos Pueblo war chief and governor, was told to Mozart Gabriel Abeyta during Abeyta's filming of *Through Eyes That Capture Us*, the short film that appeared in this exhibition. The land seizure he describes occurred in the years just before Victor Higgins made this painting of Taos. In 1970, Suazo testified in congressional hearings regarding the theft of Blue Lake, issuing the following statement: "Only when we once again have legal ownership of this land will we be assured of the undisturbed future of our beloved land. The United States goes out of its way to establish freedom, rights, and justice in many lands. Let her prove here and now that this is what the United States truly stands for. Let her prove that the rights of her first Americans are dealt with in a just way. We are not demanding land which is not ours. We are pleading for a land which our people have known as theirs since time immemorial. Please give us back our Blue Lake country."

Taos Indians—Blue Lake Amendments. Hearings, Ninety-First Congress, Second Session, on S. 750 and H.R. 471, July 9 and 10, 1970

Statement of Gilbert Suazo, President, Youth of Taos Pueblo

Mr. Chairman and members of the Senate Subcommittee on Indian Affairs, my name is Gilbert Suazo. I am a member of the Taos Pueblo Tribe, and I am a spokesman for the youth of Taos Pueblo.

I wish to present to you on this day a statement prepared by the youth of Taos Pueblo concerning the feelings of the young people of Taos Pueblo on our Blue Lake struggle.

Statement of the Youth of Taos Pueblo in Support of Bill H.R. 471, June 1970

We, the young people of the Taos Pueblo Tribe, deeply concerned about our Blue Lake land struggle, hereby reaffirm our support and endorsement for bill H.R. 471. We are behind our tribal council and tribal leaders in their efforts and leadership for our struggle for our Blue Lake land.

In the past years, we, the younger generation of Taos Pueblo, have been silently involved in this Blue Lake struggle with the feeling of conviction that our non-Indian brothers would understand the obvious fact that this has always been our tribal land, and that after necessary formalities, our land would be legally returned to us.

However, because of desperate attempts by opponents to block us from our land, we, the younger generation of Taos Pueblo, must speak out and let our support be publicly known and heard.

We have seen our grandfathers and fathers gallantly and tirelessly carry this struggle for our people.

We have heard and read baseless and false criticism thrown at our people by opponents; some who even question our aboriginal right to this land; some who even dare say all Indians are inept in the field of conversation.

We remind those who say that of the virgin condition the land occupied by Indians was in before foreign influence. Many of our opponents have no other interest in the land except for once-a-year recreation and money to be made from it through activities that are harmful to the land.

Our tribal leaders have been criticized that their tribe and traditional way of life is deteriorating, that their young people are not interested in the traditional way of life.

Let these people who voice these opinions look and listen—we are the young people of Taos Pueblo who will carry on our tribe; we will provide the generations of Taos Pueblo Indians; we and these generations will be using the Blue Lake country; and we want our generation to have the right and the environment to carry on the Indian way of life.

Our way of life is centered around this homeland which was founded by our forefathers, and we do not want to lose it for the sake of monetary, recreational, and plain landgrabbing interests of our opponents.

The Forest Service is contemplating their multiple-use policy for our homeland. This includes harvesting of timber, development for recreational purposes, and manipulation of plant life. This is wrong for a land which must remain as it was created.

A multiple-use policy, we believe, is designed as a compromise to satisfy timber industries, recreationalists, ranchers, and others who use national forest land for monetary purposes—that is, packers, guides, resort owners, and so forth.

With so many interests to satisfy and with the pressure applied by these groups, the Forest Service cannot indefinitely be the administrators of this land and still satisfy the first-priority needs of our people, who are the rightful owners.

We are convinced that the Department of Agriculture and its Forest Service will eventually force us to more and more compromises as to the use of this land with these other groups until we finally lose the land completely and are made to feel that it is we who are the intruders on this land.

Nature took care of itself through these thousands of years and can take care of itself if man respects it and does not manipulate it to suit his needs.

Our Taos Indian people have long believed that man should live in harmony with nature. Man should adapt himself to nature rather than forcing nature to adapt to man. Many people across this Nation are just now becoming aware of the importance of this way of thinking.

Our Taos Indian people are genuinely worried about what the future and the dangerously fast pace of development in this country will bring to land that we have occupied, and respected in its primitive condition, for centuries. Only when we once again have legal ownership of this land will we be assured of the undisturbed future of our beloved land.

The United States goes out of its way to establish freedom, rights, and justice in many lands. Let her prove here and now that this is what the United States truly stands for.

Let her prove that the rights of her first Americans are dealt with in a just way.

We are not demanding land which is not ours. We are pleading for a land which our people have known as theirs since time immemorial. Please give us back our Blue Lake country.

E. Irving Couse
William Herbert Dunton
Victor Higgins
Juan Pino
Roxanne Swentzell
Walter Ufer

Gallery 3

Walter Ufer
American, 1876–1936
The Fiddler of Taos, 1921
Oil on canvas
36 ¼ × 30 ⅜ in. (92.1 × 77.2 cm)
The Lunder Collection, 2013.278

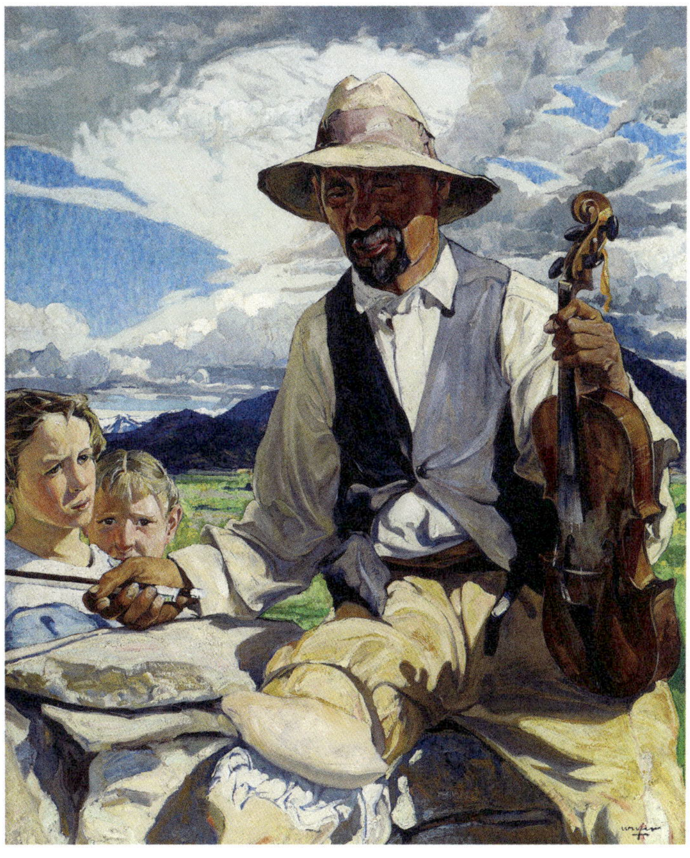

An avowed socialist, Walter Ufer often focused on the everyday routines or hardships of those he painted, reflecting his political interest in the plight of the working classes. The subject of *The Fiddler of Taos* is Don Pedro, a man who played music for the Taos community and also worked as a tailor. Pedro, who was a non-Pueblo descendant of Spanish settlers, appears in at least one other Ufer painting, which, like this one, prominently features the musician's amputated leg. In both portraits, children stand behind Pedro, intently watching his performance. This is the only TSA portrait in the Lunder Collection whose primary sitter is a non-Native person.

—Siera Hyte

Juan Pino
Tesuque Pueblo, 1896–1950
Untitled, before 1937
Woodblock prints
7 ⅞ × 10 ¼ in. (20 × 26 cm) each
Collection of the Indian Arts Research
Center, Santa Fe, New Mexico

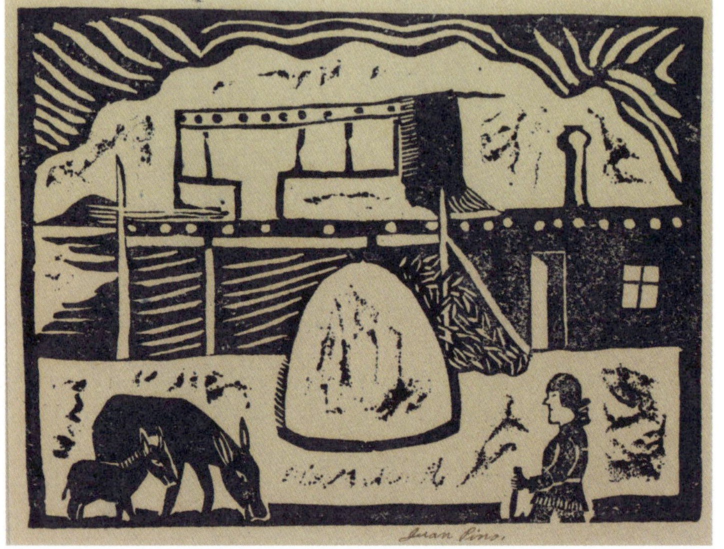

In these works, Juan Pino, a Te Tsu Geh Oweenge member, depicts the everyday and ceremonial lives of a Pueblo community from his perspective as a tribal member. Using a medium that makes his voice translatable to non-Pueblo viewers, he captures scenes that may have never been seen by outsiders. Catching and providing these glimpses into Pueblo culture highlights Pino's unique vision and artistic practice. His woodblock prints are extraordinary examples of pushing boundaries. When they were created, most Pueblo artists painted these types of images using the traditional flat techniques that Pueblo artists like Awa Tsireh (pp. 122–23) and Tonita Pena popularized in the 1920s and 1930s. Pino worked exclusively with woodblock prints and is recognized as the only Native artist to use this medium during this era.

—Juan Lucero

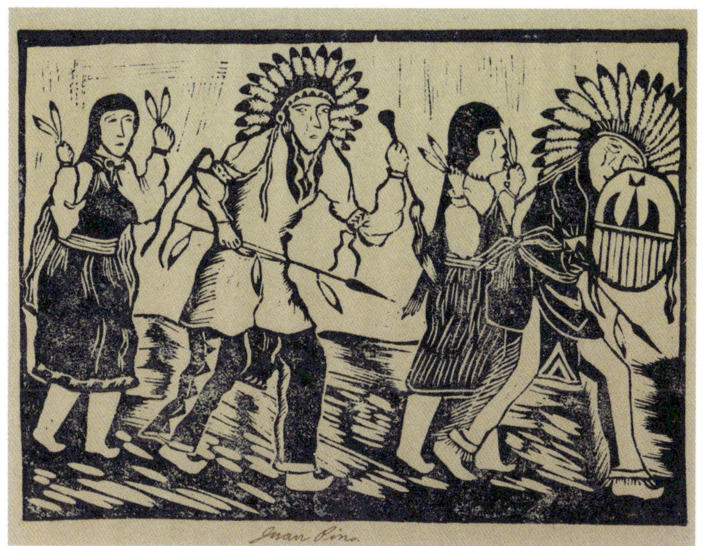
Juan Pino.

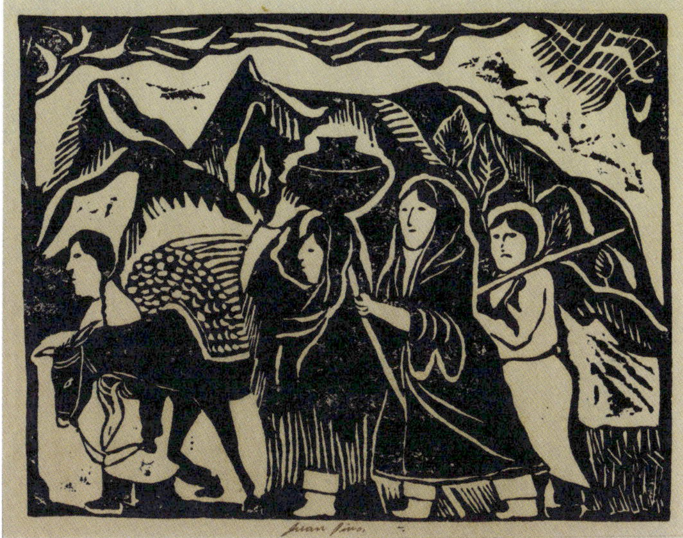
Juan Pino.

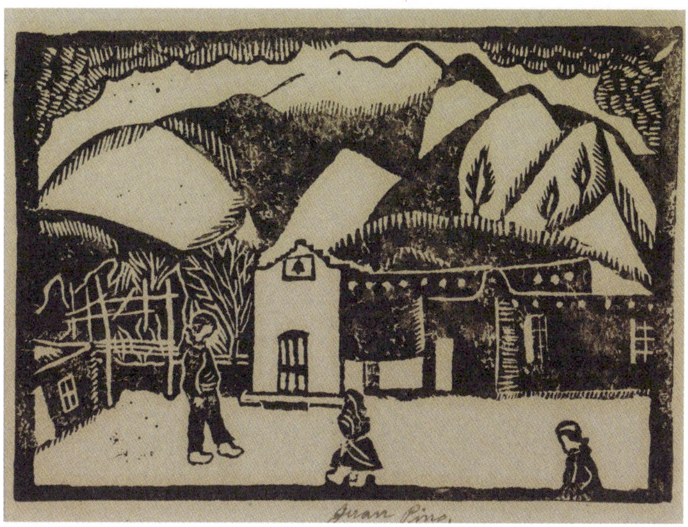
Juan Pino.

Walter Ufer
American, 1876–1936
Indian Scouts, n.d.
Oil on canvas
24 × 29 ½ in. (61 × 74.9 cm)
The Lunder Collection, 2013.277

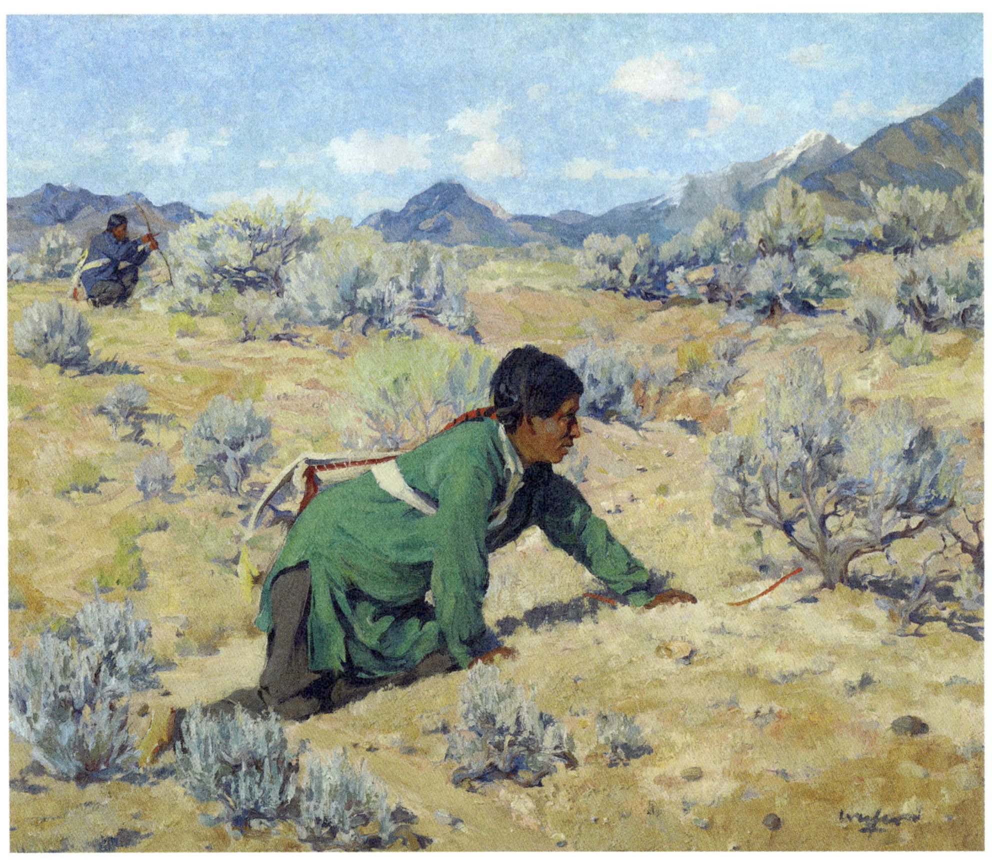

Most of Walter Ufer's paintings portray Taos Pueblo people going about everyday life outdoors—in their gardens, resting, or traveling on foot or by horseback. *Indian Scouts* depicts a man crawling on an expansive rocky surface with mountains behind. Looking closely at the background, we see another man crouching in chamisa bushes and holding a bow. The term "scouts" in the title most likely refers to scouting small animals, not people, as Ufer was committed to accurate representations of Taos Pueblo people. The period of conflict between tribes had long been over, and Pueblo people continued to practice millennia-old traditions like hunting, as did all Native people at the time.

When viewing this painting, what immediately came to mind before reading this text? What might it tell you regarding your own thinking about representations of Native peoples?

—Jill Ahlberg Yohe

How do you research someone who, outside of their painted image, has little or no presence within majority historical records or art history? Seen in the foreground of this painting is Jim Mirabal, a Taos Pueblo community member and longtime friend and model of Walter Ufer. As a curatorial intern working on this exhibition, I began the process of identifying Mirabal by investigating various historical sources. In these sources, Mirabal is consistently identified as Ufer's most frequent model and his friend of twenty years. But there is little information about Mirabal's identity independent of his work with Ufer. This is likewise the case for many other TSA models. How can museums and art historians address these gaps? And how can this archival absence be filled with perspectives and feelings that center the models and the community of Taos Pueblo?

When Mirabal worked with Ufer, the painter rarely asked him to assume specific poses or clothing. Instead, Ufer depicted Mirabal acting as himself, in his everyday attire and demeanor. According to interviews with the artist, their relationship was collaborative and built on mutual respect, but here again, I was unable to find any firsthand testaments from Mirabal about Ufer, leaving questions about Mirabal's life outside of his relationship with Ufer as yet unanswered.

—Mary Bevilacqua '23, Lunder Institute for American Art research assistant 2021–22; curatorial intern 2022–23; and Peter and Paula Lunder Colby College Museum Fellow, Couse-Sharp Historic Site 2023–24

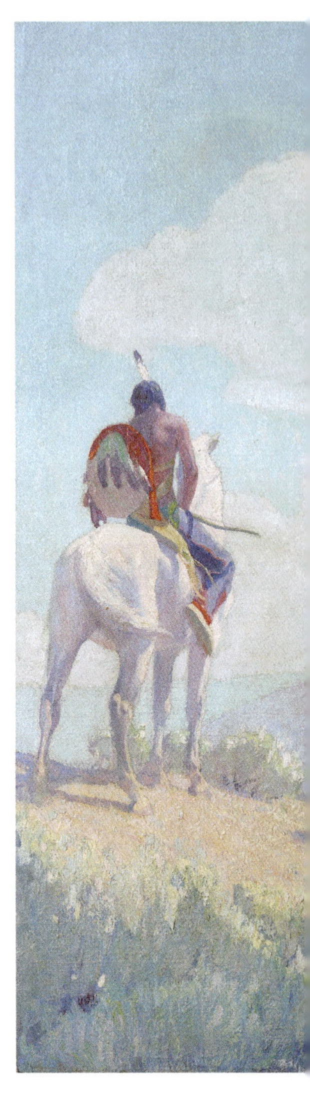

William Herbert Dunton
American, 1878–1936
Buffalo Signal, c. 1916
Oil on canvas. 34 × 51 in. (86.4 × 129.5 cm)
The Lunder Collection, 2013.115

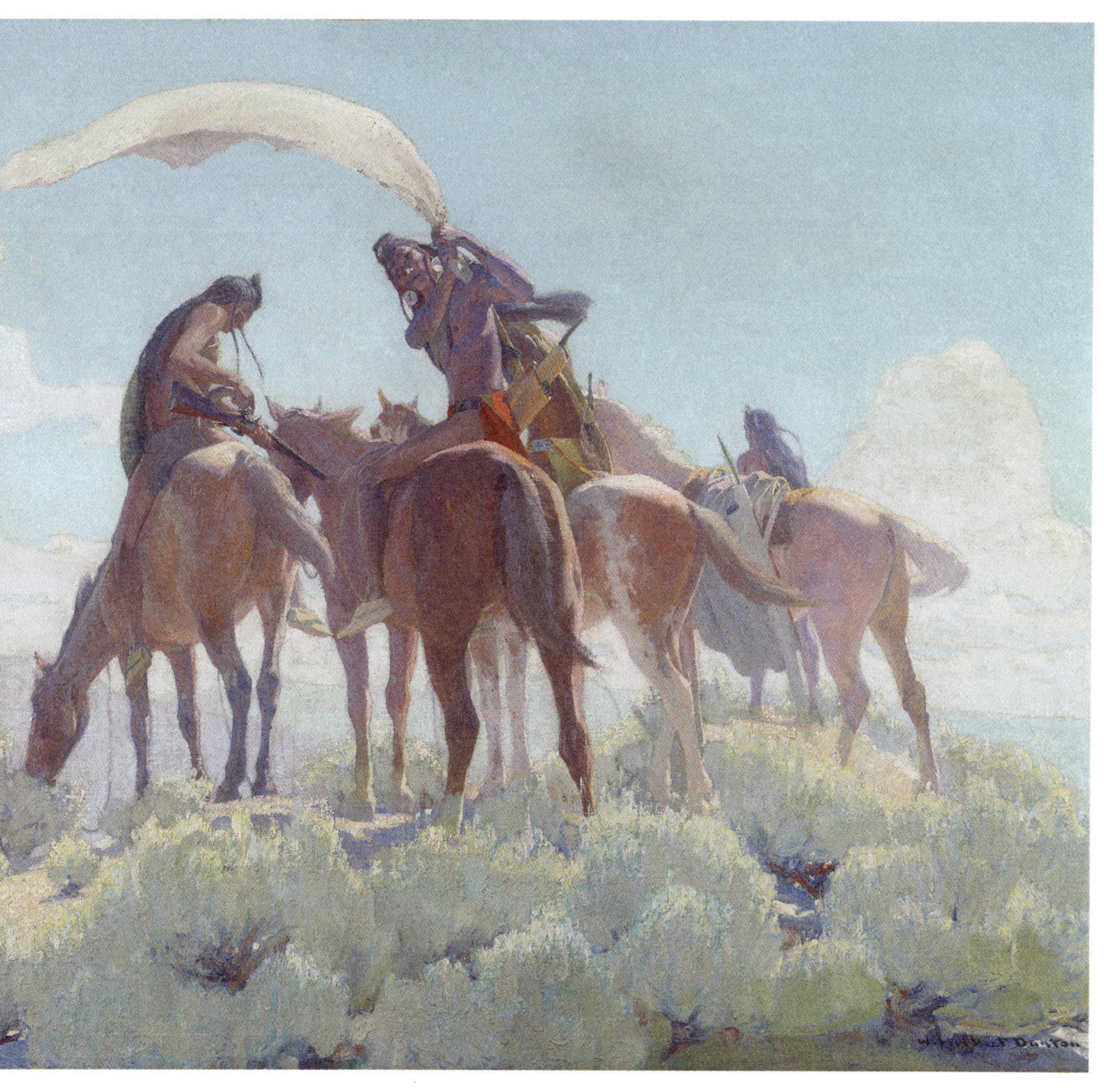

Hunting is a Pueblo practice of community betterment and empowerment. We rarely go into the wilderness without our relatives. We work together to bring food to the tables of all participating in the hunt. When one person on a journey is blessed with a bountiful harvest, we work to bring that same blessing to the rest of our party. Returning to our homes with meat is a celebration in which the entire community participates. The celebration encompasses not only the ability to feed our families, but also the life of the animal. We give thanks that they followed their journey to the hunter they were destined to meet and feed.

—Juan Lucero

Victor Higgins
American, 1884–1949
Mountain Forms III, 1924–27
Oil on canvas
24 × 27 in. (61 × 68.6 cm)
The Lunder Collection, 009.2016

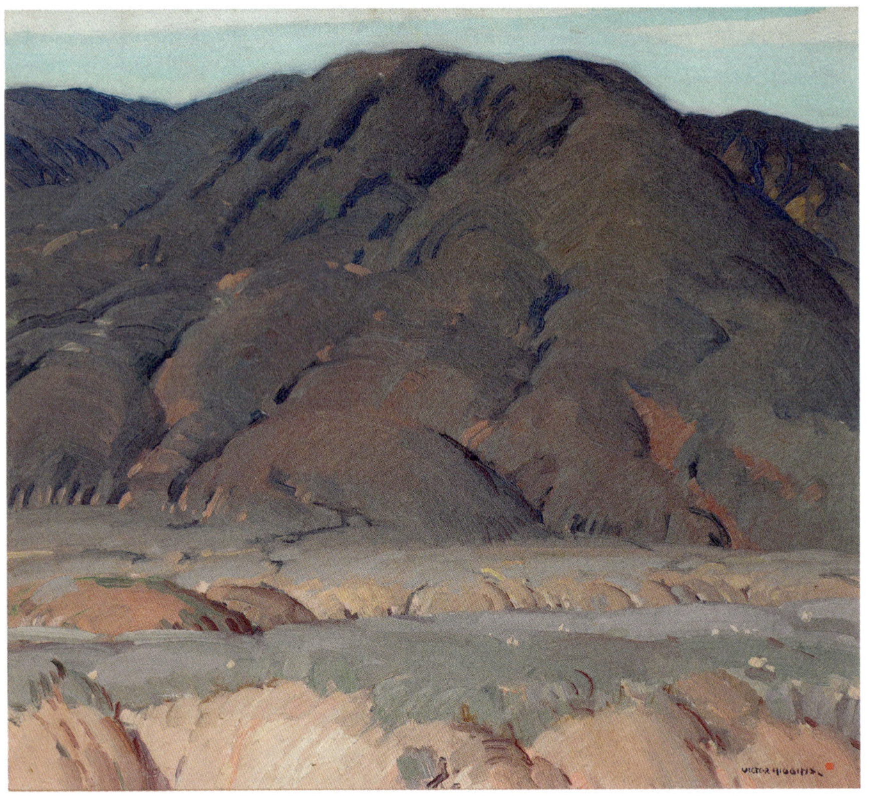

The mountain: a place of birth, a place of rest, and that which is subject to devotion. It is also a place for memories and joy. When my grandmother would take me chokecherry picking, deep in the shaded paths we would lift the bottoms of our blouses to hold the berries, staining the cotton with maroon impressions. While hauling home our treasures, she told stories of her own girlhood. When she and her friends would walk the same trails only to be met by an old brown bear, quickly they ran, as gems of red fell from their hands, rolling down the hill behind them. I would look back into that shaded path where berries grew and feel the immense power of this strange world. Falling back beside my grandmother, I knew I was safe in this place she called home.

—Margeaux Abeyta (Taos Pueblo/Diné), illustrator and designer

Right: Illustration by Margeaux Abeyta, commissioned for *Painted*, 2023

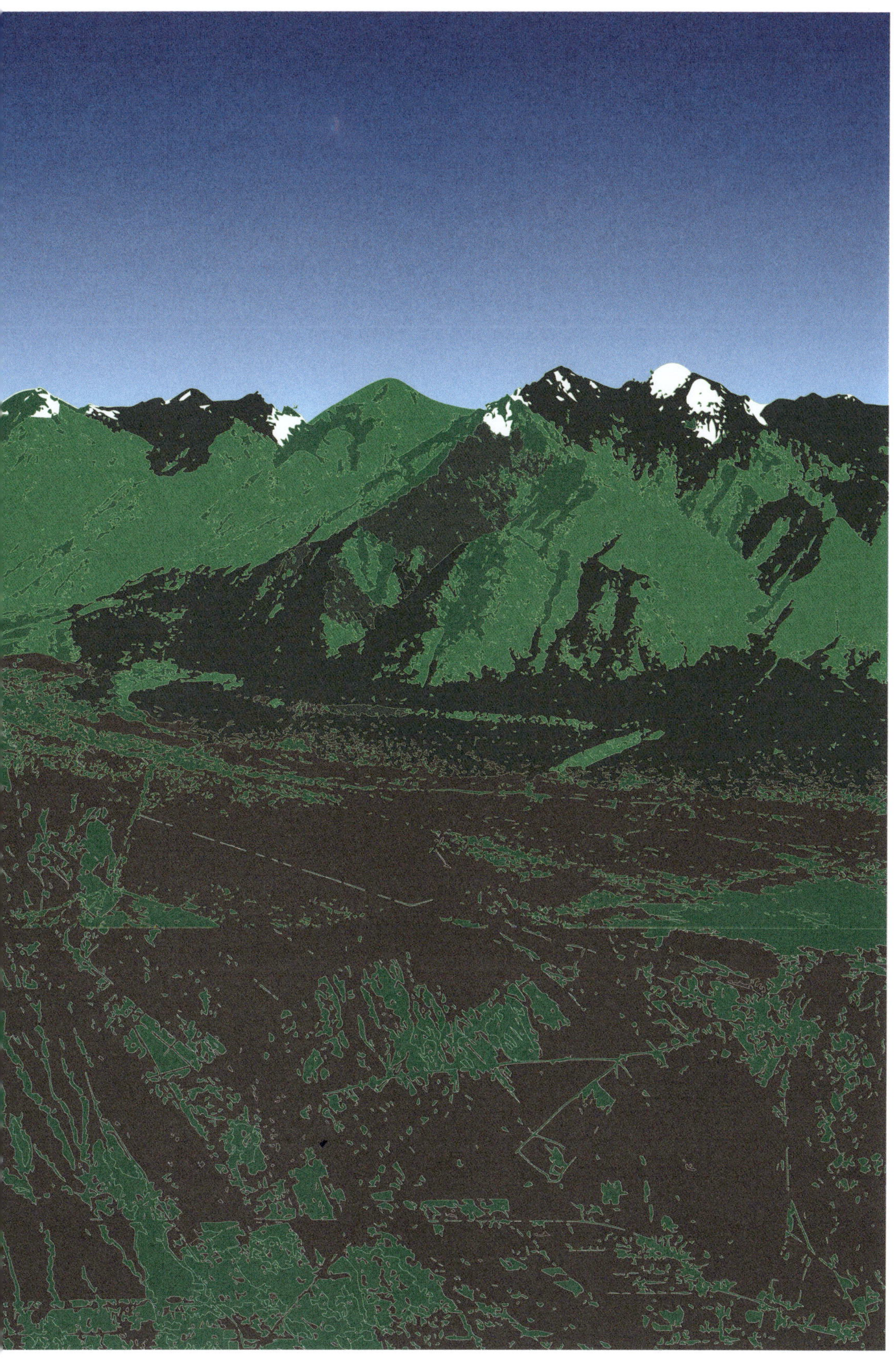

E. Irving Couse
American, 1866–1936
Flying Wedge, n.d.
Oil on canvas
29 ¼ × 24 in. (74.3 × 61 cm)
The Lunder Collection, 2013.098

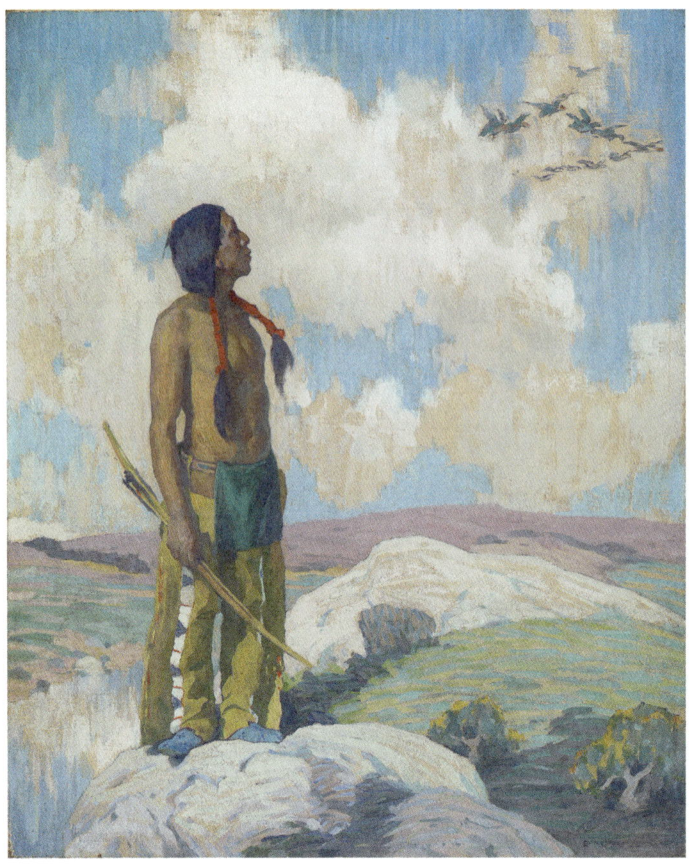

Here, Jerry Mirabal (Elkfoot), a long-standing model and friend of E. Irving Couse, wears elaborate buckskin leggings and beaded moccasins, items that would not traditionally have been worn while hunting. Couse and other TSA painters were not necessarily trying to falsely represent Taos Pueblo people; rather, they wanted to create what they believed to be more "traditional" depictions of Native American life. During and before the TSA's time period, the federal government tried to force Native people to assimilate to Anglo-American culture, disrupting Native lifeways and cultural traditions across tribes. Aware of these policies, TSA members wanted to capture what they believed to be a "vanishing race," and so they edited out signs of Anglo-American contact in their paintings.

—Alexis Kinney '22, Lunder Institute for American Art research assistant 2021–22; and Peter and Paula Lunder Colby College Museum Fellow, Couse-Sharp Historic Site 2022–23

Northern or Southern Plains artist
Leggings, c. 1900
Buckskin, glass beads, pigment, cowrie shells, tin cones, animal tail, metal thread, cotton thread
32 ½ × 16 in. (82.6 × 40.6 cm) each
Collection of the Couse-Sharp Historic Site, Taos, New Mexico

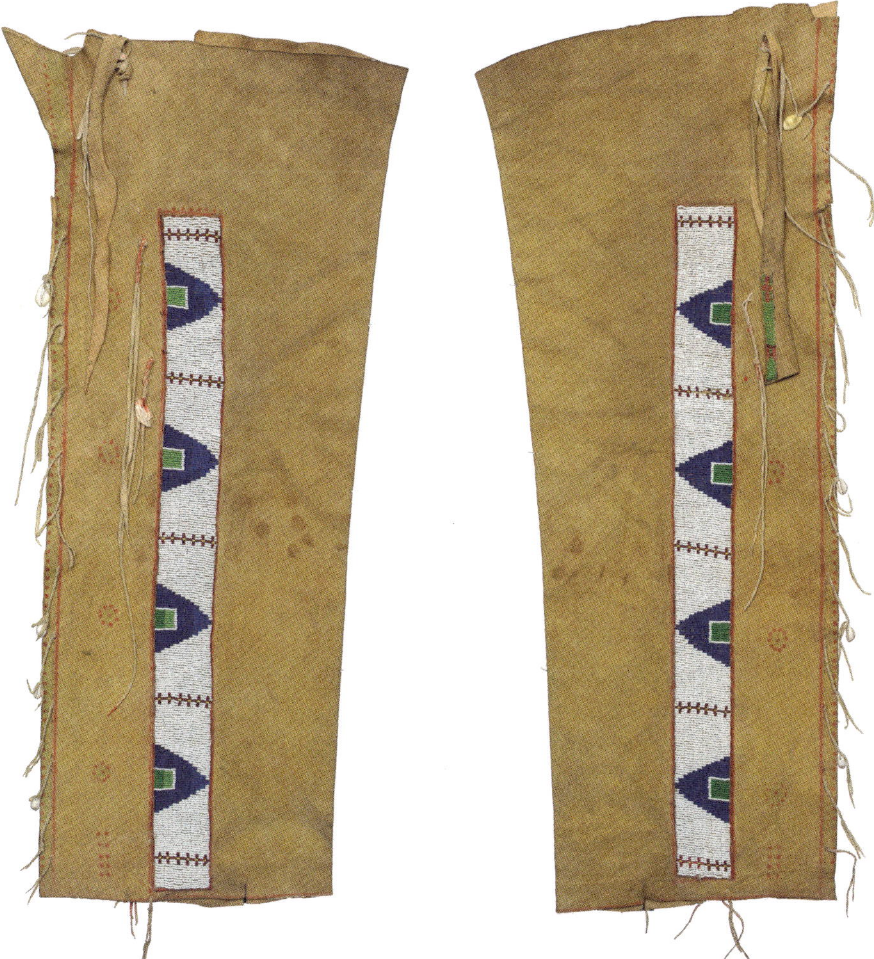

These men's buckskin leggings are typical Northern and Southern Plains regalia. The beaded strip hangs down the side of the leg; its designs are common practice because of what they signify. The blue triangles are most likely homes or lodges, which explains the green square "door" in the center of the triangle. The design was worn by men to indicate that they helped care for their home communities and perhaps had specific responsibilities for certain homes. In many ways, the design also communicates status: if a man is away from home, he is not only carrying visual representation of his home, but also signaling to others that he is honorable and holds responsibilities in his community.

—Jessa Rae Growing Thunder (Sisituwan/Wahpetuwan/Hohe), PhD, Northern Plains art historian, third-generation beadwork/quillwork artist

Victor Higgins
American, 1884–1949
The Wampum Traders, c. 1916–17
Oil on canvas
25 ⅛ × 30 ¼ in. (63.8 × 76.8 cm)
The Lunder Collection, 005.2013

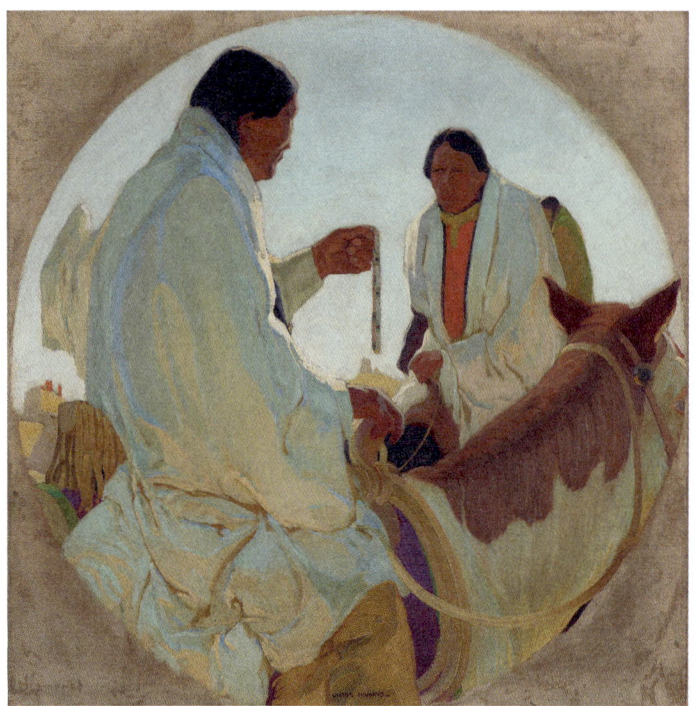

The figure in the foreground holds either a string of wampum beads or a wampum belt. Wampum beads are small cylindrical beads that were, and still are, used by Eastern Woodlands nations, including Wabanaki nations. Belts made from wampum are embedded with shared cultural meaning: their patterns record events, stories, treaties, and more. Belts aid in the telling of oral histories that illuminate complex social and political concepts for tribal members. Recognizing wampum's value to Native communities, European settlers engaged in attempts to manufacture and monetize it in exchanges with tribes. The group of traders here all wear white blankets, a garment commonly worn by Taos Pueblo men, though Pueblo people do not traditionally utilize wampum. But Taos Pueblo has been an intertribal trading site for a thousand-plus years, serving as a central gathering place along many historic travel routes. Native people from different tribes had personal, political, and trading relationships with each other long before colonial contact. Though it is likely that Victor Higgins invented this scene by overlaying elements from different Native cultures, it is possible that Taos Pueblo community members acquired or were gifted wampum through relations with other tribes.

—Siera Hyte

Roxanne Swentzell
Santa Clara Pueblo, born 1962
Indian on the Edge, 2000
Clay, parrot feathers
21 × 12 ½ × 14 in. (53.3 × 31.8 × 35.6 cm)
Museum purchase from the Robert Cross Vergobbi '51 Museum Acquisition Fund, 2024.009

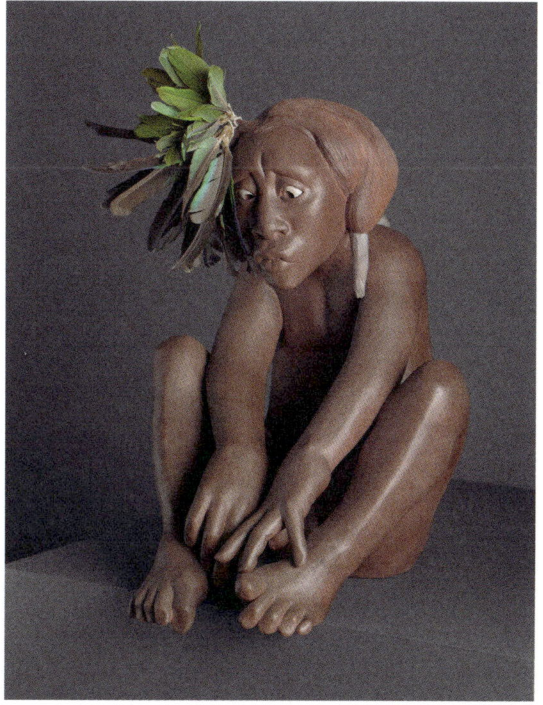

In ceremony, Pueblo people sit in prayer and contemplation. They approach everyday life as a ceremonial practice. From a parent cooking dinner, to an artist beginning their creative process, a ritual begins anytime a prayer is said. The moment a clay artist places their hands on the earth, ceremony begins. Deep within prayer, artists allow their inner vulnerabilities to communicate through their creations. Human languages limit one's ability to translate emotions, but through ceremonial design, an artist can create empathy by showing viewers exactly how they feel, without words. Roxanne Swentzell is a contemporary clay artist from Kah'p'oo Owinge who comes from a long line of celebrated clay artists. From an early age she used her work to communicate emotions she could not convey otherwise. With *Indian on the Edge*, we see a figure in a state of prayer or reflection. When encountered in the gallery, he is balanced precariously, his vulnerable position creating a sense of viewer encroachment on a moment of unguarded interiority. Swentzell's clay figures often upend representations of Native people created by non-Native people, telling her own stories. Her work is a powerful tool in the re-matriation process for Pueblo culture.

—Juan Lucero

Ernest L. Blumenschein
E. Irving Couse
Jessa Rae Growing Thunder
Ernest Martin Hennings
Seferina Herrera
Bert Geer Phillips
William Robinson Leigh
Diego Romero
Joseph Henry Sharp
Awa Tsireh

Gallery 4

Whose Story?

Within the exhibition, the curatorial team filled one gallery in particular with paintings of Pueblo people made in the first quarter of the twentieth century. The space featured large portraits of Taos Pueblo individuals, primarily Ben Lujan and Jerry Mirabal, two models who worked closely with the TSA. Visitors were invited to absorb and ponder these works of art, perhaps looking for deeper meanings, matters of representation, and the intentions of the artists.

Who tells the story of these paintings? In the first half of the twentieth century, an art historian or a curator might have suggested that the TSA paintings depict an American story, one unique to this continent, and are therefore a primary source in the creation of an American art history. He (nearly all art historians in the early twentieth century were white and male) might describe the "authenticity" of the artworks, or the beauty and "simplicity" of life they evoke, as a counterpoint to the "progress" and industrialization of the time. He would likely not consider the work of Awa Tsireh, a Pueblo painter contemporaneous with the TSA, as art with a capital *A*, nor would he situate Tsireh's work in conversation with the TSA paintings. But this would miss an opportunity to appreciate intricate and accurate renderings of Pueblo people by a Pueblo artist.

In the latter half of the twentieth century and into the twenty-first, an art historian might delve into the subjugation of the sitters, or inaccuracies in the clothing and regalia (for instance, beadwork and bonnets that are Plains material, not Taos Pueblo adornments), or the "inauthenticity" and "invented-ness" of the scenarios TSA painters produced. But as we will see, this would again be inaccurate, given that Taos was an epicenter for trade with Plains people.

Taos Pueblo people have rarely if ever been asked to tell their own stories, their thoughts and feelings, about these representations of community members. Art history has thus far silenced their perspectives, instead speaking for and about the people pictured. A Taos Pueblo advisor for this project shared with us that "we as Taos people are capable of providing our own story." And indeed, our advisors shared many stories of strong connections with the people in the artworks. They described the accuracies and inaccuracies, and offered glimpses into a millennia-old place for artistic production and exchange. They expressed their responsibility for sharing their perspectives within galleries depicting Taos people.

—Jill Ahlberg Yohe

William Robinson Leigh
American, 1866–1955
Zuni Pottery Maker, 1907
Oil on canvas
25 × 30 ¼ in. (63.5 × 76.8 cm)
The Lunder Collection, 2013.188

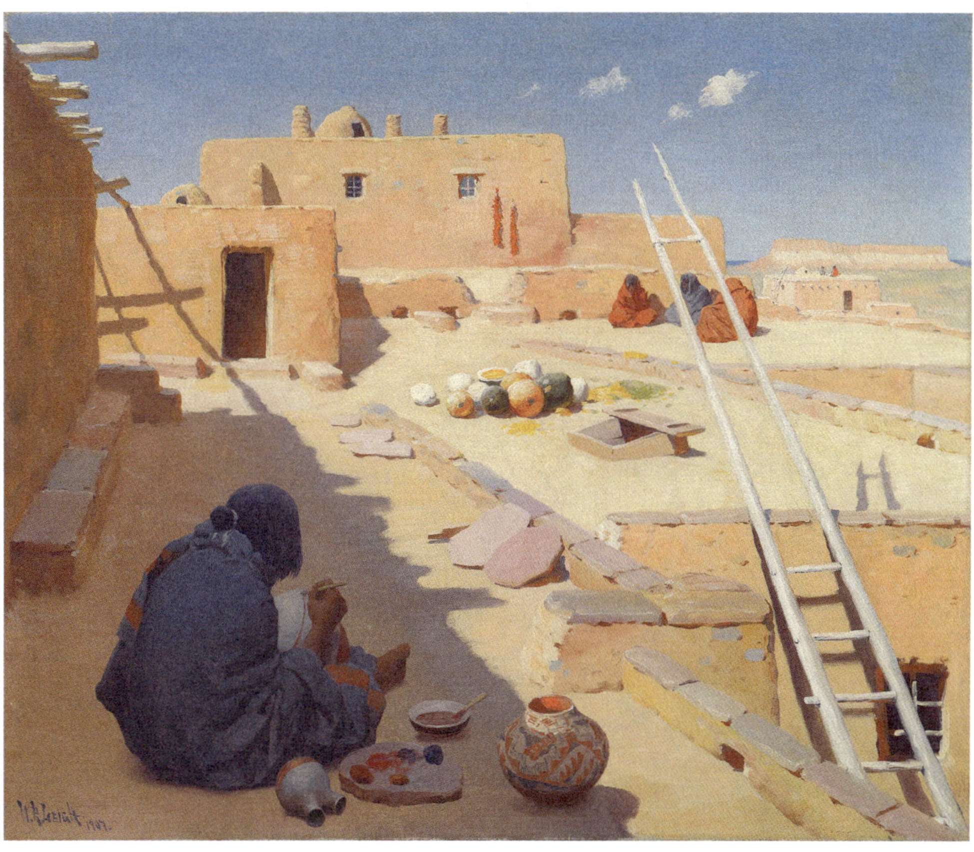

One of the greatest contributions art brings to the world is the ability for all viewers to look at a painting such as William Robinson Leigh's *Zuni Pottery Maker* and absorb, think, and feel for themselves. The foreground features warm-toned pueblos and individuals wrapped in blankets painting pottery, with a group of people gathered in the background and a crisp blue sky behind. Viewing this painting for the first time, my eyes seek place, orientation, and meaning. I stare at the mesa in the distance, and then I focus on the pottery vessel. It is a beautifully sculpted and painted pot made in Acoma, nearly one hundred miles from Zuni Pueblo. Yet the title is *Zuni Pottery Maker*. Do I critique the artist for inaccuracies, even dismiss the painting as "wrong"? Do I look for other cultural elements Leigh incorporates, like the bread ovens in the distance? Or do I turn my attention to the feelings evoked—fond memories, warm sunshine, vast skies, and the knowledge that Pueblo people will forever be present and thriving in our world? I think and feel all of these.

—Jill Ahlberg Yohe

E. Irving Couse
American, 1866–1936
Sacred Birds, 1910
Oil on canvas
46 ½ × 35 ½ in. (118.1 × 90.2 cm)
The Lunder Collection, 2013.100

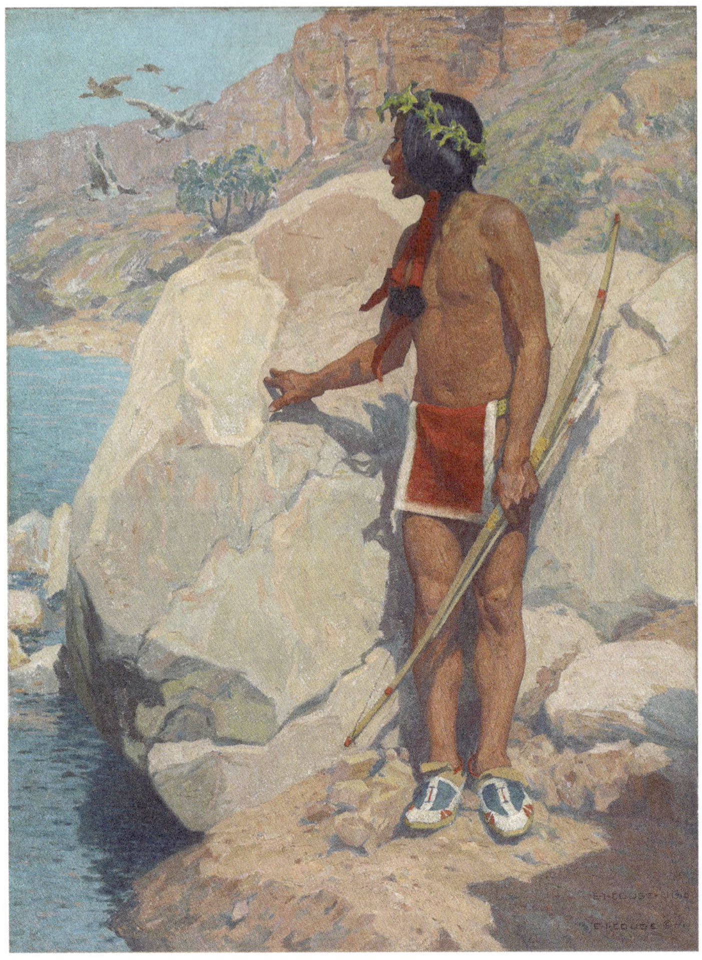

In *Sacred Birds*, Jerry Mirabal (Elkfoot), a Taos Pueblo model who posed for many of E. Irving Couse's paintings, is pictured with clothing and props from the artist's studio. Couse made frequent use of photography as an efficient tool for creating compositions that he would then transfer to canvas using the grid method (unintentional traces of this technique are visible in the even spacing of the painting's vertical lines). Couse stitched together images of Mirabal in his studio with photographs he took of the Rio Grande Gorge to create this imaginative hunting scene.

—Caroline Jean Fernald, executive director of the Phoebe A. Hearst Museum of Anthropology, and Lunder Institute for American Art research fellow 2021–22

Arapaho artist
Moccasins, c. 1900
Buckskin, glass beads, sinew thread
4 × 3 ½ × 10 ¼ in. (10.2 × 8.9 × 26 cm) each
Collection of the Couse–Sharp Historic Site, Taos, New Mexico

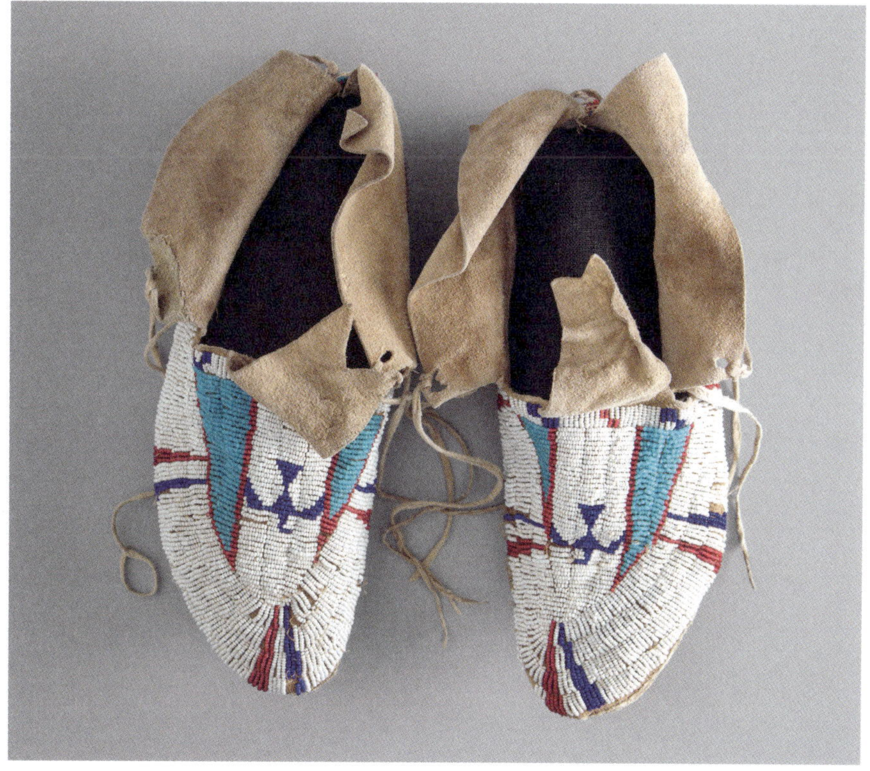

Beaded thunderbird motifs are common throughout Cheyenne and Arapaho territory, making this pair of moccasins, which are beaded with this marker, classic examples of the region. A beaded white background for the border allows for a strategic use of reds and blues to highlight the design components. In this case, the red and blue elongated triangles draw attention to the thunderbird. The stitching technique used is called hump-stitch and requires one needle and thread. A beadworker must have excellent math and design skills (counting beads and determining their reach before they are stitched) to execute a pair of moccasins in this style because the border typically takes up the most space, and it must remain even and consistent across the two moccasins in the pair.

—Jessa Rae Growing Thunder (Sisituwan/Wahpetuwan/Hohe), PhD, Northern Plains art historian, third-generation beadwork/quillwork artist

Arapaho artist
Moccasins, c. 1890
Buckskin, glass beads, sinew thread
4 × 3 ¾ × 10 ½ in. (10.2 × 9.5 × 26.7 cm)
Collection of the Couse–Sharp Historic Site, Taos, New Mexico

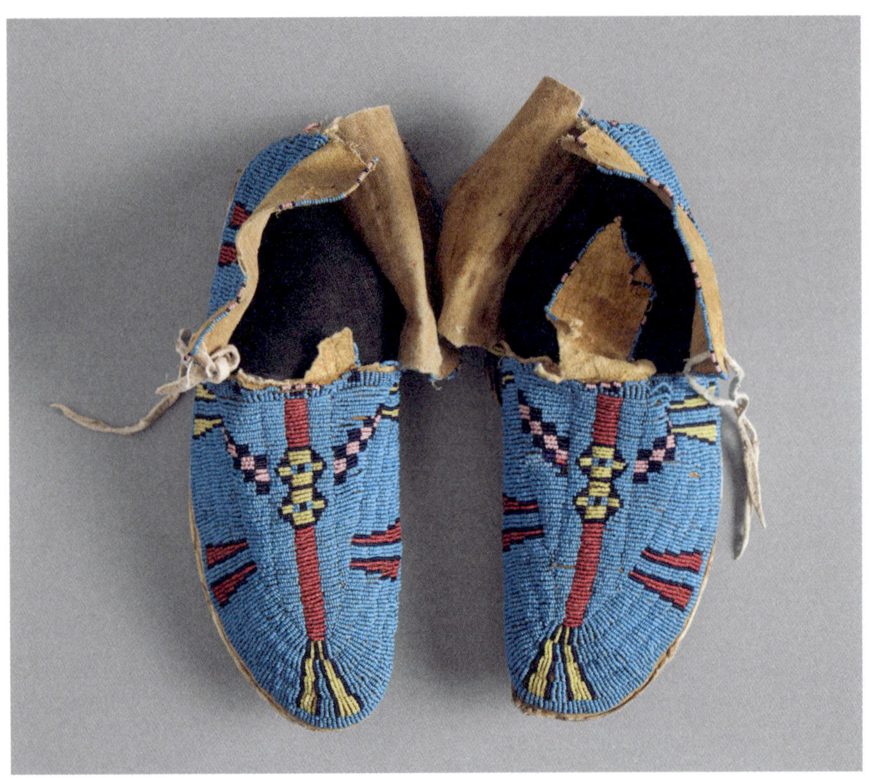

Arapaho beadworkers are brilliant color theorists, and the blue moccasins presented here are a prime example of those skills. The vibrant background color of a greasy pony-trader blue necessitates other color choices that complement and contrast its boldness. An added layer of strategy is how the beadworker outlined the red, yellow, and pink designs in navy blue—a brief separation between background and design. This strategy helps guarantee that colors with similar tones don't blend together. Masterful beadworkers are always thinking about how colors work in close-up as well as distant views. As viewers, observing beadwork from several steps back helps us think about color theory in this medium. What color draws your eye first? What other colors stand out? In what ways does color separate design components?

—Jessa Rae Growing Thunder (Sisituwan/Wahpetuwan/Hohe), PhD, Northern Plains art historian, third-generation beadwork/quillwork artist

E. Irving Couse
American, 1866–1936
Indian Weaver, c. 1933–34
Oil on canvas
24 × 29 in. (61 × 73.7 cm)
The Lunder Collection, 2013.099

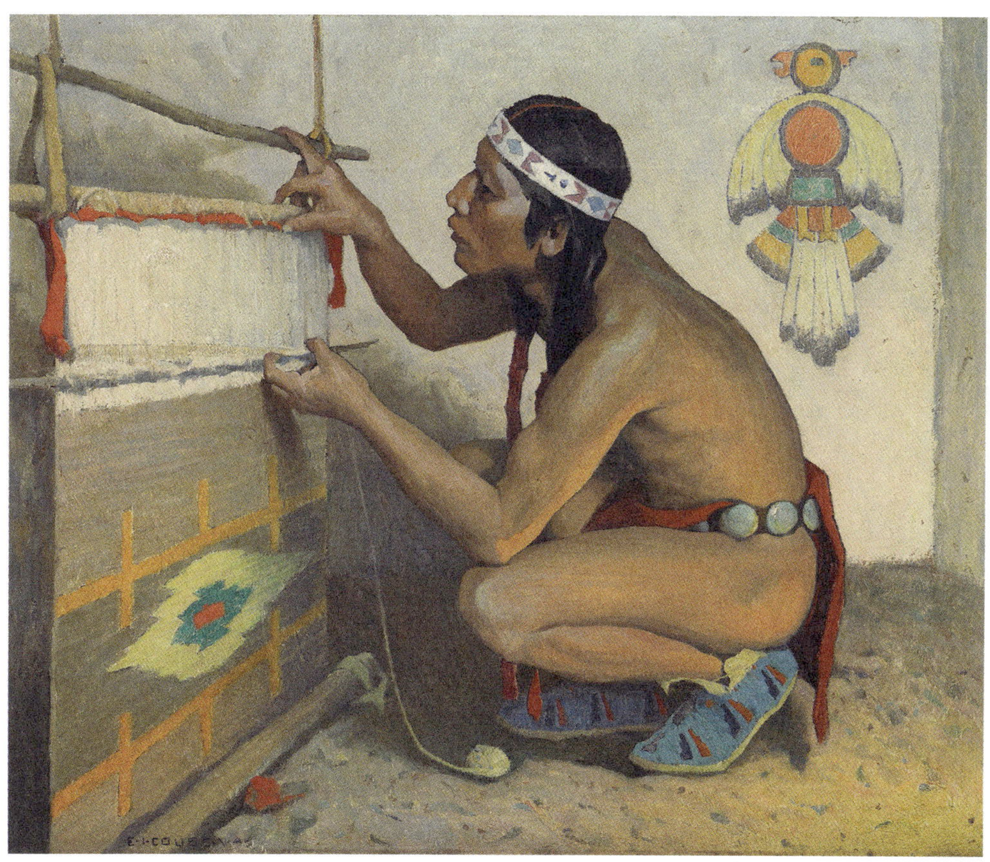

Not long after his first sojourn to Taos in 1902, E. Irving Couse took up the subject of the Indigenous weaver and painted numerous versions over the next thirty years. He regularly worked with models from Taos Pueblo, including Jerry Mirabal (Elkfoot), featured here. Mirabal played a crucial role in Couse's compositions, many of which present romanticized versions of a seemingly timeless pan-Indigenous culture. This tension between Indigenous agency and objectification speaks to the complexities of early-twentieth-century Taos, which was marked by economic imbalance and opportunity, cultural respect and appropriation, and interracial relationships.

—J. R. Henneman, director and curator of the Petrie Institute of Western American Art, Denver Art Museum

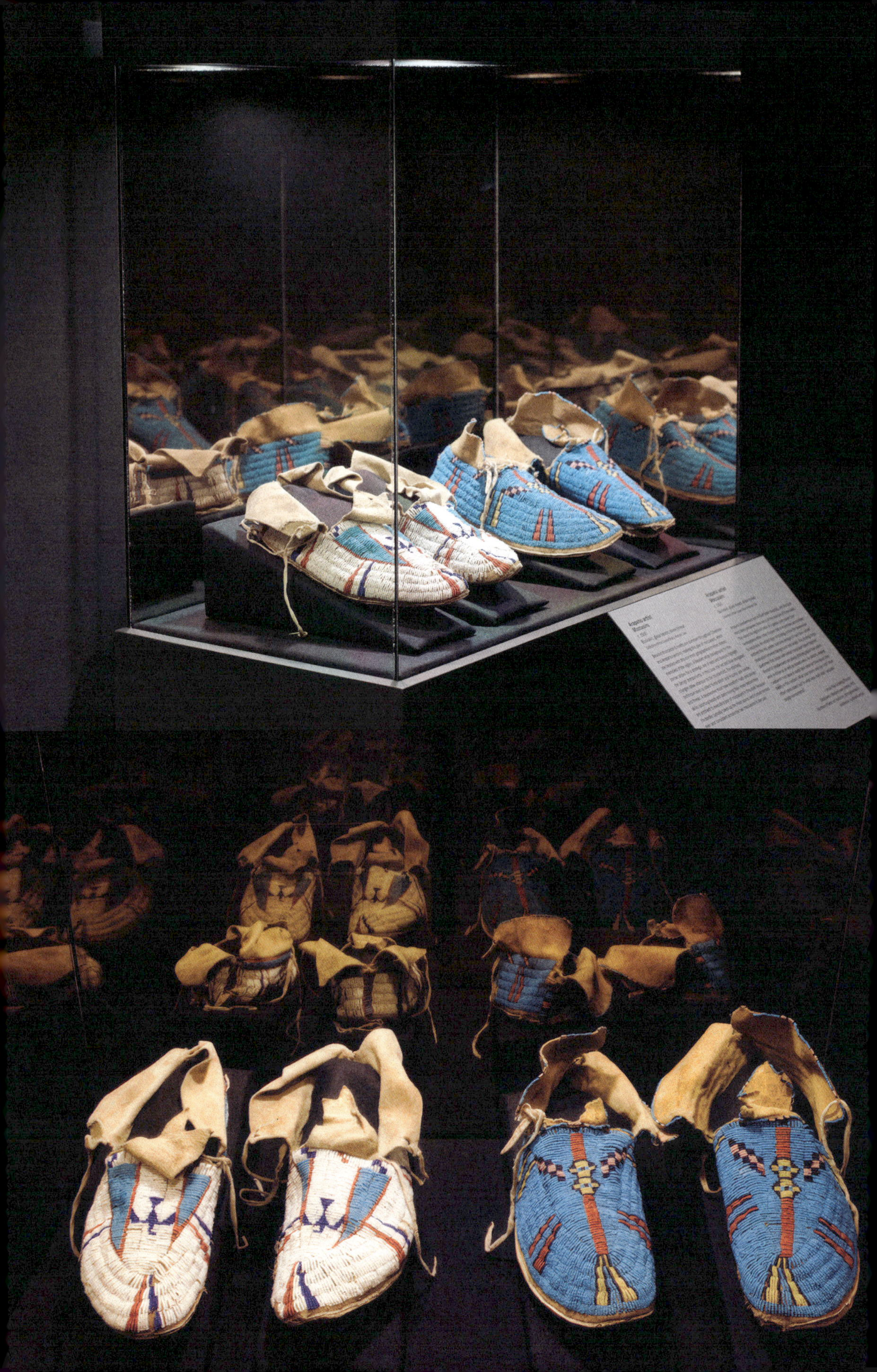

Jessa Rae Growing Thunder
Sisituwan/Wahpetuwan/Hohe, born 1989
Assiniboine (Nakoda) Pipe Bag, 2022
Smoked brain-tanned buckskin, antique seed beads, wool, brass bells, brass beads
27 ½ × 5 ½ in. (69.9 × 14 cm)
Museum purchase from the Jere Abbott Acquisitions Fund, 2022.068

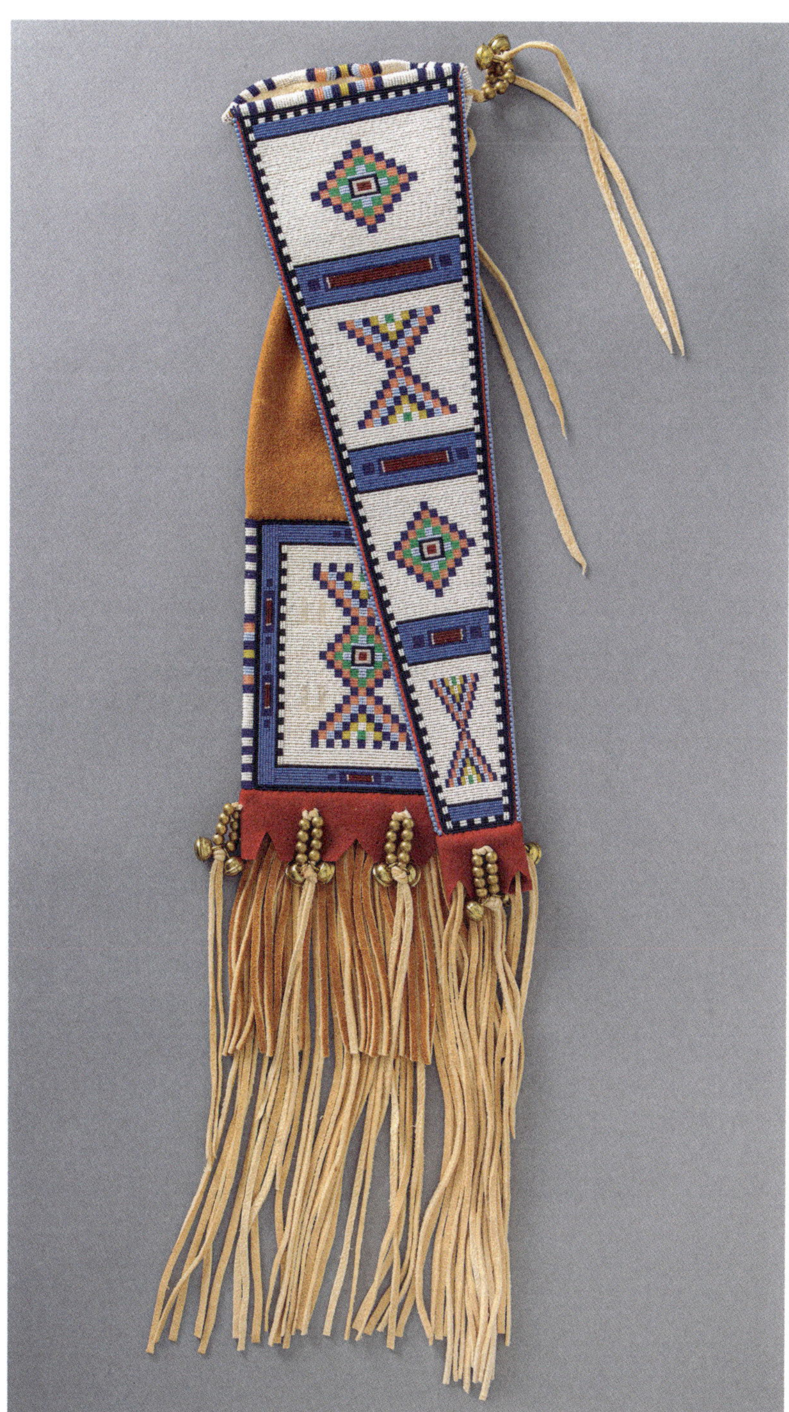

Jessa Rae Growing Thunder
From the artist's talk at the Painted *symposium, November 2023*

Good day, to all my relations, how are we doing? Museum spaces, gallery spaces, are usually a very quiet experience, but I'm personally always trying to communicate a feeling of, "Let's talk, let's vibe, let's visit, let's share." That's what these spaces are for—to learn and engage. So I want you all to take a deep breath with me. I ask that you bring only good energy into this group. Good feelings, good intentions. We all have different experiences. We all bring such good experiences and perspectives into these spaces and into *Painted: Our Bodies, Hearts, and Village*.

I'm going to speak from my truth and my experience. I come from the Buffalo Nation. I am Sisituwan/Wahpetuwan/Hohe, and I come from the far northeast corner of Montana. We sit right on the border of Canada and North Dakota. I'm a Northern girl, and occasionally that comes out; bear with me if it does. I am a wife, I am a mother, I'm an aunt, I'm a sister, I'm a daughter, and I'm a granddaughter. I am a third-generation artist. And I say "third generation" with the understanding that I have learned from the hands of my mother and the hands of my grandmother. But of course, my grandmother learned from her grandmothers, who learned from their grandmothers, and their grandmothers before them. So even though I am the one who made the decisions here, I carry the truth, the honor, the respect, and the love of all of my *uncis* and all of my grandmothers. That is how I was raised and that is how I navigate through this world. I also hold a master's and a doctorate from UC Davis—this is my life's work, y'all. This is it, the heart-work. It's been a true honor working with this show, with Colby. It's been a real honor and a privilege to be part of this experience.

Now that you all have taken a deep breath and are bringing only good intentions and energy into this room, I want you all to look around. Everything on the walls and in the cases—these are all relatives to me and all the other artists who are here with us. And to those who cannot be here with us, these represent relationships and living beings. My grandpa was a fine-art painter in the Western style. So I have a little bit of history, a little bit of background and experience with the style of the TSA paintings. I love experiencing works like this because we all know that the models were posed. But the thing that I bring to the table, what I look at, is the other relatives in the paintings, namely the moccasins, the beadwork on the belts, the leggings.

All are relatives who are also being represented. And so for me, giving them the honor of inclusion in this exhibition and working with these amazing people across these many different spaces gives a little bit of perspective and a little bit of agency to the work represented—that makes me feel good. It means that they're loved and they're respected enough that they have been sustained throughout all of the changes.

I want to give a warm, warm thank you to this amazing team for allowing me to do that and to have a little bit of voice because, like I said, my voice is not much my voice. I carry the voice of my *uncis* and *unkanas* and all of my *tiwahe*, all of my grandmas. So I thank you for that. It is an honor that my work is on this wall with so many amazing other artists and histories and experiences presented in the show. This piece is actually one of my favorites that I've ever created.

I'm a mom. I have two beautiful little girls who are three years old, and I've grown up with this practice and this way of life. My mom and my grandma, they are living artists, they bead every single day. They wake up at three in the morning and bead continuously until about four or five in the afternoon, then they have dinner and go to sleep by seven. This is the life they live every day. They don't take vacations, they don't take breaks. If they travel, they travel with suitcases full of beads, I kid you not. This is the life I grew up with.

When I was six years old—and I talk about this a lot, because it was a pivotal moment in my story—I went to my friend Kayla's house. I understood that I was Native, and Kayla was not. But for the life of me, I could not understand why her mom didn't bead. I could not get my head around it! I went home and asked my mom, "Why are you beading every day? Why can't you have a normal job?" I remember this very vividly. This is the moment, right? This is the moment in my movie that set the tone for everything that followed. She explained to me, "We pick up our needle and our thread every day so that your grandchildren and their grandchildren—whether they pick up a needle and thread, whether they dance, or sing, or pray, whatever it is—those little actions guarantee that they survive. That is our responsibility in this life." I picked up my first needle and thread at three years old and I have never put it down. My daughter Nuna actually picked up her first needle when she was two. Which is good—you all want that for your kids.

I've been beading my entire life. As a young person, as a bead worker and quill worker, I thought to myself: "I'm going to make a name for myself, y'all. I'm going to stand out." I mean my grandma, she is a legacy and a master. And as a young person, I was like, "I'm going to create my own path, I'm going to push the limits." And then I became a mother, and something shifted in me. All the moms in the room can understand this, and I'm sure all the fathers as well. The way I work with my materials and the way I gauge my color palette and aesthetics all changed. All of a sudden, my practice felt like home. It was a thing with my work that I had never previously experienced. I began to see my mom and my grandma in my work, and feel how they influenced me.

This piece right here represents one of those moments. It started as an entirely different piece. I laid it out, I started stitching, and as I was beading, it was effortless, it was easy, nothing fought with me, nothing challenged me. As I was stitching, I realized it wasn't doing what I wanted it to do, but I had to trust it. And in the end it was an entirely different piece. It was still a bag, but instead of a contemporary exploration of color, it takes a historical approach to our pipe bags.

This is a rare, rare style, it is Nakoda, it is Assiniboine. There's not many historical pieces related to the Assiniboine people in institutions or in private collections anymore in great part because the Assiniboine, the Nakoda, endured three smallpox epidemics. We were once one of the largest peoples in the Northern Plains, at one time expanding from Wyoming and Montana up into Canada. But because of the smallpox epidemics—you have to consider that they didn't know how to eradicate smallpox, they didn't know how to protect people—they were not only burning and burying bodies, but also doing that to all their clothing and accoutrements.

Because of this there are incredibly few Nakoda/Assiniboine pieces out there in the world. So if you find one, take advantage of it, really truly visit with it. The style I rarely come across, not a lot of people are familiar with it. My grandma did only about two of this style of bag in her long, long career. When this bag decided to be this style, oh, I was excited. And then I stepped back and realized: my grandmother is all over this, she's present in all of it. Not only the construction of it, but the boldness of the red wool against those brass beads. See the two details there? I wanted that boldness of the red wool. I felt in tune. I was thrilled when I got to pull it out and show it to her for the first time. That's one of my favorite things to do: show her a piece that I haven't told her about, that she hasn't seen me work on. That's when I know if I get the stamp of approval. To this one, she gave an "Oh!" So it's a special piece to me. And I could not be more thrilled and happy that it is here, at Colby, because I know that it's going to be cared for, that it's going to continue to share a story, continue to share feelings and experiences.

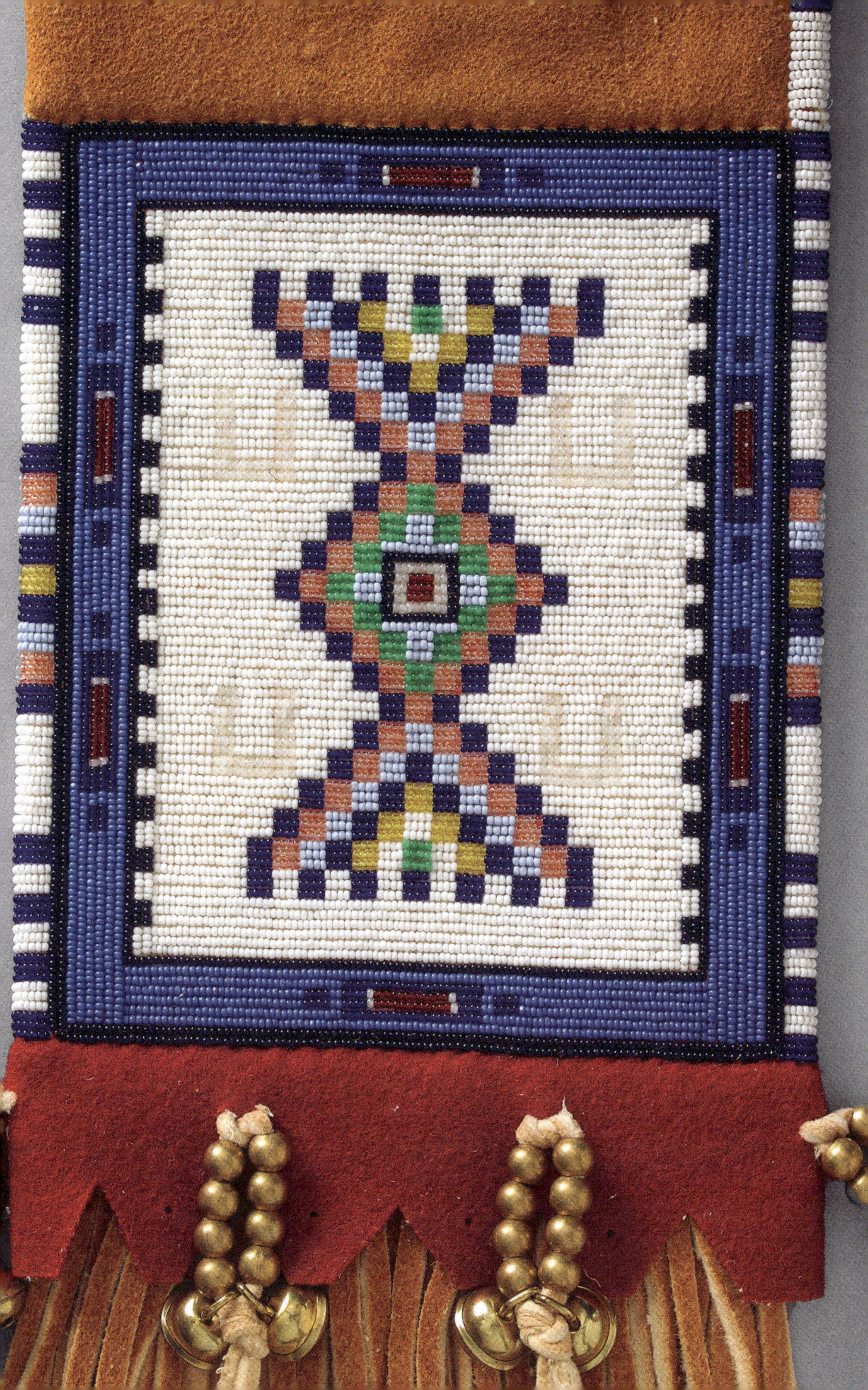

Joseph Henry Sharp
American, 1859–1953
Jerry Elkfoot, n.d.
Oil on canvas
24 × 20 in. (61 × 50.8 cm)
The Lunder Collection, 2013.261

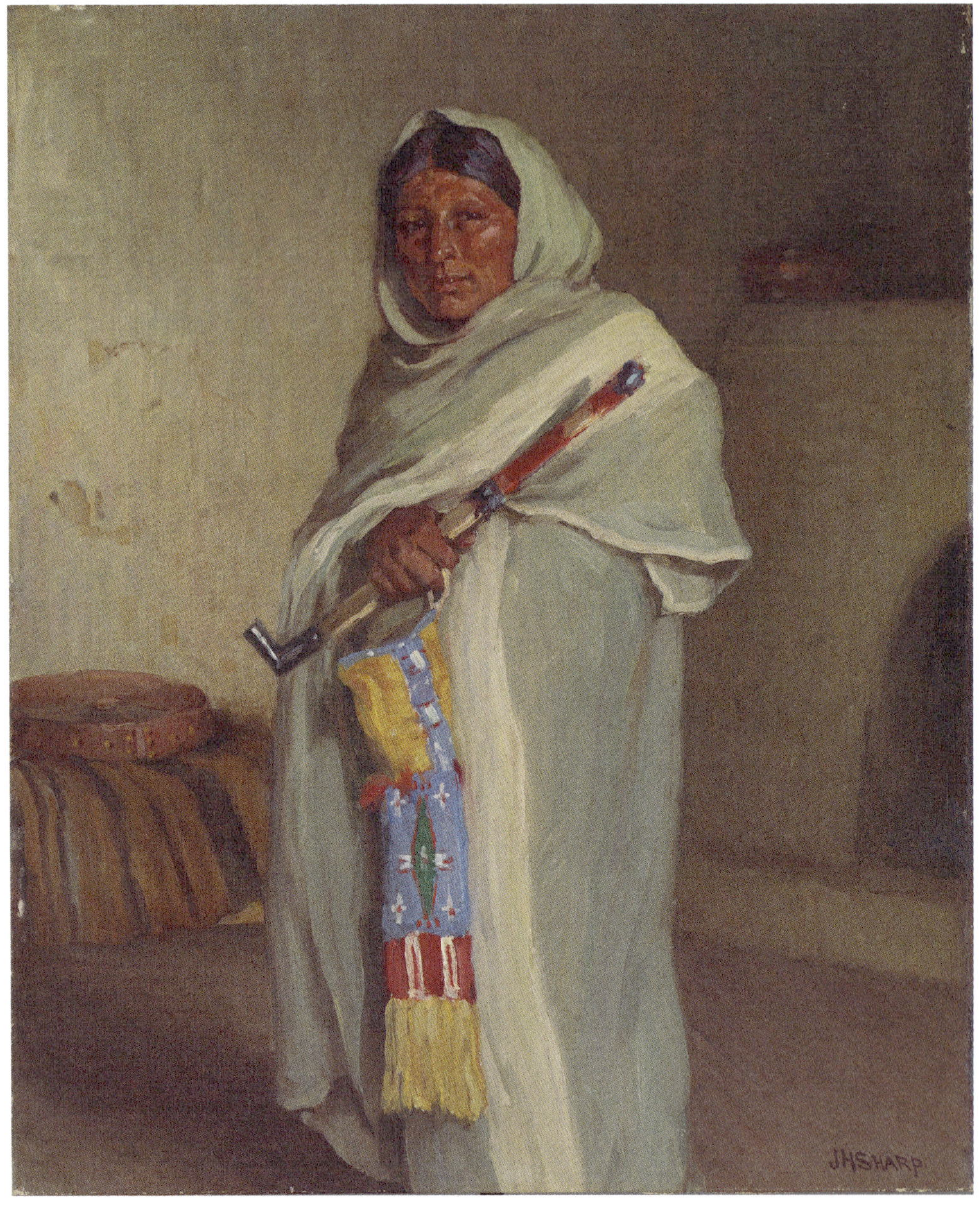

The following quote by Joseph Sharp, one of the TSA's cofounders, may be upsetting for Native readers. But our curatorial team and advisory council collectively agreed that it provides important first-person context on societal attitudes toward Native people during the TSA's historical moment. The repugnant belief that Anglo-Americans were morally and intellectually superior to Native people, widely held in Sharp's time, was used to justify violence against Native people and continues to cause harm to Native communities to this day. Our curatorial team chooses to read agency and Native resistance between the lines of Sharp's description of his sitters. The models Sharp refers to stood tall, comfortable in their own stillness, and, after working with Sharp for a few sessions, decided of their own accord to refuse further contact with the artist.

—Juan Lucero, Siera Hyte, and Jill Ahlberg Yohe

"As a model the Indian is not a great success. After various tribulations to get him to pose, it is impossible to make him unbend. If it is his first attempt he will invariably take [a] pose of majestic and often ludicrous stiffness. Having used much persuasion, time and patience in breaking one in, he soon becomes indifferent, often gets too familiar, goes on strike for more pay, or stays away altogether; so at times one is tempted to take Dooley's advice, 'give him 10 dollars, let him go off and drink himself to death.'"

—Joseph Henry Sharp, 1899 article in *Brush and Pencil* magazine

Awa Tsireh
San Ildefonso Pueblo, 1898–1955
War Dance, c. 1930s
Zuni Dance, c. 1955
Watercolor on paper
5 1/2 × 3 9/16 in. (14 × 9.1 cm)
8 11/16 × 5 7/8 in. (20.1 × 14.9 cm)
Collection of the Indian Arts Research
Center, Santa Fe, New Mexico

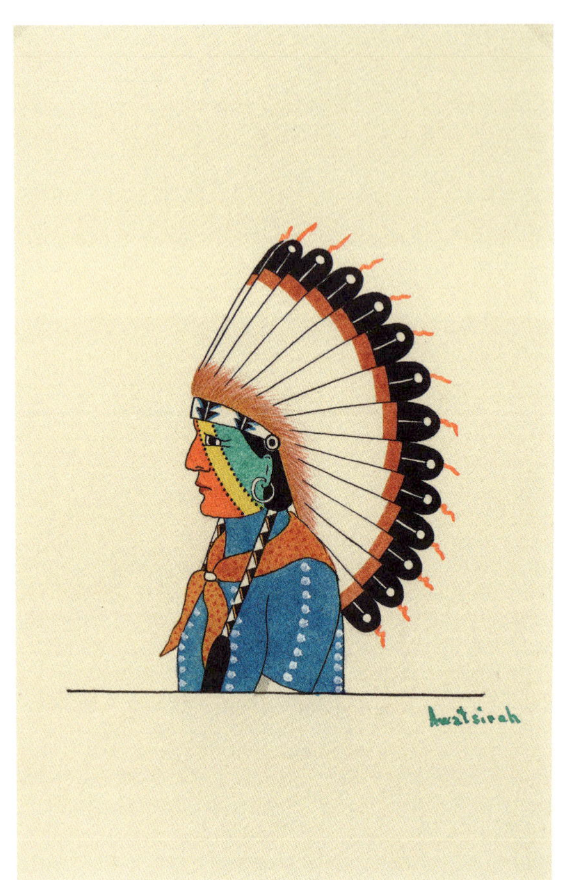

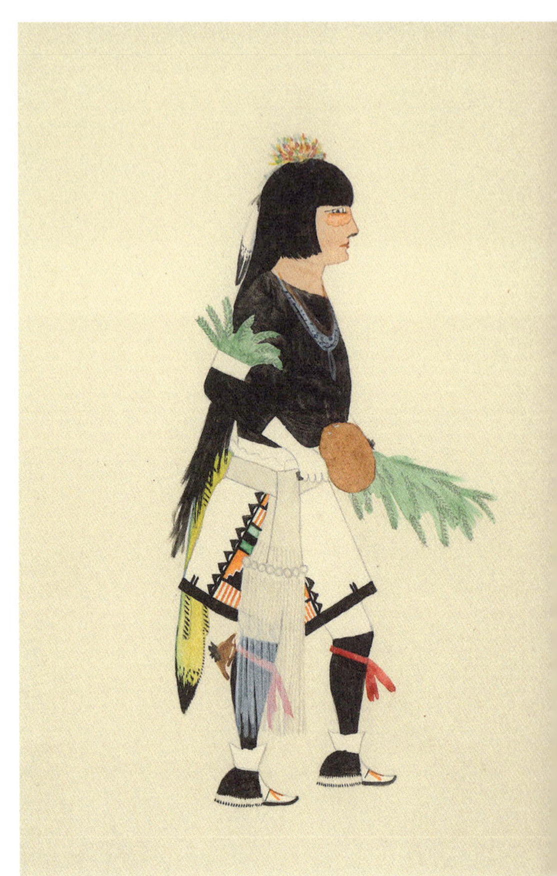

Awa Tsireh
San Ildefonso Pueblo, 1898–1955
Antelope Dance, c. 1930s
Slow Dance, n.d.
Watercolor on paper
5 1/2 × 3 9/16 in. (14 × 9.1 cm)
8 7/16 × 5 7/8 in. (21.4 × 14.9 cm)
Collection of the Indian Arts Research Center, Santa Fe, New Mexico

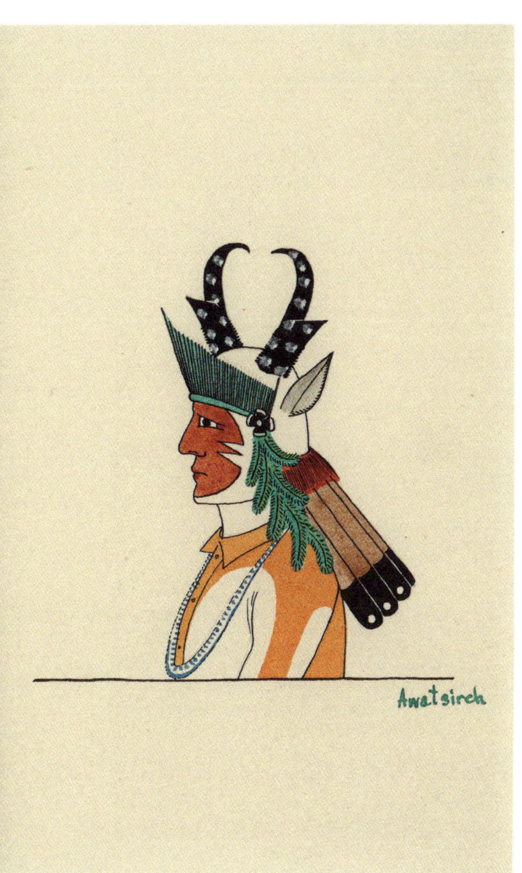

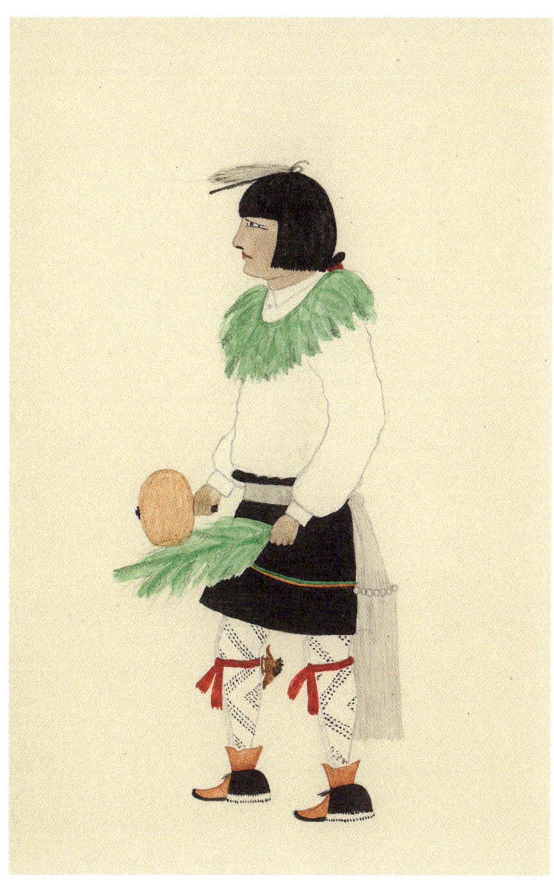

Awa Tsireh's highly detailed and empathetic approach includes details of dancers that only a member of the community would be able to create. The artist highlights important aspects of the regalia while omitting elements that may be culturally sensitive. Evergreen needles are individually painted, highlighting their significance in Pueblo dances. Also known as Alfonso Roybal, Tsireh began his career in the early 1900s. He took inspiration from his upbringing in Po-Woh-Geh-Owingeh and drew upon his experience as a painter of pottery. He was one of the first Pueblo painters to be widely recognized by the Santa Fe arts community, and sometimes included aspects of contemporary non-Native art in his cultural imagery.

—Juan Lucero

Joseph Henry Sharp
American, 1859–1953
Testing the Shaft, c. 1920
Oil on canvas
25 × 30 ¼ in. (63.5 × 76.8 cm)
The Lunder Collection, 2013.262

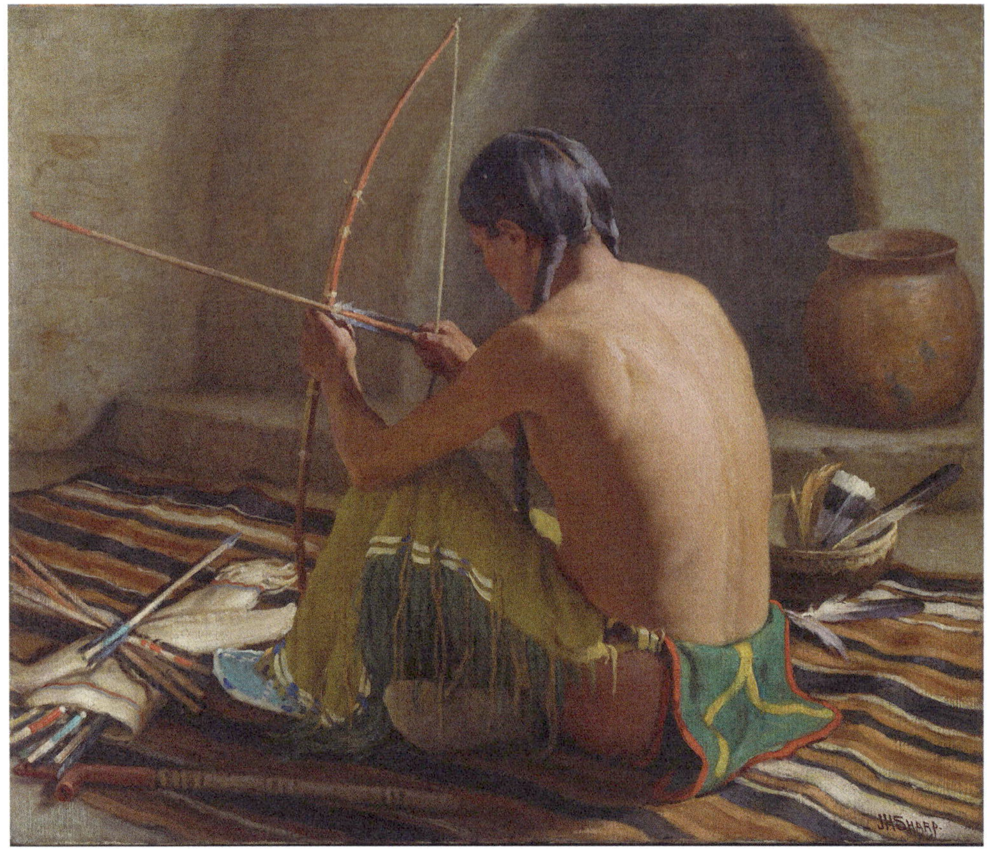

In the early twentieth century, US federal policy restricted Native peoples' rights to their own land and traditional ways of living, necessitating increased reliance on a cash economy. Though there are few historic records pertaining to the average wages of artists' models, *The Manual of Occupations* (1929), a guidebook for job seekers, counseled aspiring sitters to expect one dollar an hour, while photographer's models might demand as much as five or ten dollars for a session. The TSA paid the Taos Pueblo models who sat for them twenty-five cents per hour. In 1920, Native American workers averaged an income of around one hundred dollars per year, compared to $1,350 for white, Anglo-American workers.

This exhibition's advisory council challenged our curatorial team to "tell the whole story" of encounters between the TSA and Taos Pueblo. The following text, written by TSA cofounder E. Irving Couse, provides insight into the economic dynamics behind these portraits. The story of this moment in Taos Pueblo's long history includes financial and power disparities, along with present-day recollections by Taos Pueblo community members of friendships between their ancestors and the TSA painters. To hear the "whole story," we must hold different, sometimes conflicting, truths at the same time.

—Siera Hyte

"A clipping from the *Santa Fe New Mexican* was sent [to] me containing an article on the coming exhibition of the Taos Society of Artists in which values & prices of certain paintings were published.

'During the past couple of years, we at Taos have been experiencing difficulties in getting models owing to the belief among the Indian that we get huge prices for our pictures in which they should at least get half. The established rate for models is 25 cents per hour which is more than twice as much as the Indians can make in other work.... I firmly believe they get their ideas from the Indians who can read English & from similar articles to the above mentioned. Last summer our secretary [TSA painter Bert Geer Phillips] was instructed by our society to write you a letter requesting you where possible [avoid] having prices published. I do not know if you received such a letter.... I hope you will see the wisdom of our request as I firmly believe that unless these impressions are nipped in the bud the whole future of the Santa Fe Taos Art movement will be seriously handicapped & that the artists will be compelled to go elsewhere for models.'"

—E. Irving Couse, 1920 letter to a Santa Fe gallery owner

Ernest L. Blumenschein
American, 1874–1960
Eagle Feather Prayer Chant, c. 1915
Oil on canvas. 34 × 30 in. (86.4 × 76.2 cm)
The Lunder Collection, 2013.018

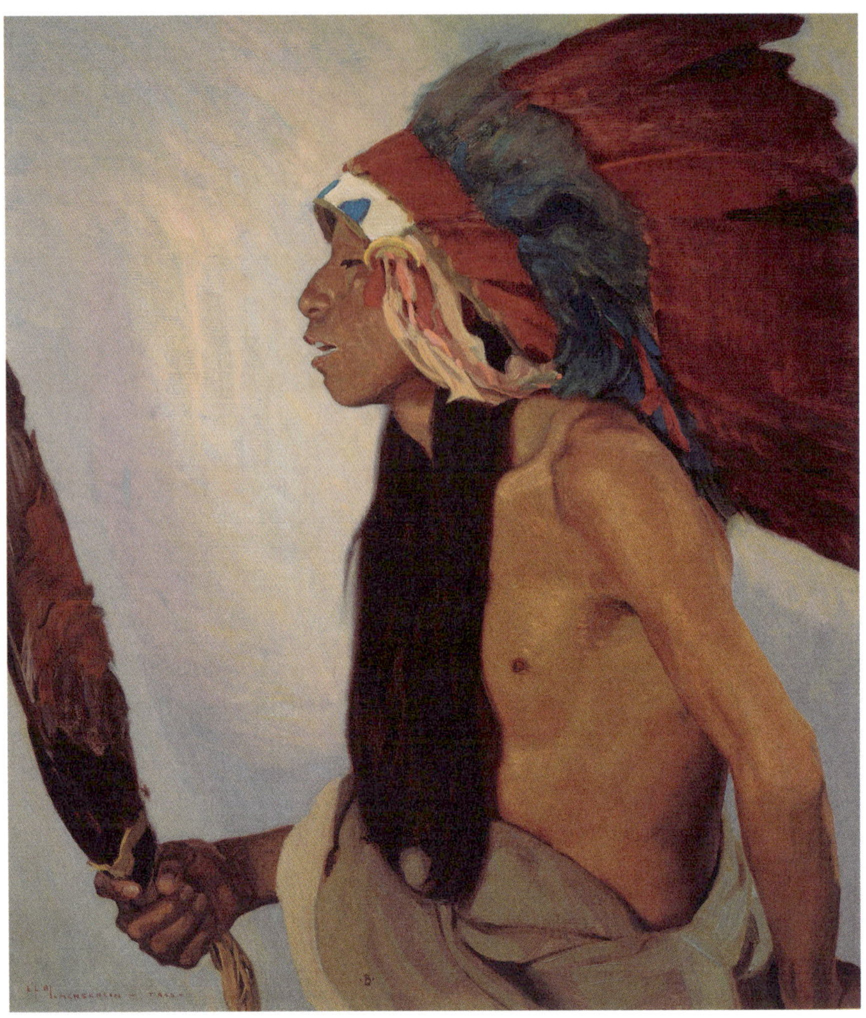

Created in 1915, this painting was originally part of a larger composition titled *The Chief's Two Sons* that featured two men in headdresses holding eagle feather fans and looking toward each other in front of a landscape of trees and adobe dwellings. Sometime after 1920, Blumenschein cut the painting in half and layered muted colors over the background of each. The other "chief's son" now resides at the Denver Art Museum. This history reminds us of the malleable nature of artworks—they may say more about the artist and their choices than about the people or cultures represented.

—J. R. Henneman, director and curator of the Petrie Institute of Western American Art, Denver Art Museum

Bert Geer Phillips
American, 1868–1956
The War Captain, Taos Pueblo, n.d.
Oil on canvas. 24 × 20 in. (61 × 50.8 cm)
The Lunder Collection, 2013.226

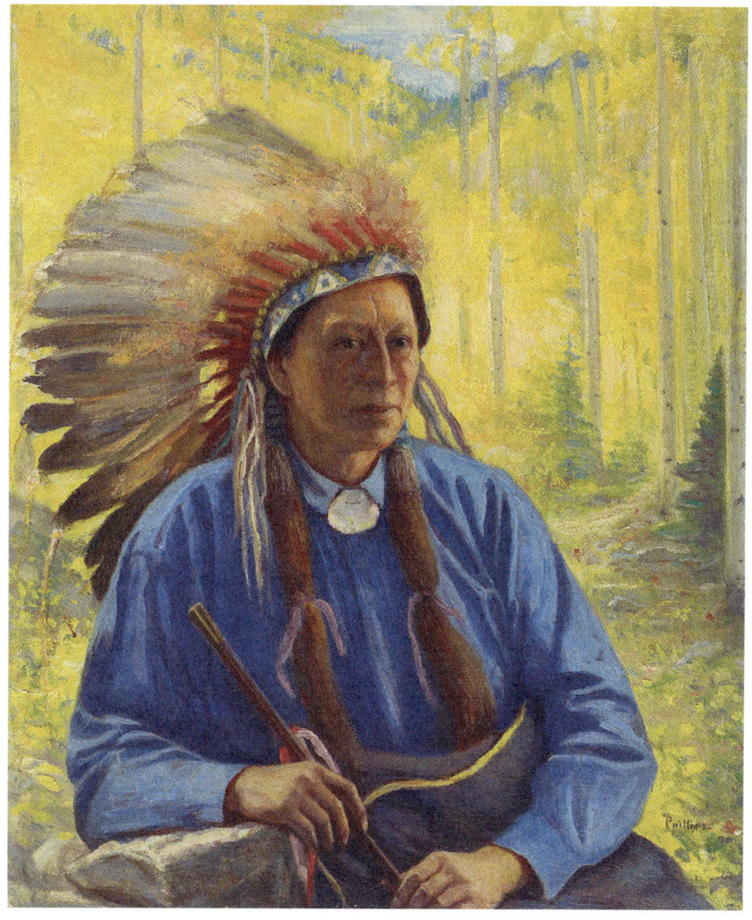

In congressional hearings on the seizure of Blue Lake, the lead counsel representing Taos Pueblo read a statement by TSA painter Bert Geer Phillips recounting a conversation with portrait sitter Manuel Mondragon, the likely subject of *The War Captain*, in which Mondragon stated his "fear that non-Indians would move up the Rio Pueblo canyon…thus contaminating Pueblo water and taking over lands used only by the Pueblo as far back as any man knows." Mondragon modeled for both Phillips and Ernest L. Blumenschein, another TSA contemporary, and knew them well enough to spend time in their homes. Mondragon and other sitters may have been instrumental in gaining support regarding federal policies that impacted tribal sovereignty. By some historical accounts, the TSA generally affirmed Taos Pueblo's legal stewardship of Blue Lake and promoted this opinion within their social circles. Mondragon's worries about unsafe water and violations of Native land rights echo contemporary issues affecting Native peoples today.

—Siera Hyte

Ernest Martin Hennings
American, 1886–1956
Young Taos Chief, n.d.
Oil on canvas
30 × 30 in. (76.2 × 76.2 cm)
The Lunder Collection, 2013.136

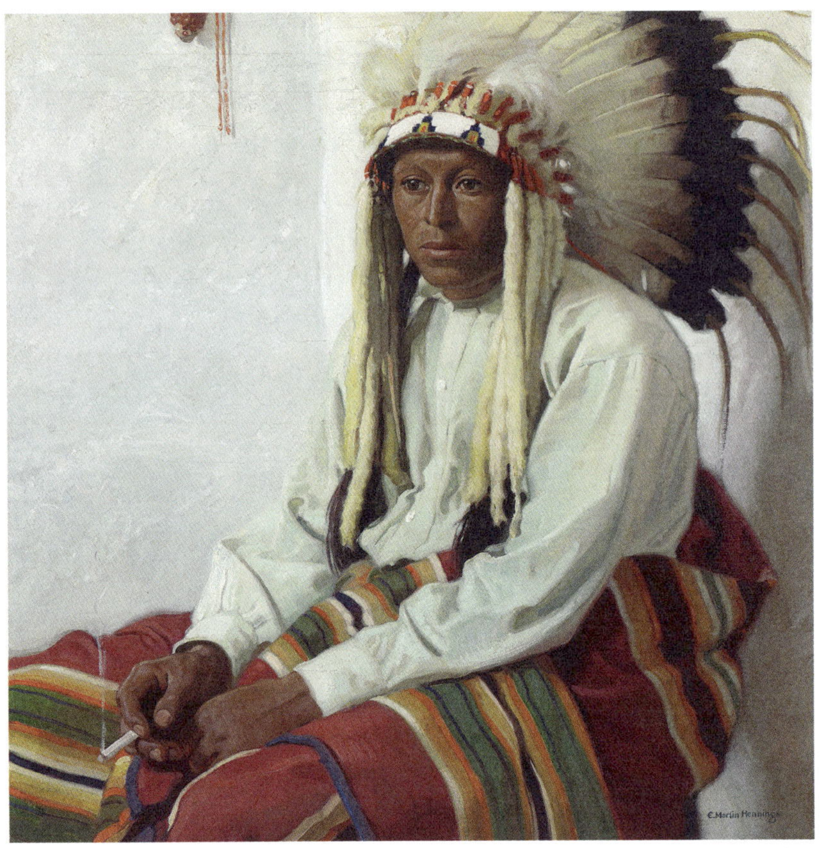

128

Seferina Herrera
Cochiti Pueblo, dates unknown
Cochiti Priest Mono, c. 1885–90
Clay, paint
16 15/16 × 8 1/4 × 6 1/4 in. (43 × 21 × 15.9 cm)
Collection of the Indian Arts Research Center, Santa Fe, New Mexico

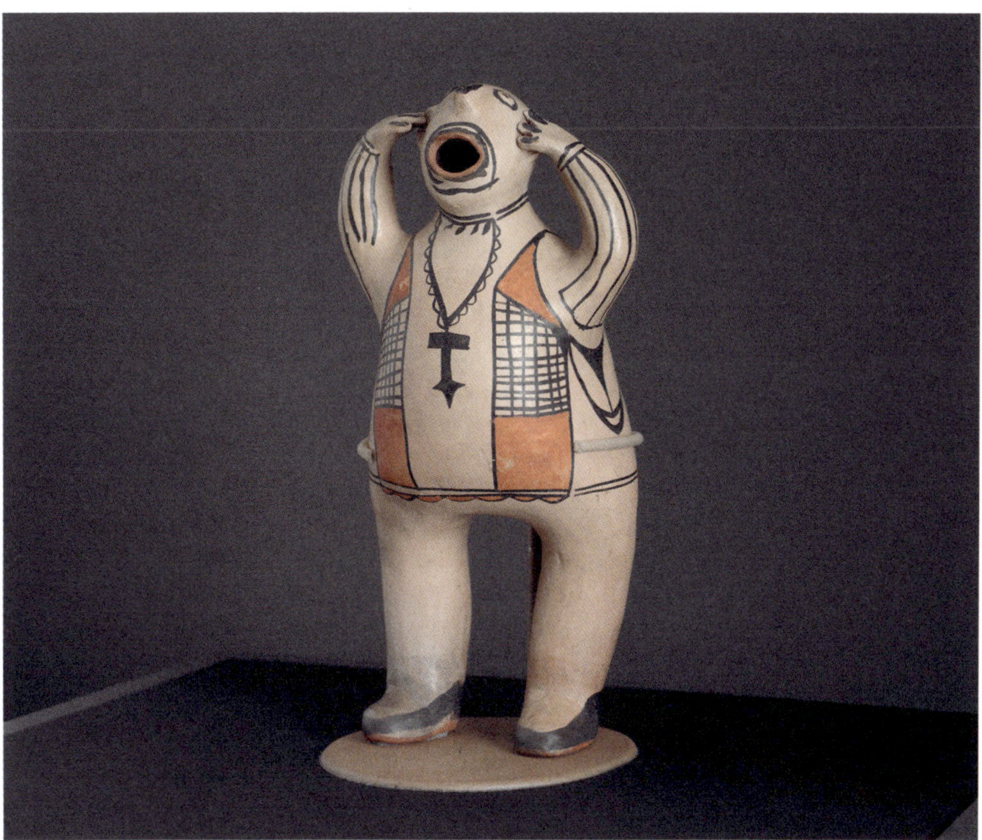

Seferina Herrera was a Cochiti potter who, like many Cochiti artists of her time, engaged in social critique through parodying settler occupants of Pueblo lands. Artist Virgil Ortiz, the designer of the *Painted* exhibition, encouraged the curatorial team to include one of these historic Cochiti figures, called Monos, in the show. Ortiz cites this satirical tradition within his community as a source of inspiration for his own work:

"I think my role now is to help be a part of the continuation, part of the timeline. I want to open minds of individuals who stereotype Cochiti figures as storytellers (a term that refers to a better-known style of figurative Cochiti pottery) and expose them to the humorous figures of the past. I want to make that link and spread it to the younger generation."

—Siera Hyte

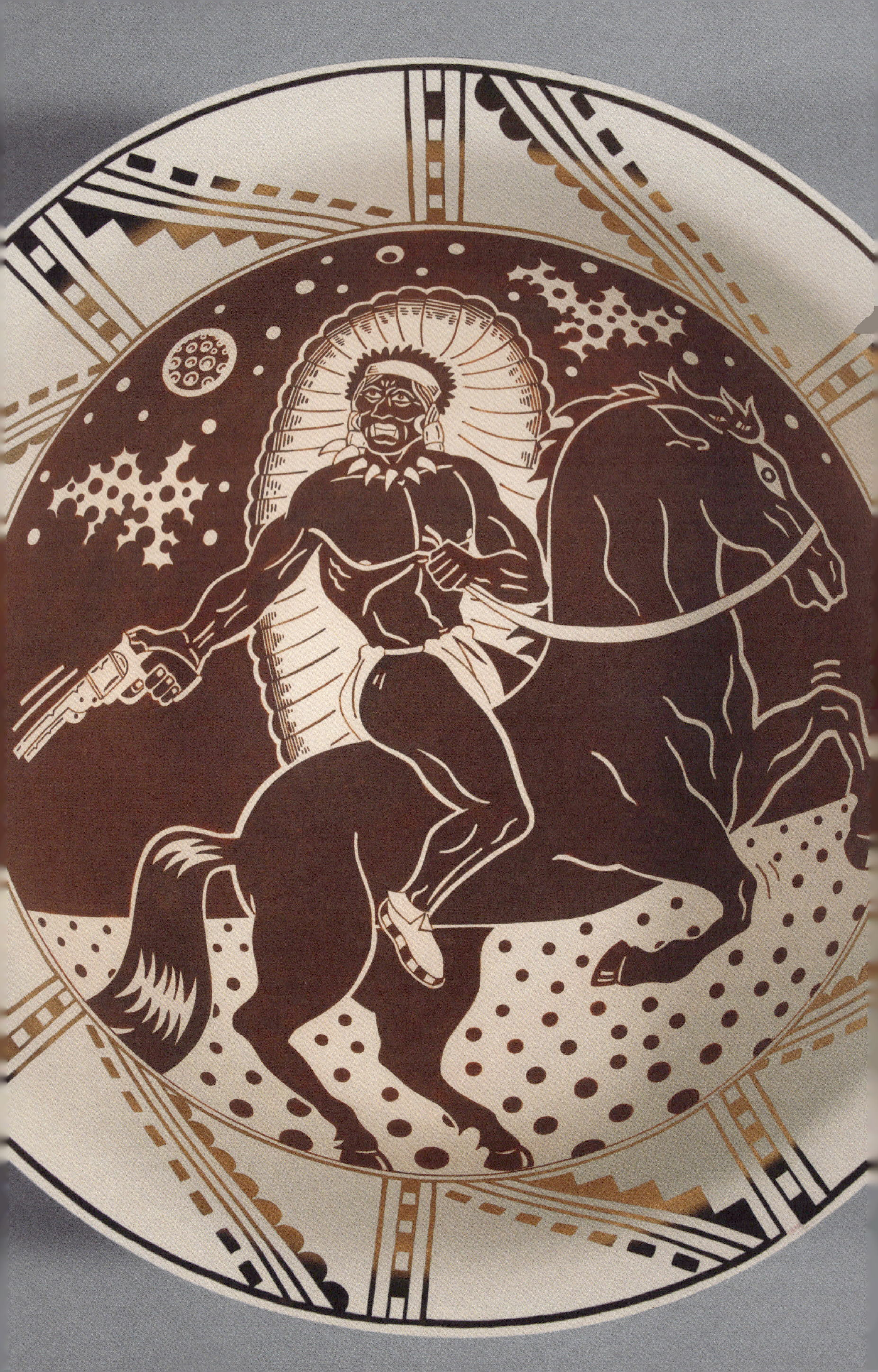

Diego Romero
Cochiti Pueblo, born 1964
Comanche Moon, 2023
Native mineral paint, commercial slip, and gold luster on clay
7 × 16 × 16 in. (17.9 × 40.6 × 40.6 cm)
Museum commission from the Jere Abbott Acquisitions Fund, 2023.294

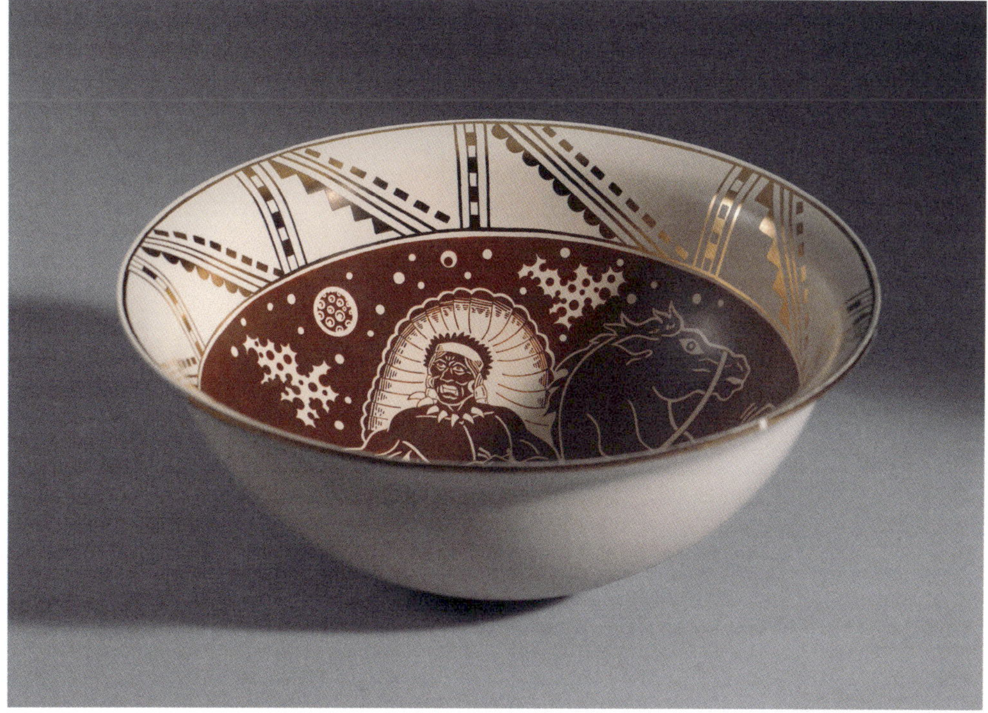

Sincerity in Consultation

Brian Vallo

At the end of each year, the hierarchy of our clan system at the Pueblo of Acoma engages in an ancient process of appointing men from the community to serve as leaders of both the secular and traditional governance structures. Members of the Antelope Clan are exclusively entrusted to fulfill this responsibility, and it is also the responsibility of male members of the community to accept the appointment of leadership in the spirit of *Ustithu'gai'l*, a term and revered value encompassing the concepts of respect, responsibility, upholding culture, and care for the people, land, and animals.

On December 29, 1991, while away from college on winter break, I was appointed to serve my community as a tribal official and First Lieutenant Governor. I was reappointed twice and served three years as both the Tribal Secretary and First Lieutenant Governor. On that early morning, my father, Fred (who himself has served four terms as Governor), phoned to inform me of the appointment. I was in Albuquerque visiting friends, very much a free-spirited student, and looking forward to returning soon to New Mexico State University, where I was studying business administration and marketing. The news indicated that my immediate future would change in a very significant way. While driving back to Acoma, I questioned why the Antelope Clan would appoint me, knowing that I was in college. And why would they choose someone so young (I was twenty-three years old) and inexperienced? Upon arriving at my family home, I found it filled with maternal family and clan elders who expressed their gratitude for the appointment and instructed me on the process for accepting the position. Their words, conveyed to me in the Acoma language, were simple and powerful. I realized at that moment the significance of the appointment and the fact that my personal ambitions had to be placed on hold for a year to serve on behalf of my people, our culture, our land, and its resources.

I was very young and inexperienced. My family and clan elders encouraged and advised me throughout my time in office, though much of the learning occurred via hands-on experience. I was grateful for my upbringing and having spent a great deal of my childhood with my paternal grandparents, my maternal clan elders, and other older members of my tribe who had relationships with my family elders. I found myself surrounded by a wealth of traditional knowledge and endless stories of lived experiences, and in settings where I gained ever more knowledge of Acoma culture, the natural environment, and tribal history. All of this had a profound impact on my development as an Acoma man. Had I not been exposed to such a wealth of traditional knowledge and other historical information, my ability to fulfill the responsibilities associated with tribal leadership would have been far more challenging.

The one-year appointment turned into three consecutive years of service. I am grateful for the experience, as I gained an even greater respect and understanding for our ancient traditional governance system and its critical role in upholding our culture. The process is intentional, and in fact lays a path for those of us who are identified to serve in leadership positions. My own path emerged because of this experience.

During this time, my Pueblo was engaged in many significant issues, including long-standing involvement in cultural preservation initiatives. Acoma was and remains recognized as a leader, along with other Pueblos in New Mexico, in asserting its sovereignty where federal policy, economic self-sufficiency, and access to and protection of land, water, resources, and education are concerned. With cultural preservation as a priority (an inherent responsibility, really), Acoma was also actively involved in developing innovative and effective initiatives related to language immersion, historic preservation, and repatriation. Even prior to the enactment of the Native American Graves Protection and Repatriation Act (NAGPRA) in 1990, Acoma had previous experience with repatriation of ancestors and culturally significant items, while being actively involved in consultations associated with federal and state policies designed to address environmental concerns as well as inadvertent discovery of ancestral sites both on and outside tribal lands. In addition, Acoma was at the forefront of protecting sacred sites and landscapes that are culturally significant to the ongoing practice of Acoma culture. During my term as a tribal leader, the Governor and Tribal Council charged me with overseeing activities associated with these critical issues and developing a more comprehensive framework for how the tribe would respond to and organize work specifically related to the implementation of NAGPRA.

It was this introduction to NAGPRA and the vastness and complexity of the associated implementation issues that provided me with insight into the "white tape" (a former Acoma Governor's term), or federal bureaucracy, that often complicates and/or creates barriers to achieving successful outcomes. It was clear that other tribes across the country were experiencing similar challenges during this initial implementation of NAGPRA, and we worked in partnership to advocate for, and sometimes demand, improved processes for consultation. We realized the magnitude of the problem and were overwhelmed by the tremendous amount of time and resources that would be required to support this long-term effort. As we reviewed some of the first inventories sent from museums and other repositories (one of the requirements stipulated in NAGPRA for institutions that receive federal funding), we were confronted with the sheer magnitude of ancestors, objects of cultural patrimony, and material culture in the possession of museums, universities, and federal and state agency collections. For the first time in our tribe's history, we found ourselves in a very difficult and uncomfortable circumstance where cultural and spiritual leaders, elders, and tribal government officials were forced to engage in discussions about the sensitivities involved with NAGPRA-related work, including the inevitable need to identify a process for reburying ancestors and their funerary items once they were repatriated back to the Pueblo.

As Lieutenant Governor, I was directly involved in consultations with museums, government agencies, and universities concerning our NAGPRA claims. Many of the consultations were one-sided, as federal processes did not always consider tribal needs or provide opportunities for tribes, including Acoma, to have direct influence in shaping the consultations and ultimately the decision-making. Moreover, many institutions had very little familiarity with Acoma culture and Native culture and history more broadly, which made the consultation process even more challenging. For our part, we too realized we might not have all the tools and expertise to fully engage in the NAGPRA process, and thus needed to be concerned about contentious relations and unfavorable outcomes. It became evident that if Acoma was to continue its work on repatriation using NAGPRA, we needed to invest resources to establish an office with personnel qualified to work on NAGPRA and other significant issues related to safeguarding Acoma culture. With the support of cultural leaders and the Tribal Council, a plan emerged to establish such an office.

Another piece of legislation that was making its way through the federal process at this time was the Native American Free Exercise of Religion Act (NAFERA), a proposed revision to the 1978 American Indian Religious Freedom Act. The associated legislative process, which included internal research and dialogue, development of official testimony, lobbying congressional representatives, and consultations, also consumed much of my time. I learned that almost every issue that involves our government-to-government relationship with the federal government calls for continuous analysis, internal and external consultation, and a need for our own tribal laws and systems to evolve in order to protect tribal sovereignty and realize favorable outcomes for Acoma people—both those alive at that moment and those not yet born.

At the end of 1994, my third appointment was coming to an end and I was eager to resume my college education. But my experience as a tribal official had influenced my pursuits and shifted my interests. My introduction to museum operations as they related to NAGPRA, combined with the profound impact of working on a government-to-government basis with federal agencies on policy and issues related to sacred sites and cultural resource protection, placed me on a new career path. I had the privilege of serving as both Director of the Acoma Historic Preservation Office and Founding Director of the Sky City Cultural Center and Haak'u Museum, where much of what I learned outside of university was highly valuable. I remain committed to these processes today in my work as an independent consultant.

I have been extremely excited to witness the evolution of Tribal Historic Preservation Offices and tribal museums throughout the country, who are providing expert guidance to their respective tribal leaders on complex issues impacting repatriation and cultural resources management. These entities work closely with tribal community experts in the development of policies and laws. Most tribes, even if they do not have a formal historic preservation office, designated Tribal Historic Preservation Officer, or museum, have organized internal processes and systems that allow for their involvement in consultation where cultural (or other) resources are concerned. Many tribes have organized cultural advisory committees and councils comprised of tribal elders, cultural and spiritual leaders, scholars, artists, and others who are experts in traditional knowledge and history. While the establishment of said internal structures has secured "seats at the table" and voices that render favorable outcomes for tribes, many of these offices find themselves overwhelmed with requests for consultation. Each tribe sets their priorities for this cultural work and navigates the federal, state, and (more recently) private systems to determine what to prioritize and with whom they will engage.

This is part of my personal story. Tribal community representatives (most of whom are also cultural and spiritual leaders) who serve as expert advisors on behalf of their respective tribes all have their own stories and experiences. These tribal experts take time away from family and cultural responsibilities to engage in the work, which can oftentimes be demanding and occurring on an inconvenient schedule. Tribal leaders also play a significant role in consultation and other related work, as they are official government representatives who may be called upon to provide recommendations and/or final decisions. It is especially refreshing to see more tribal scholars and artists finding their place in the consultation process. A growing number of tribal artists and scholars are working within both Native and non-Native spheres to advance scholarship, contribute toward changing colonial practices in academia and museology, and grow awareness of Native contemporary art. This work is being recognized by tribal governments and cultural leaders as critically important to cultural preservation initiatives. Some tribal leaders who are organized under both traditional and secular governments work with community representatives who participate in consultation and other collaborative projects outside of tribal advisory groups (publications, research, commissioned art projects, exhibitions, etc.) and establish mutual understanding for this type of engagement for the purpose of protecting traditional knowledge, cultural patrimony, tribal sovereignty, and other intellectual property.

I am encouraged by the capacity building that is occurring in our tribal nations. Investing in initiatives that encourage higher education for tribal members in fields that are critical to the cultural work (for instance, law, anthropology, archaeology, museology, library science, history, and the arts) is a profound act of sovereignty and preservation. Institutions and agencies are also direct beneficiaries of this growth, as it provides for more active involvement at all levels, and on all issues that are important to our tribes. Furthermore, this advancement is acknowledged by some tribes as a realized prophecy, an answer to prayers, and a step toward a more sustainable and successful future. Native people are contributing to the greater society in many significant ways, and we are laying a foundation for increased visibility in federal and state government and corporate America.

I first heard of *Painted: Our Bodies, Hearts, and Village* from a representative of Colby College Museum of Art at a meeting we were both attending. When the collaborative process employed by the museum was mentioned, I was immediately interested to know more. I was excited to learn of the many Pueblo and other Native artists, several of whom were immediately known to me, who were directly involved in developing the presentation. I further learned that the curatorial approach centered on bestowing agency to each Native contributor, acknowledging them as the expert and trusted resource to narrate the story of the Taos Society of Artists, and to extend the storyline to include other important issues of interest to each Native artist. These include sovereignty of Pueblo people, self-representation, settler colonialism, and misrepresentation of Pueblo people through art of the TSA and other non-Native artists, to name a few. This was all exciting and groundbreaking to me.

Shortly thereafter, I received an invitation to offer a keynote address during a symposium held in conjunction with the show. While I was somewhat surprised to be asked to deliver such a prestigious talk, I gave the invitation careful consideration, and decided to accept and honor the important work of the museum and the Native artists. My presentation centered on collaboration between museums and tribal communities. I shared examples of exhibition projects where similar, meaningful processes served as the basis for the curating, versus projects where the curating was absent those essential elements of relationship building, trust, and granting freedom and authority to Native collaborators. I also shared aspects of my personal experiences working for my Pueblo in various capacities, and my observations on tribal consultations associated with NAGPRA, other federal undertakings, and, more recently, museum exhibitions and collections. I offered these thoughts in hopes of conveying some of the positive outcomes resulting from consultation.

Most important is to remind ourselves that to ensure access to collections, expand opportunities for repatriation via NAGPRA and otherwise, and influence the ways museums present Native peoples, belongings, and art as well as the diverse menu of issues relevant to contemporary Native people, we must remain steadfast in shifting obsolete paradigms while securing our place in the collaborative process. Many US museums remain noncompliant with NAGPRA, including some who outright refuse to abide by the law. Even as the symposium was taking place, federal officials were organizing input offered by tribal leaders, federal agents, museum administrators, Tribal Historic Preservation Officers, NGOs, collectors, and other participants in a series of consultations surrounding the original NAGPRA law. For years, tribal leaders and federal officials have been in dialogue about the problems associated with the repatriation process as dictated in the original NAGPRA. This prompted the need for the tribal consultations that took place in 2021. It is likely that by the time this exhibition catalogue is published, a revised law will have been released from the US Department of the Interior's National Park Service. More to come.

As I walked through the gallery spaces devoted to *Painted: Our Bodies, Hearts, and Village*, I felt embraced by the stories, the diverse modes of artistic expression, and the lived truths of Native people conveyed by the Native collaborators. This exhibition is a testament to meaningful collaboration and the commitment of Colby College to providing Native people with access and opportunities for meaningful engagement. *Painted* reminds us of the importance and beauty of storytelling through the cultural lens of the innovative and thriving descendants of the ancestral Pueblo people.

On December 29, 2018, during a traditional meeting of community elders and cultural leaders in which I accepted an appointment to serve as Governor of my Pueblo, I reiterated my commitment to cultural resources protection, which would be one of many priorities that my administration and I would be entrusted to uphold. Elders offered words of encouragement and reminded me and the other appointees to embrace the sacred core values and cultural teachings that have always guided the paths of our people and sustained our way of life. This experience proved significantly different from what we expected, as my administration and the Tribal Council had to deal with the global COVID-19 pandemic. This experience shifted the way we conducted business and interacted not only with our own community, but with the world outside Acoma.

Interestingly, one issue that did not lose traction was related to culture and resources protection. We had a fight on our hands, and it wasn't just against the virus. We found ourselves in elevated dialogue with the federal government concerning sacred sites protection and rights to water and land. If that wasn't enough, the federal government also informed us that it was closing our hospital—in the middle of a global pandemic. This is when my toolbox became critical to my ability to lead my people in these fights. I am grateful that my community remained resilient and is recovering from the impacts of the pandemic on our cultural, social, and economic structures. Our collective prayers and wisdom ensured we would prevail in the unforeseen challenges posed by the "White Father" during such an unprecedented time in our living history.

As happened in the early 1990s, my one-year appointment as Governor was extended to three. These life-changing experiences, combined with teachings associated with my role as a cultural leader in various capacities at the Pueblo, are what guide me as an Acoma man who lives in two very different worlds simultaneously. I am strengthened by the fact that Native people in this time all have stories to tell—that we all have our own culture, language, history, and set of inherited values and responsibilities that inform our being and purpose on this Earth. We contribute these Indigenous qualities and acquired wisdom to the greater society in many different ways. Even as our culture and languages are continually at risk of being lost, the spirit of Native people remains and will ultimately sustain future generations. Those of us who engage in cultural work with museums and other entities are mindful of this critical moment that fuels our commitment to sincerity in consultation and collaboration. As so beautifully presented in *Painted: Our Bodies, Hearts, and Village*, the spirit and creativity of Native people endures and is ever changing.

Brian Vallo (Acoma Pueblo) served as Governor of Acoma Pueblo in 2019–21, formerly directed the Indian Arts Research Center, and was the Founding Director of the Sky City Cultural Center and Haak'u Museum. He has spent more than thirty years working in museum development, repatriation of ancestors and cultural patrimony, cultural preservation, the arts, and tourism.

Robert Mirabal and the Rare Tribal Mob

Robert Mirabal (Taos Pueblo) is an artist whose sound piece *The Society* (2023) was commissioned for *Painted*. Mirabal's band, Robert Mirabal and the Rare Tribal Mob, performed at Colby College's Gordon Center for Performing Arts in Waterville, Maine, on October 13, 2023. Additional band members include Arnaldo Acosta, Ryan Clement, Artha Meadors, Kona Mirabal (Taos Pueblo), and Randy Sanchez, along with the dancer Fabian Fontenelle (Zuni/Omaha).

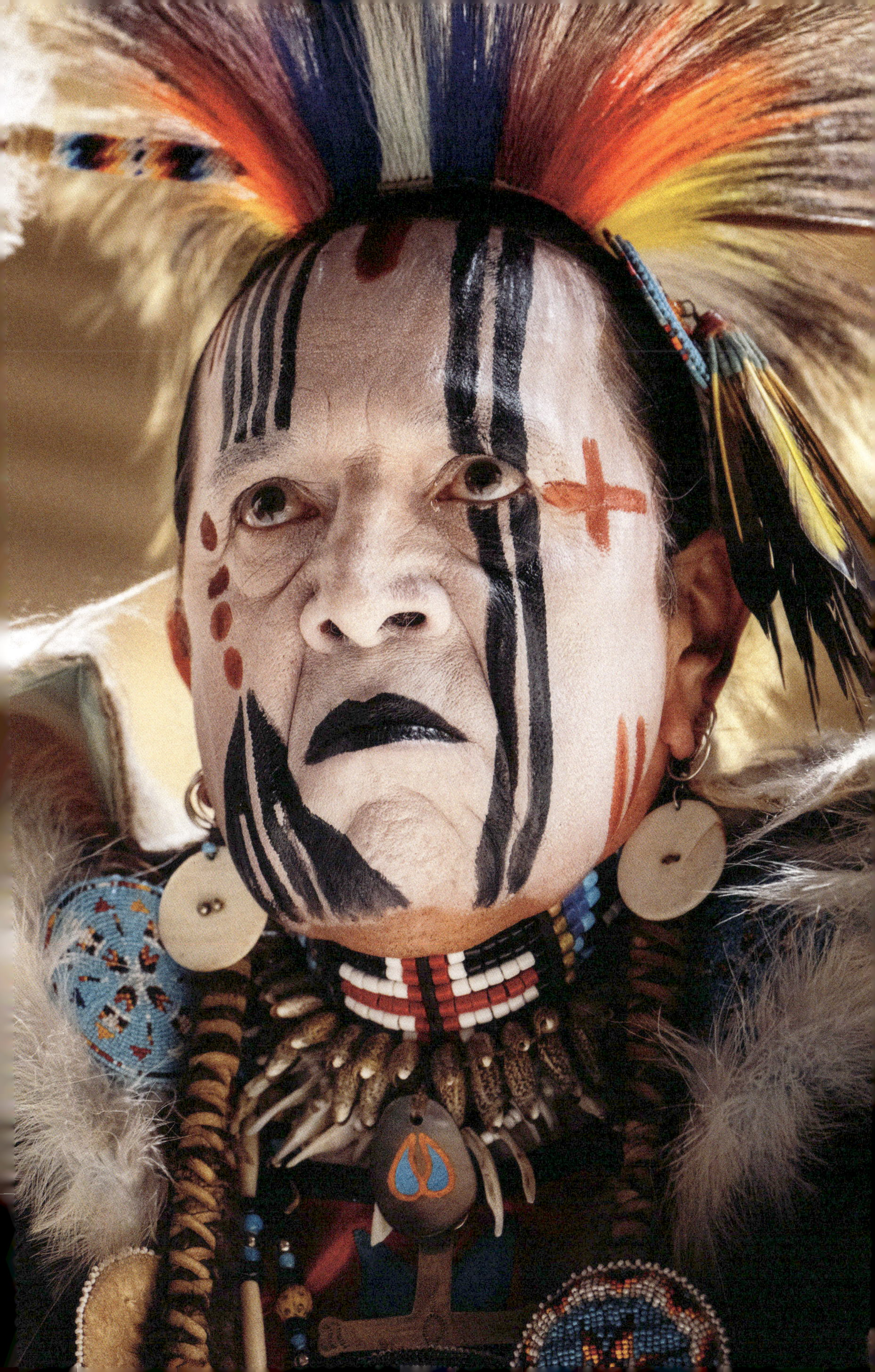

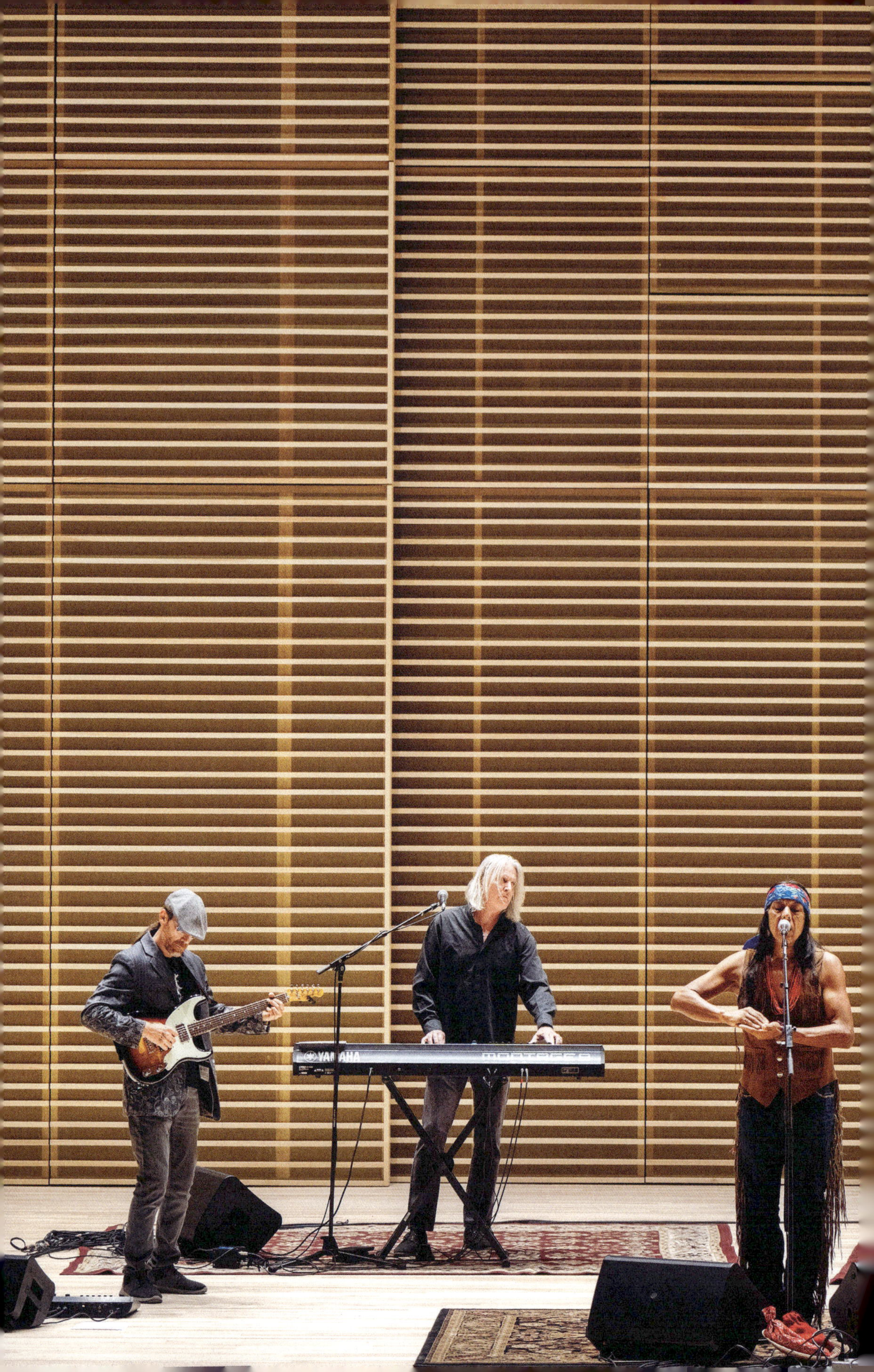
YAMAHA

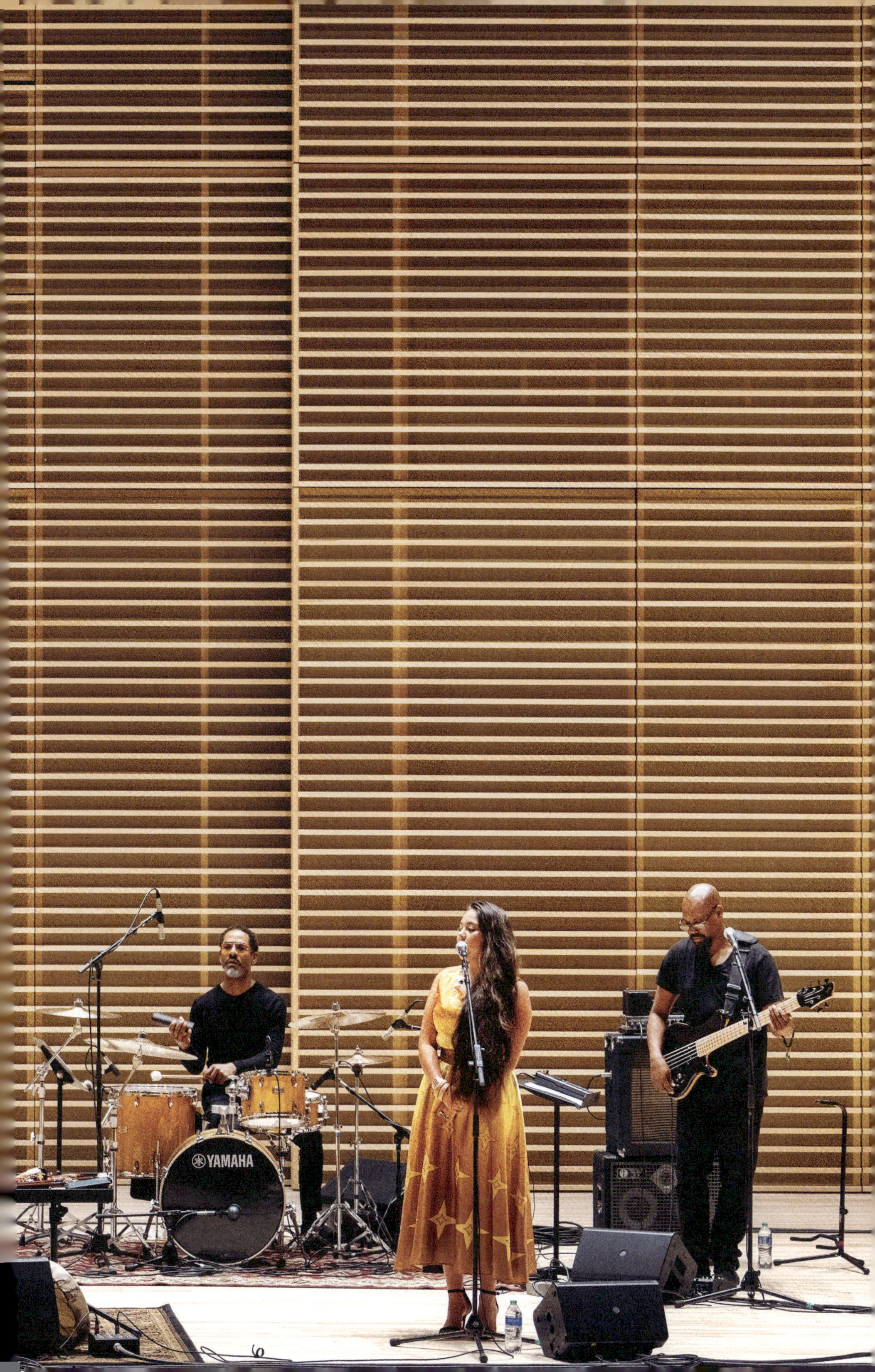
YAMAHA

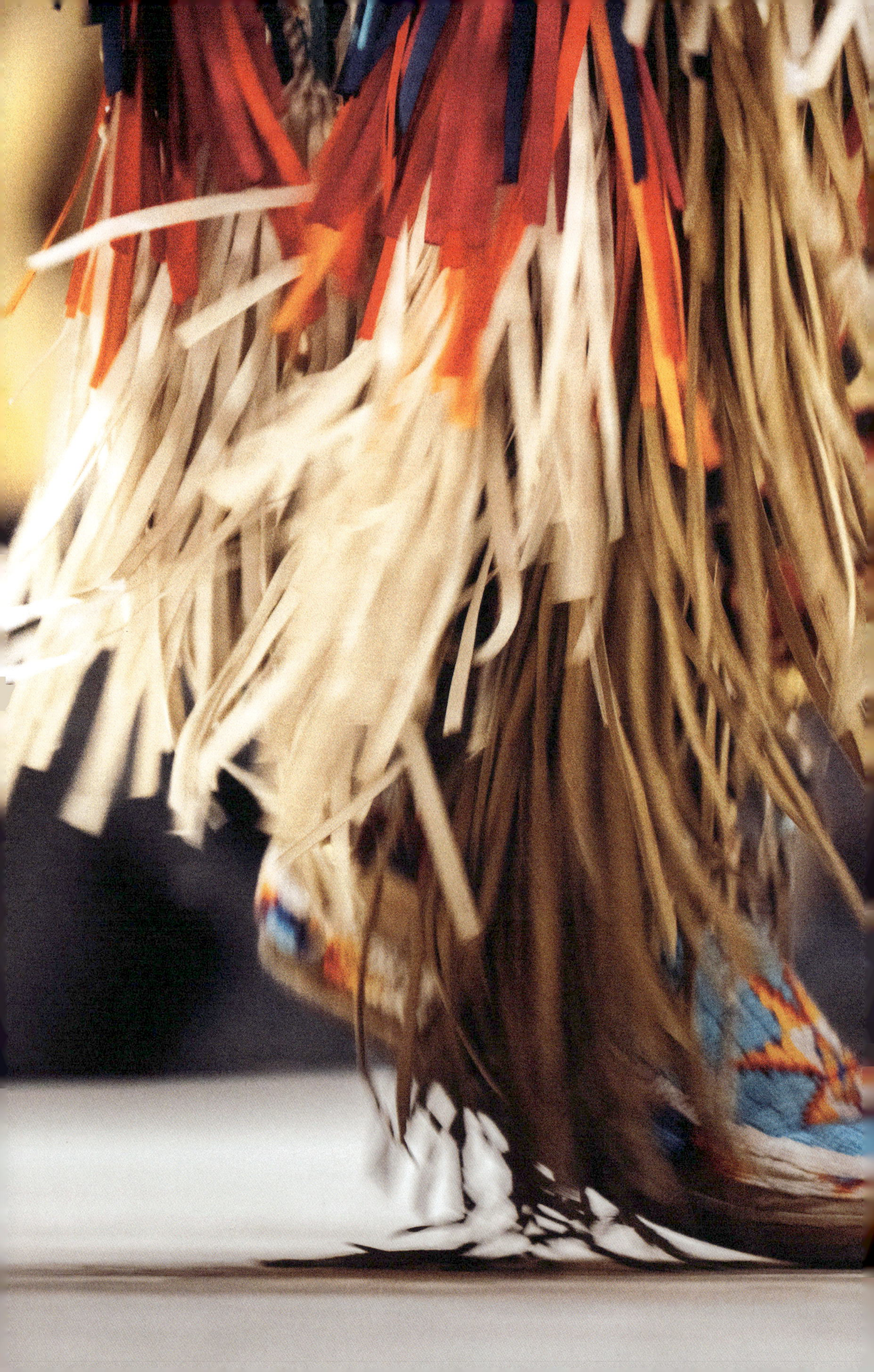

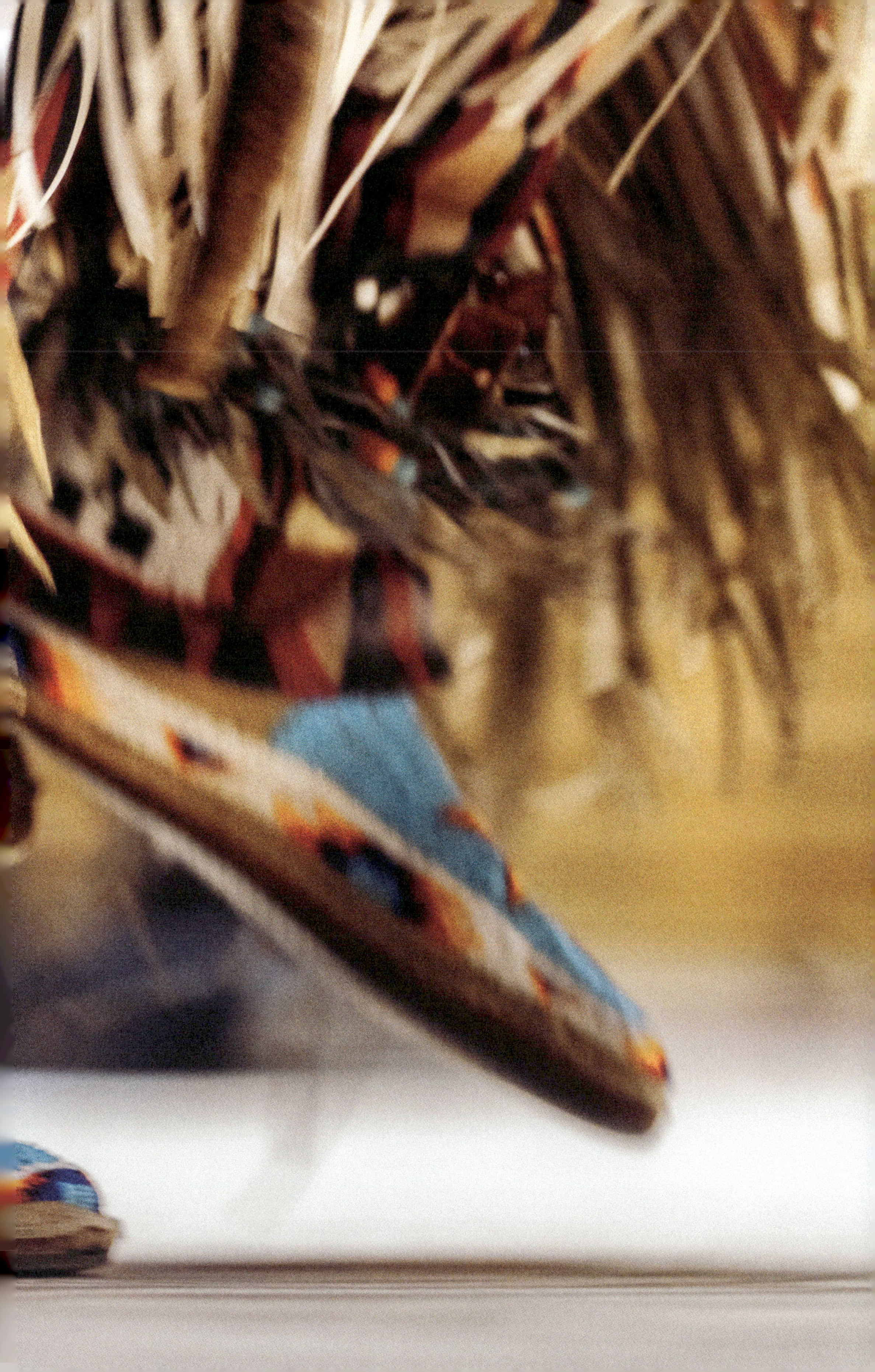

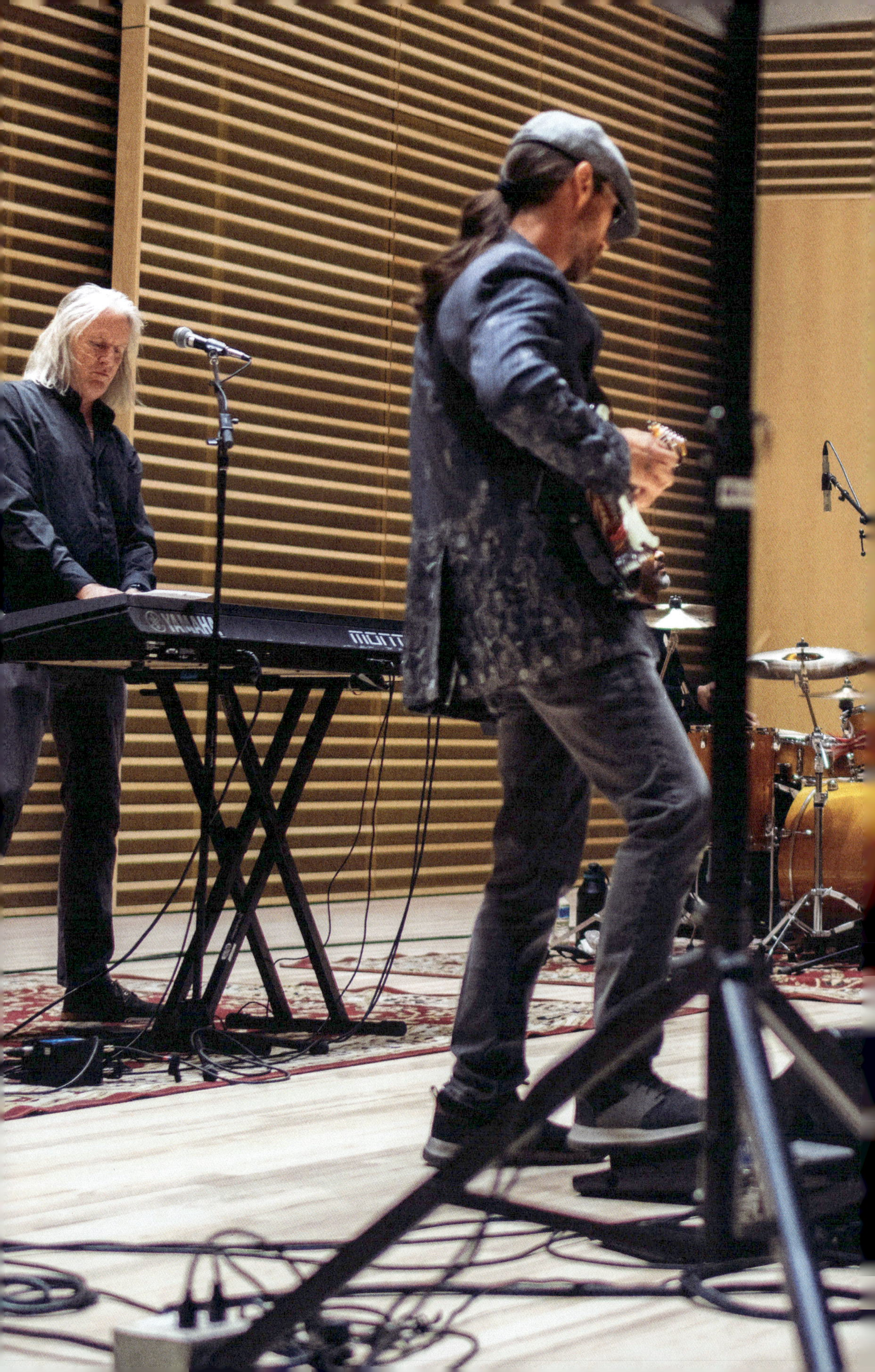

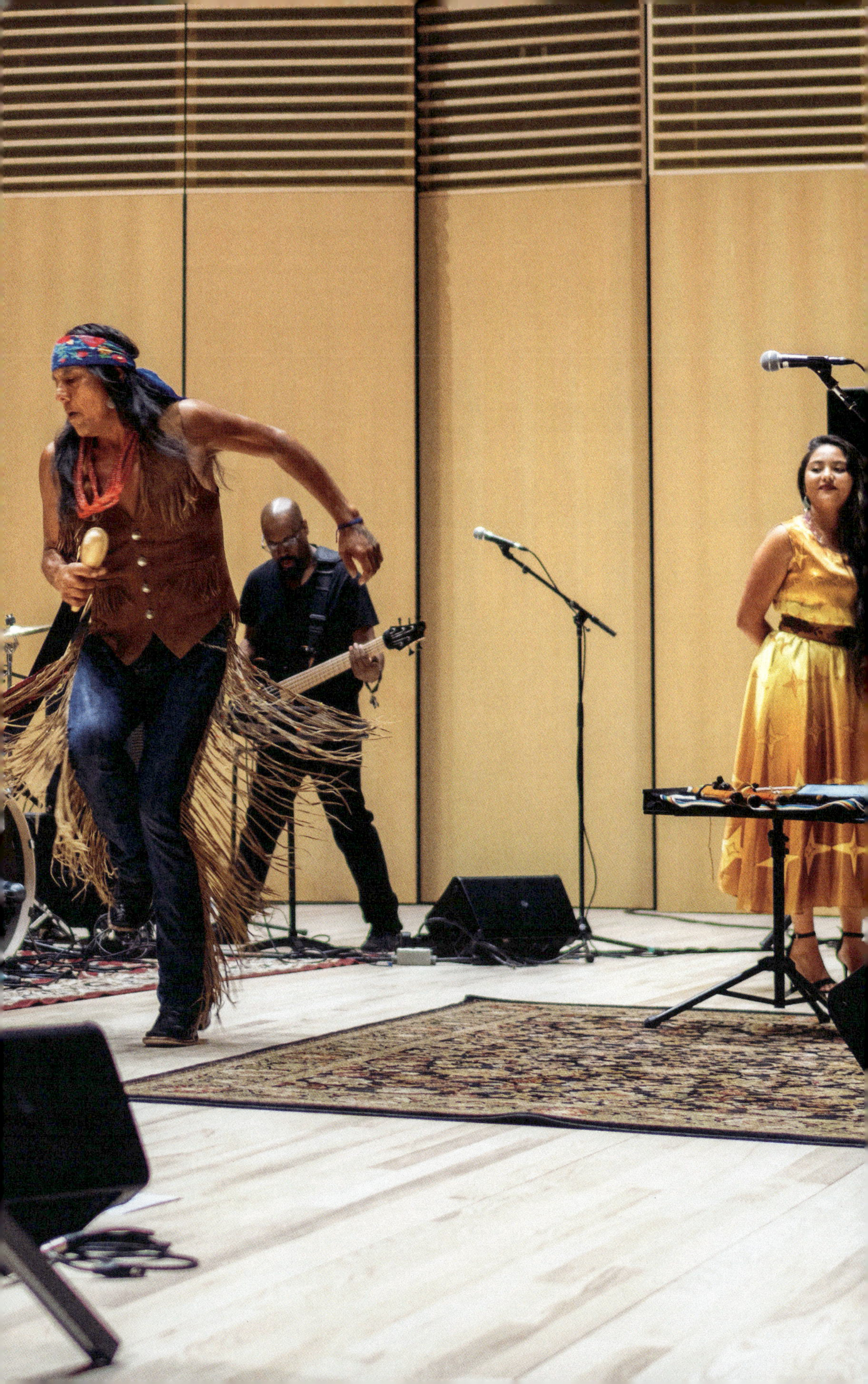

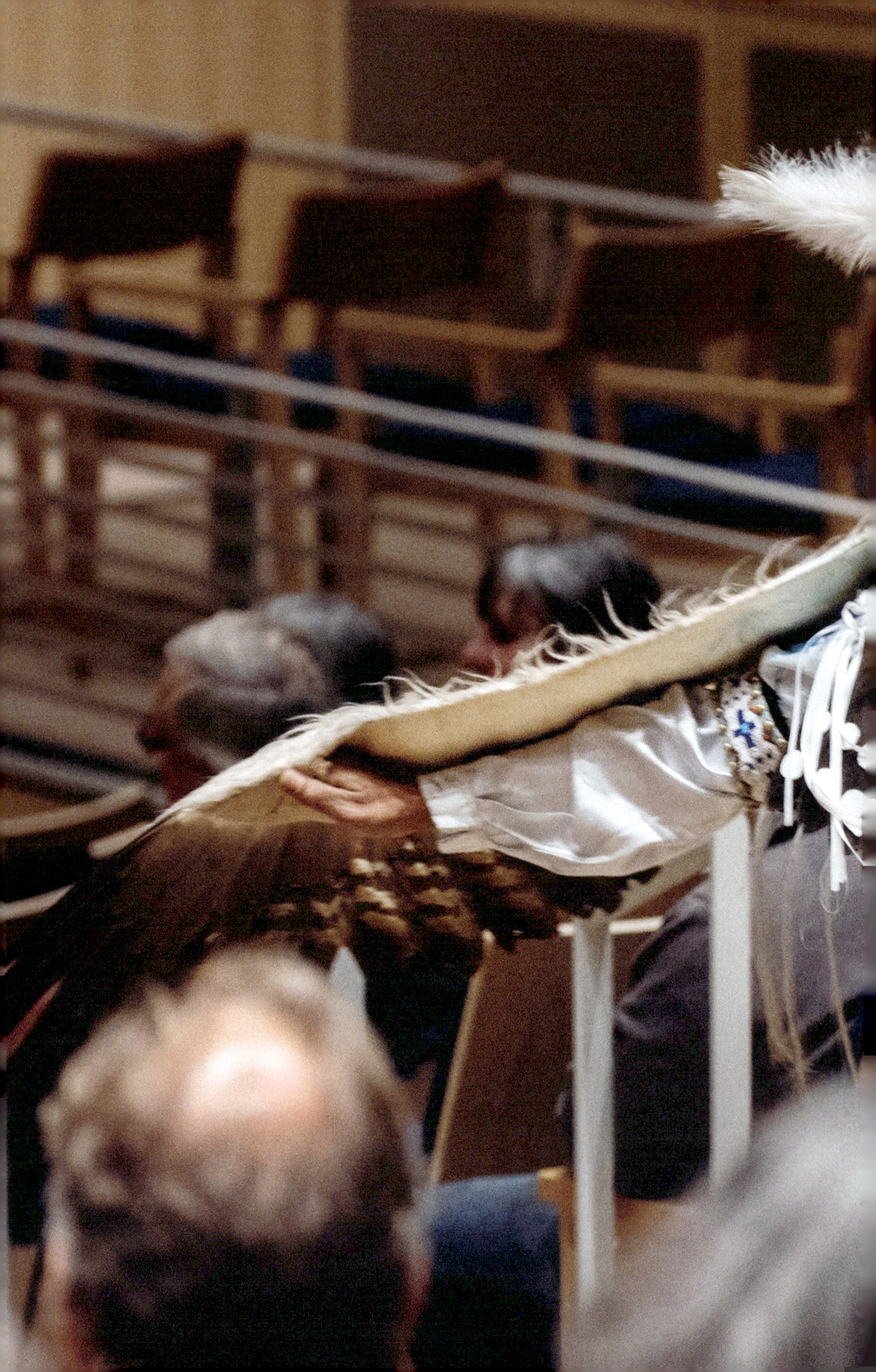

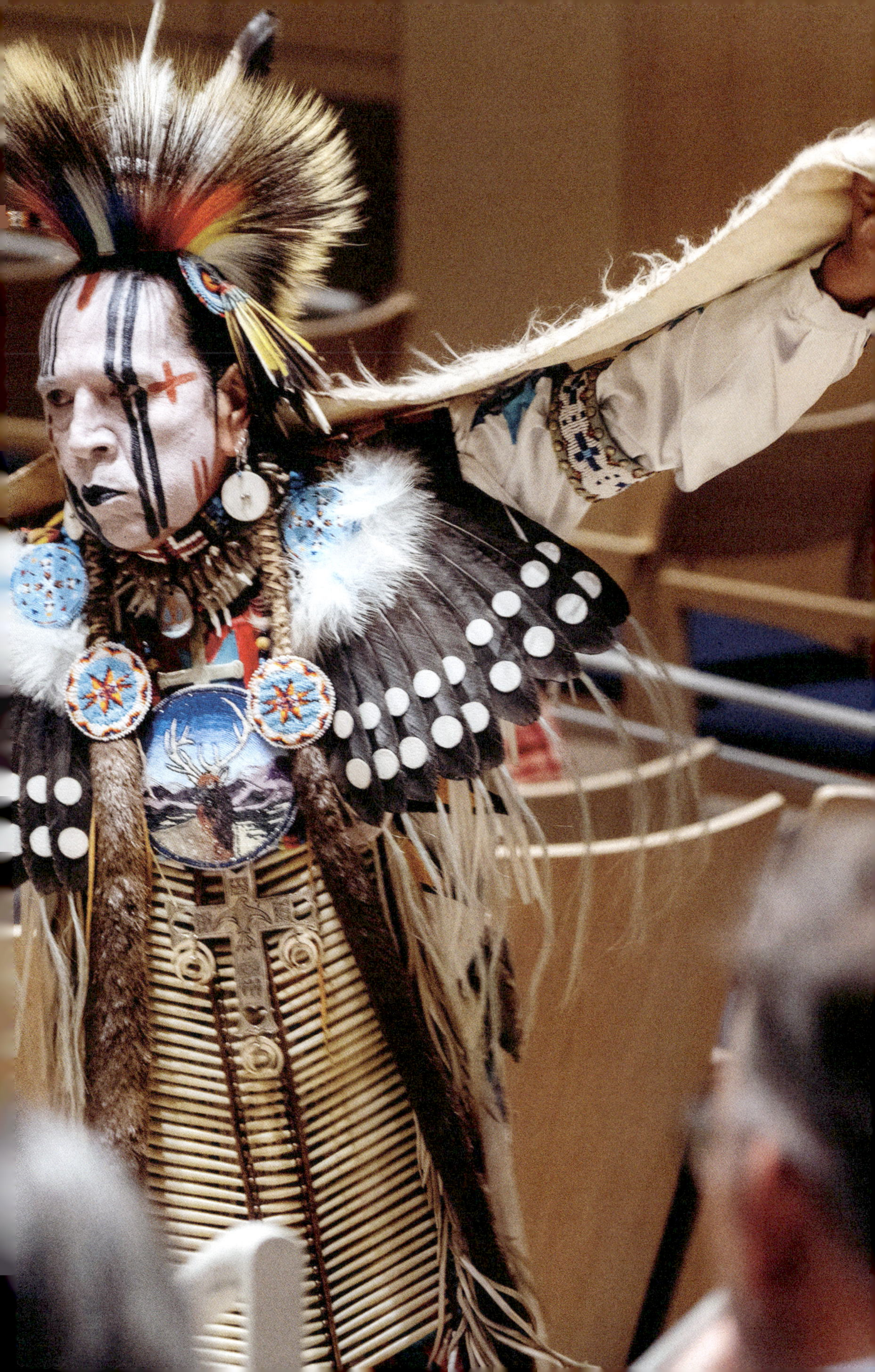

Anglo Artists and the Creation of Pueblo Worlds

Rina Swentzell

I am an Indian person from Santa Clara Pueblo in northern New Mexico. However, when I was in the tenth grade, my family moved to Taos, which is about an hour north of Santa Clara. We did not move into Taos Pueblo, but rather lived on the boundary between the pueblo and the town of Taos. During the 1950s, when I lived there, the legacy of the early society of Taos artists was very real. The artists of the 1950s were still mostly painting in the romantic style of the early-1900s Taos colony. The works in the galleries were of archetypical and idealized Indians—mostly Indian men. The artists still gathered in the dark lobby of the Don Fernando Hotel on the plaza. We Indians seldom went in there, and if we did, it was for very short times. We were not comfortable. We felt that we did not belong even though the paintings hanging on the walls were of us.

The paintings, however, were interesting to us because we would look to see who we could recognize. They were distant images of relatives or people connected to a particular family within the Pueblo. We would move away, not always sure how to feel or react because we could not be comfortable in those strange places, yet it was the paintings of us or pots made by us that really made those places what they were. They set the tone for those places. The pots, drums, and paintings made them special—different—and, moreover, gave them a feeling of well-being and status. Those items, paintings, pots, et cetera, obviously reminded the white people of why they had moved to this place of romance, "this haven of happy, peaceful Indians."

We Indians (and I would guess everybody else) knew that the people in the paintings were not the simple Indians who were portrayed. Outside the Don Fernando Hotel was a parking lot that served a grocery store, and this was where the drunks—drunk Indian men—gathered. They'd sit against the wall of the hotel until they passed out, strewn in the dirt alongside the hotel wall. Even in the early 1900s, when Anglo-American artists began painting the Taos Indians, alcoholism and cultural depression were already problems. So why were we being presented only as happy and noble people? The paintings, it seems, were really about what those Anglos needed to see for themselves. Their paintings were efforts to fill a need inside themselves. They wanted assurance that the technological and consumeristic world that was growing around them had not yet pervaded every corner of the globe.

E. Irving Couse, for instance, who in 1912 became the first president of the Taos Society of Artists, had been intrigued with Indians even when he lived in the East. Born in 1866, he belonged nonetheless to the tradition of Emerson and Thoreau, who also yearned for unspoiled nature and untouched natives. The Indians back East, however, already lived very disjunctive and disrupted lives and were a disappointment to lovers of nature and Indians. Couse, and other artists with his sensibilities, found the Pueblo communities to be more cohesive. There was still some semblance of what the Pueblo people's lives might have been like in the not too distant past. Particularly at Taos, the Pueblo community was architecturally intact and gave the feeling of a place where daily life was lived in a different rhythm than the Anglo artists had experienced elsewhere. Dances in the plazas and ceremonies in the kivas were still common practices. The men still draped themselves in blankets, and the women wore wide-legged moccasin boots and mantas, or cloth-draped dresses tied at the waist with a woven belt. Travel was by foot or wagon. Hunting, gathering, and farming were the primary means of providing food and items for trade.

The greatest attraction that the Pueblo Indians of that time held for the Anglo artists was their belief system, which stressed the connectedness of humans to the natural world. Pueblo people believed that they were given birth by the mother, the earth, who was impregnated by the sky. The entire cosmos is bounded by the far mountains and enclosed by the sky. The people lived in this bounded world knowing that they were dependent on the trees, rocks, and other animals for their survival. The sun was greeted and talked to every day, and at Taos footraces were run to give energy to the sun when it was at its lowest point in the sky. Interaction of humans with the sun and with all other beings was accepted. At Taos Pueblo there is still a quiet season during the wintertime when the people take off their shoes and do not drive cars or make loud noises because the mother, the earth, is resting. As they ask for consideration from the earth and the sky, the parents of all life, they also must give consideration. Nature is an organic being with people only one part. There is no superhuman god. All other creatures, rocks, animals, and plants are considered by humans to be brothers and sisters.

Those early artists who gathered in Taos were, I believe, sincerely searching for an alternative lifestyle that would give promise and hope for their own lives within American culture and society. E. Irving Couse "charmingly and poetically presented the American Indian at peace in his habitat." He wanted so much to see peace and human oneness with the natural world. He was biased toward painting Pueblo men in peaceful and thoughtful poses, and I think not only because men would pose with fewer clothes than the women would, but also because he knew that in Anglo culture, aggressive and socially disruptive activities are generally initiated by men. If he could find peaceful, loving, gentle men in the world, there was hope for where he saw modern life going.

How did his seemingly innocent motivations to paint Indians influence the lives and the world of the Indians themselves? During those years that I was a teenager, I worked at a tourist gift shop in downtown Taos. I visited galleries during my breaks and lunch hours because it was all very intriguing—the paintings, artifacts, as well as the people who ran the galleries. (And it was really very different than Santa Clara Pueblo and Española, the closest town to Santa Clara. Española was and is not a place that the Anglo painters or romantics took a liking to. Española is a typical Chicano town—poor and without the upper-class Anglo tastes in clothes and buildings.) Taos was different. The wealthy Anglos really did set the tone for the place. As we looked at those images of who we were supposed to be—and really, no one living in Taos or Taos Pueblo could escape seeing these renderings from the late 1800s to the 1950s of images of Indians because they were everywhere in Taos—we felt idealized, yet unworthy of that adoration. There was always the feeling that we were not good enough or could not measure up to how we were represented. As people saw us, their questions and interactions with us suggested that we were what those images presented. And what was presented, underneath it all, were values, attitudes, and relationships.

Art does communicate all those things: values, attitudes, and models for relationships. We talk about colors having value—and they do. Colors and the curve of a line do set a mood, a tone, for what to feel and a way to know what is more important. In Couse's work, we have soft, muted colors representing warm, romantic feelings. They are feelings of a good, faraway place that we all began to claim for ourselves. But for Indians, it sets the standards for what one is supposed to be like. Granted that what Couse was proposing for the Indian was not bad in terms of who we once were—or still might work toward being. It does manipulate conformity to another's ideas of our behavior, actions, and even dress. It does what Rousseau felt about himself having to accept other men's definitions of one's self. Rousseau said it leads to inauthenticity. But Rousseau, writing in the mid-1700s, saw no way out of it and saw no hope for authenticity in the world he lived in. He longed to stop time at the moment when "he was drunk in the charms of nature."

Members of the Taos Society of Artists, so well exemplified by Couse, were of that vein. In their enthusiasm over the discovery of a cultural group that possessed characteristics they were looking for, they wanted to prolong, revive, and protect it. In their eagerness to do so, they forgot they were dealing with people and not objects. Or perhaps they were really acting as products of a worldview in which objects are the end rather than a by-product of striving for some greater end. In any case, they could not truly relate to the values they sensed as valuable in the other group and, consequently, imposed the values that they were themselves trying to escape. It is like the Heisenberg principle in modern quantum science that says whatever is observed is changed by the act of observation—and by the observer.

And then there is the issue of what happened to those renderings—those paintings. They, of course, were sold for a lot of money—a whole lot of money, especially to us, Indians, who had so little. We could not afford those representations of ourselves. They went to people out there in the other world—into that other world that had economic means that we, Indians, were already yearning for. As these artists themselves struggled to enter the commercial art world through advertising with the Fred Harvey system, commercialization of art was the model to be emulated by Indians and non-Indians alike. Remember that during those years, around the 1920s, romantic Indian organizations were forming, such as the New Mexico Association on Indian Affairs, later known as the Southwest Association on Indian Affairs, which runs the very popular Indian Market in Santa Fe. Their goal was to work for fair prices, to establish markets, and to collect artifacts. As a result of all that was happening for their benefit, Indians very soon found, as had the Taos artists, that the economic reasons were very compelling for the creation of art. Functional and ceremonial art is almost nonexistent today in the Pueblo communities. Undeniably, modern Indian art has a strong veneer of money and fame.

Paintings by artists such as Couse were done in a representational manner that also influenced how art was to be approached but, more importantly, how reality was to be known and defined. Indian people, traditionally, expressed themselves in symbolic and metaphorical ways. Designs, which represented clouds, mountains, the sun, the earth, snakes, lightning, were all symbols pointing to forces larger than the individual. They pointed to connecting energies in the world. The lightning moves from the sky to the earth, from the male to the female, connecting them. The content of petroglyphs and designs on pots encouraged people to remember nonphysical forces, energies, in the world. Their gaze was not to stop at the physical form. Reality was in the movement of the clouds, the water, and the wind; human creations were a way of realigning with the formless. The act of creation was to use the form as a way to see beyond the form itself. Art was not done for art's sake. It was a means to experience the power beyond the actual creation.

In the realistic paintings of Couse's era, we have a focus on the very real human individuals doing very real things in very specific places. Moreover, the focus on the skin tone and texture of the individuals sends the message that this physical human world is of primary, utmost importance. It is almost as if these artists wanted to make what they found so attractive about the Indians as real for themselves as possible.

Again, in traditional Pueblo thought we have many realities, many realms of existence, simultaneously. This realm in which we live is only one of four realms that we acknowledge, and we have the capability to move between those realms. Additionally, the human realm is only one level of reality and therefore is not where primary meaningfulness lies. As we work within our very mundane lives we are always conscious of the movement that can take us into the clouds and into the worlds under the lake.

For Pueblo people, explicitness of form and subject matter also limits the possibility of interpretations. These artists were very explicit about what they wanted to communicate. We Pueblo people are uneasy with one interpretation of anything, maybe because we are part of an oral tradition where the written or even spoken word does not limit our communication. In an oral tradition, interpretation of song, story, or design by one person does not become standardized. Even songs and stories are given the respect of being alive because they change. For instance, the borrowing of songs, stories, and myths between Pueblo communities is a common event. In the Tewa communities, which is where I come from because the Santa Clara people speak Tewa, we often "borrowed" songs from the Hopis in Arizona. Such songs are recognizable by the Hopi people, but everyone understands that when a Tewa group sings the song, it will become Tewa because it moves with the rhythms of the Tewa people.

And so also with the Taos artists? Or whoever else takes on the work of painting another group of people—or writing about them? They paint or write with the ideas that have been formed in their head, with the sensibilities in their fingers and with the rhythms of their soul. In the case of Couse, it is no wonder that people talked about "Couse's Indians."

And so we are. As the Hopi songs transform in Tewa voices, so have we Indians been transformed by Couse's paintings. It is part of the movement of life—we Indians find ourselves valuing realism over spiritualism, individualism over community and connectedness, explicitness over subtle interpretations—creating for money, running after recognition and fame, and wanting to possess objects, things, paintings for ourselves. We want to be like the rest of the world and collect our own works now because that represents well-being.

But of course, who we are as Indians can't all be laid at the feet of Couse and his contemporaries. However, they are undeniably part of that Western world that is so alluring. So alluring that the options we Indians once offered in terms of alternative lifeways, ways of thinking, and understandings of the world have been transforming into something closer to what we know as Western ways and thinking. On the other hand, we Indians and non-Indians are all continuously creating our own worlds, given all the influences and thoughts and values we choose to take in. Pueblo thought tells us that this is exactly what should be happening. Yet one always wonders. What if that person didn't impose those images, values, and thoughts? What kind of world might we have created for ourselves through today? What possibilities have been closed?

There has been much tension in the Taos community through the years because of the alignments between the Anglo artists and the Indians. And usually, these alignments have been initiated by the Anglos. The Hispanics in the area have felt left out because they were not seen or regarded as special as the Indians by the Anglos. But really, in the end, who are the more fortunate people? Those who can move and grow more with their own rhythm, or those who do not know their own rhythm anymore because of overpowering outside impositions and expectations?

Rina Swentzell (1939–2015, Santa Clara Pueblo) held an MA in architecture and a PhD in American Studies from the University of New Mexico. A weaver and potter, she also lectured and wrote about Pueblo architecture, culture, and art. Her books include *Younger–Older Ones* (2001), *Children of Clay* (1992), and, co–authored with J. J. Brody, *To Touch the Past: The Painted Pottery of the Mimbres People* (1996).

"Anglo Artists and the Creation of Pueblo Worlds" is reprinted from *The Culture of Tourism, the Tourism of Culture: Selling the Past to the Present in the American Southwest*, edited by Hal Rothman. University of New Mexico Press, 2003.

Ernest L. Blumenschein
Gerald Cassidy
Theresa Neptune Gardner
Honyumptewa family
Ahkima Honyumptewa
Clara Neptune Keezer
Madeline Naranjo
Virgil Ortiz
Molly Neptune Parker
Cara Romero
Mary Sanipass

San Ildefonso Pueblo artist,
possibly Ramona Sanchez Gonzales
(1885–1934)
Plate, early twentieth century
Clay and slip
11 ¾ × 11 ¾ × 1 ¾ in. (29.8 × 29.8 × 4.5 cm)
Gift of Adelaide Pearson, 1960.145

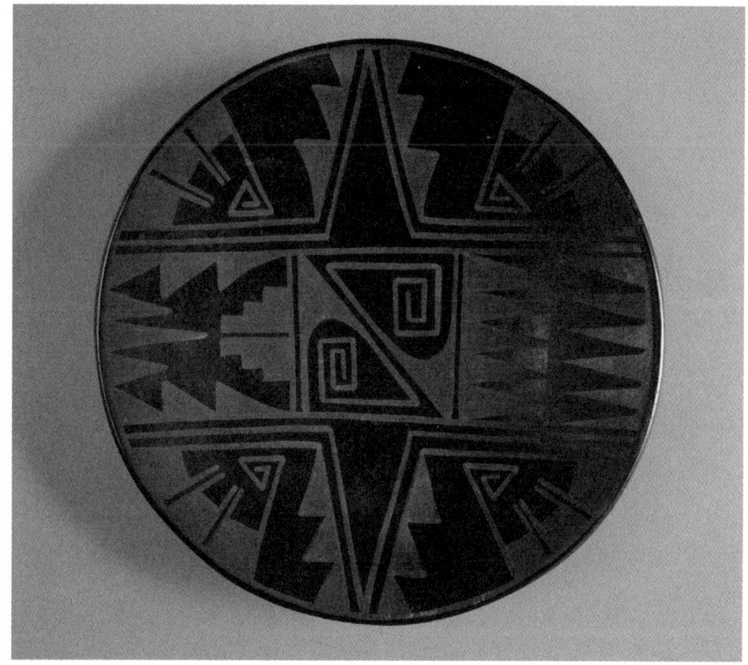

One of the most highly respected innovators and teachers of Pueblo pottery, Ramona Sanchez Gonzales practiced polychrome, red-on-red, black-on-black reduction, and natural slip techniques. The artist was born on the more conservative south end of San Ildefonso Pueblo, which impacted public recognition of her work, and she was overshadowed throughout her career by her more popular colleagues Maria and Julián Martinez. Early in her career, Sanchez Gonzales recognized the importance of sustaining pottery production for the well-being of her community. She is credited with training and inspiring multiple generations of celebrated artists, including Rose Gonzales, Tse-Pé Gonzales, Blue Corn (Crucita Gonzales Calabaza), and the award-winning Russell Sanchez.

Created using locally hand-harvested clay, this black-on-black plate features representations of clouds, mountains, and natural environments. The clay preparation includes the addition of sand and crushed rock, hand coiling, then scraping and smoothing with river stones or shells. A natural slip glaze was applied before pit firing using an oxygen reduction process to achieve the matte surface designs.

—Dr. Patricia Norby (Purépecha), associate curator of Native American Art, Metropolitan Museum of Art, and Lunder Institute for American Art research fellow 2021–22

Cara Romero
Chemehuevi, born 1977
Crickett, 2014
Archival inkjet print. 40 × 27 in. (101.6 × 68.6 cm)
Museum purchase from the Jere Abbott
Acquisitions Fund, 2022.067

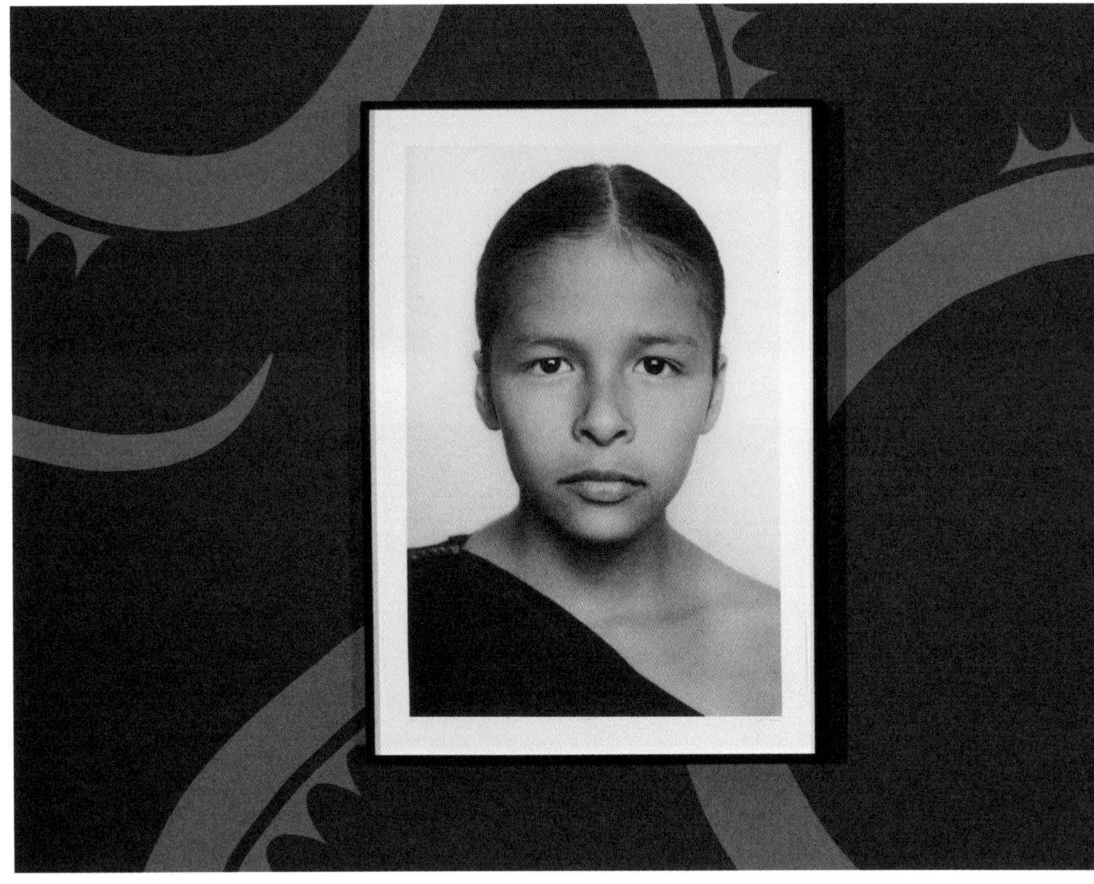

A brief moment marks the passage between girl and young woman. My stepdaughter was at this transition when I photographed her in the dining room. As I have observed her fondly over the years, she strikes me as one of the most remarkable women I have ever met. She has also always been wise beyond her years—an "old soul," if you will. Her mother has HIV/AIDS and Parkinson's; Crickett was conceived by artificial insemination, and a careful delivery by a specialist ensured she was HIV-free at birth. She has inherited a life of hardship and was born of a miracle. She lives each day with grace and strength. She has been her mother's primary caretaker since about this age. When I photographed her, I said, "Look fierce."

—Cara Romero

Ernest L. Blumenschein
American, 1874–1960
Girl in Rose, 1926
Oil on canvas. 30 ¼ × 25 in. (76.8 × 63.5 cm)
The Lunder Collection, 2013.019

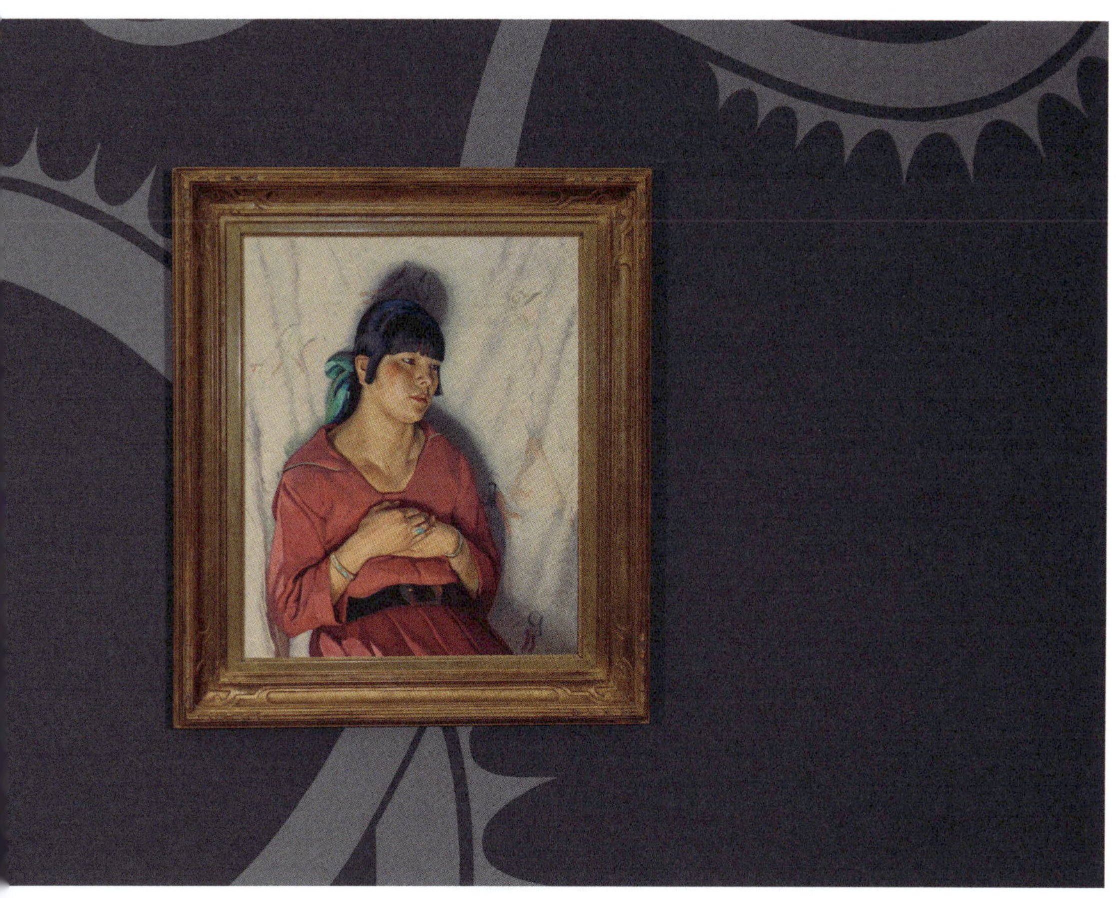

The sitter here is most likely Maria Mondragon, a Taos Pueblo community member whose husband, Don Mondragon, also modeled for Blumenschein and other TSA artists. Though the title refers to a girl, Maria was already a married young woman by the time she posed for Blumenschein. In general, the TSA painters depicted and hired men to sit for them, though in any case many TSA portrait sitters are still as yet unidentified. It was in part because it was rare for women to pose that we were able to narrow down Mondragon's identity here.

What story might we read in the sitter's expression? She looks away from the artist and, by extension, the viewer—a gesture historically employed by many painters to communicate a type of feminine docility. We could also read her pose as a personal refusal to meet our gaze, a retaining of privacy that is reinforced by her arms, which encircle her own body in what may be a protective embrace or simply a strategy to stay comfortable during a long modeling session.

—Siera Hyte

Ahkima Honyumptewa
Hopi, born 1981
Orayvi kenel kwasa, 2022
Wool, natural dye
43 × 20 × 20 in.
(109.2 × 50.8 × 50.8 cm)
Private collection

Honyumptewa family
Moccasins, 2023
Cotton, hide, silver
10 × 5 × 9 in. (25.4 × 12.7 × 22.9 cm) each

Stockings, 2023
Cotton
20 × 5 × 5 in. (50.8 × 12.7 × 12.7 cm) each
Private collection

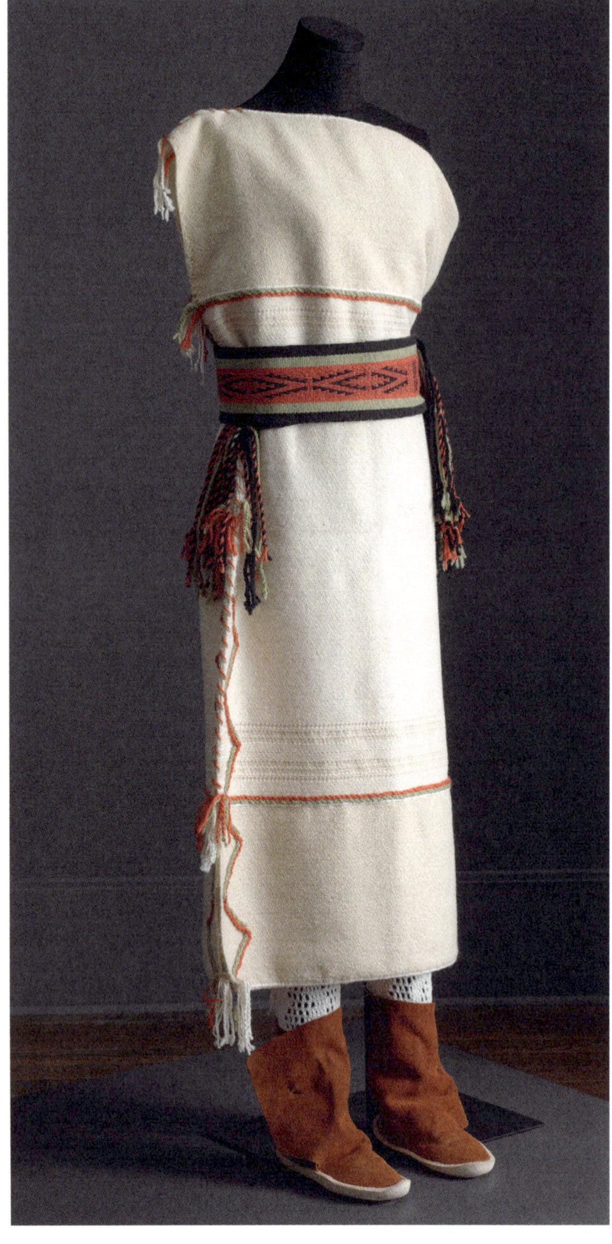

A white *orayvi kenel kwasa* (wool dress) is woven with diamond and diagonal twills. Hills and valleys are the ribs just above the diamond twill. It has natural white in the middle, and off-white for the diamond twill. It is embroidered with light green and cochineal red, and has a matching belt. The original style of *orayvi kenel kwasa* is indigo and black with the same weave. Pueblo women from all Pueblo tribes wear this style of dress, going back thousands of years, with a *kwewa* (belt) to hold the garment in place. This is just one of many contemporary styles that can be in different colors, but all with the same style of weaving.

—Ahkima Honyumptewa

Gerald Cassidy
American, 1879–1934
Pueblo Priestesses, c. 1930
Oil on canvas
40 × 30 in. (101.6 × 76.2 cm)
The Lunder Collection, 2013.039

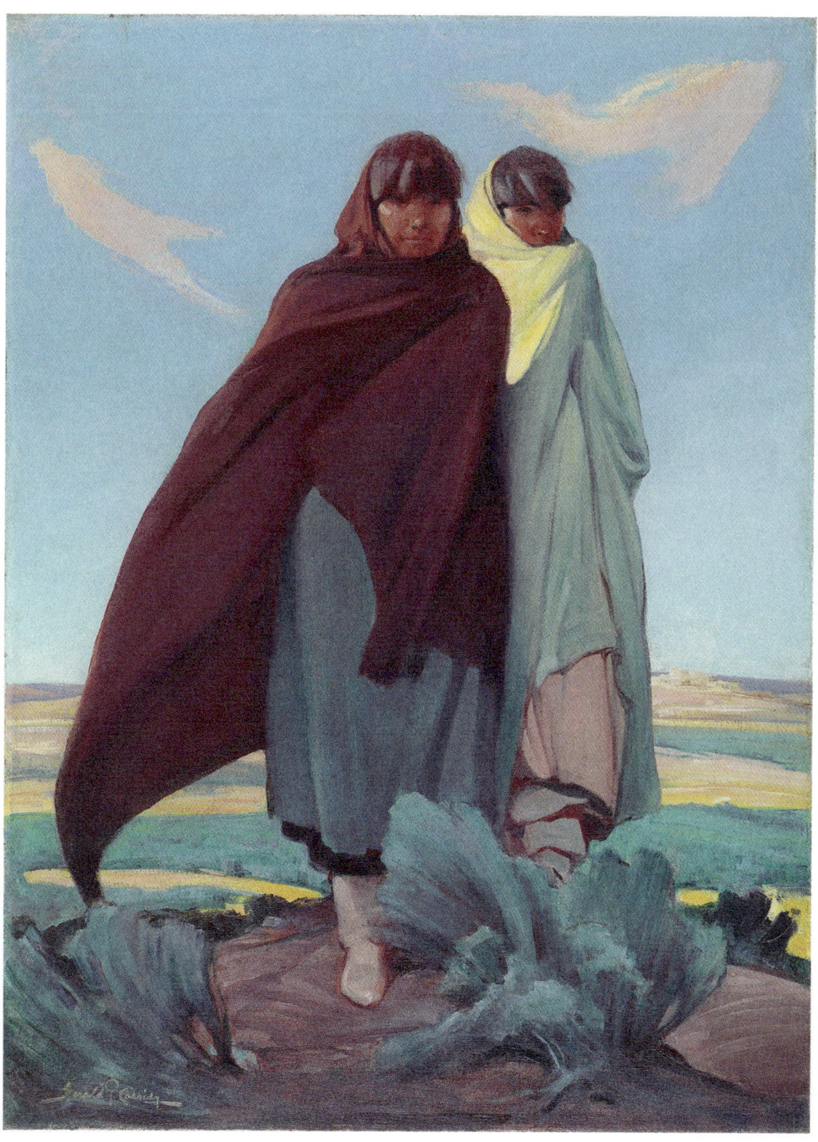

This spread, top to bottom, left to right:

Molly Neptune Parker
Passamaquoddy, 1939–2020
Flower-Top Basket, 2002
Brown ash, sweetgrass, commercial dye
7 ¼ × 6 ½ × 6 ½ in. (18.4 × 16.5 × 16.5 cm)
Anonymous gift, 2019.068

Acoma Pueblo artist
Water Vessel, n.d.
Earthenware
8 × 9 ½ × 9 ½ in. (20.3 × 24.1 × 24.1 cm)
Gift of Adelaide Pearson, 1960.146

Theresa Neptune Gardner
Passamaquoddy, 1935–2004
Pineapple Basket, n.d.
Brown ash, sweetgrass, commercial dye
7 ½ × 4 × 4 in. (19.1 × 10.2 × 10.2 cm)
Anonymous gift, 2019.064

Clara Neptune Keezer
Passamaquoddy, 1930–2016
Drum Basket with Swirl Curls, 1999
Brown ash, sweetgrass, commercial dye
4 ⅞ × 3 ⅝ × 3 ⅝ in. (12.4 × 9.2 × 9.2 cm)
Anonymous gift, 2019.052

Kewa Pueblo artist
Dough Bowl, n.d.
Earthenware
4 ¼ × 7 ¼ × 7 ¼ in. (10.8 × 18.4 × 18.4 cm)
Gift of Adelaide Pearson, 1960.144

Cochiti Pueblo artist
Water Vessel, n.d.
Ceramic
6 ⅜ × 6 ½ × 6 ½ in. (16.2 × 16.5 × 16.5 cm)
Gift of Adelaide Pearson, 1960.150

Mary Sanipass
Mi'kmaq, 1935–2020
Shopper Basket, 2012
Brown ash, commercial dye
14 × 13 × 8 ½ in. (35.6 × 33 × 21.6 cm)
Anonymous gift, 2019.071

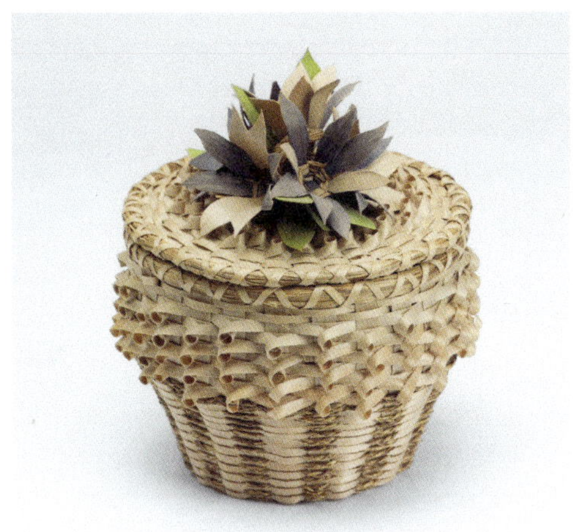

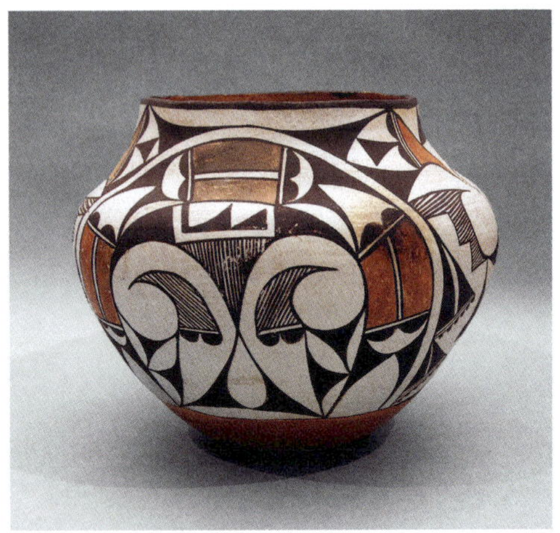

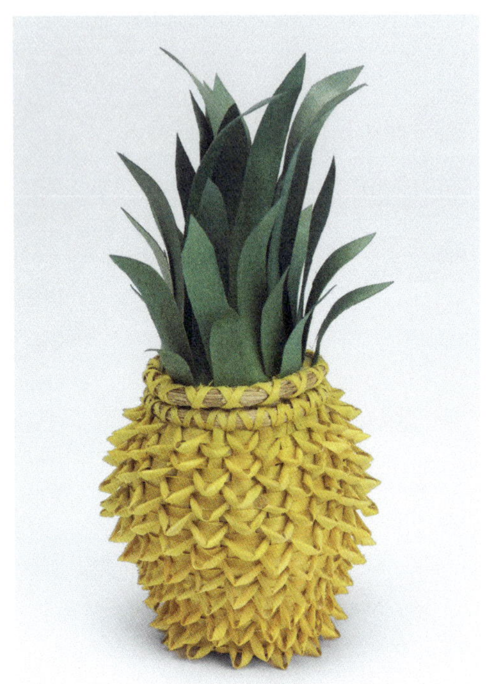

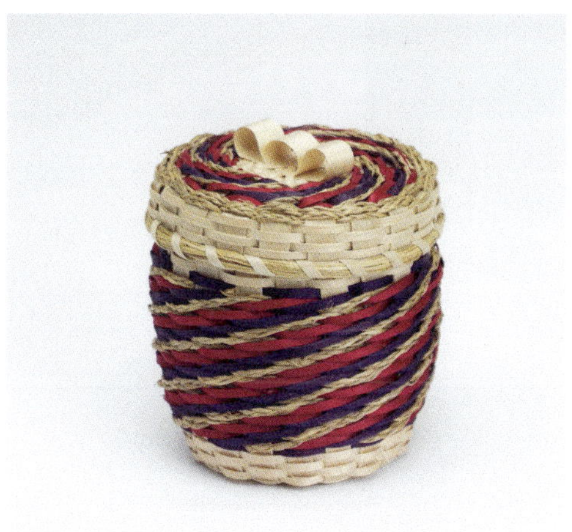

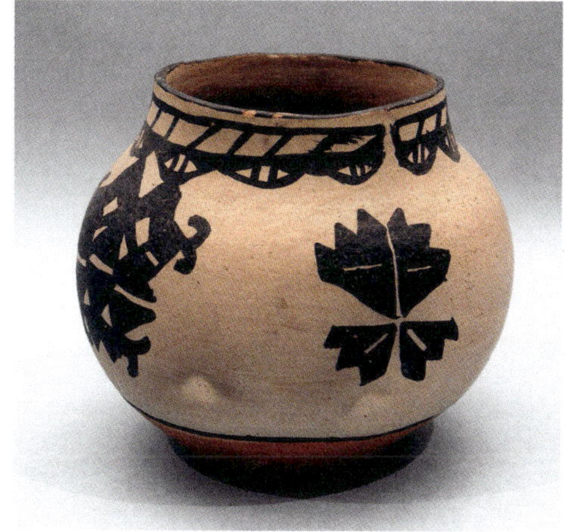

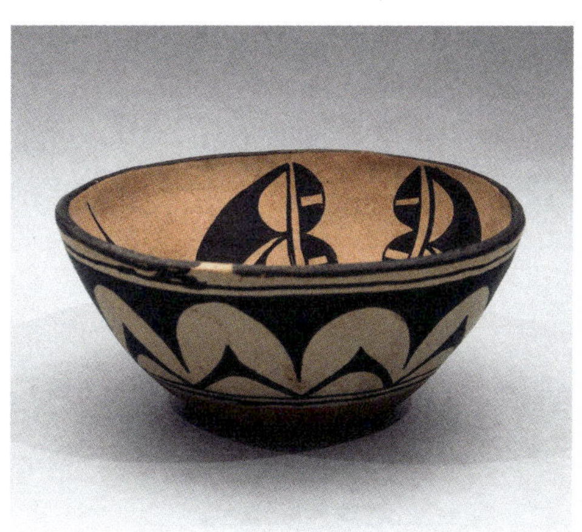

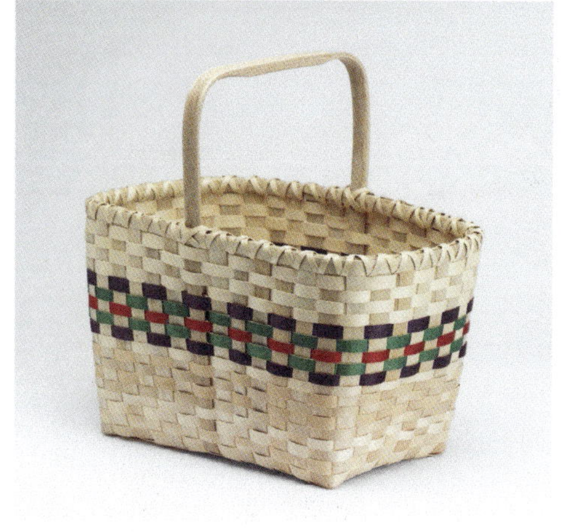

On living-room shelves and in kitchen cabinets in Pueblo homes you will find the greatest collections of pottery, baskets, storytellers, and trinkets. These collections are glimpses into private lives. Each work holds stories and fingerprints of relatives—both the living and those who have passed on. The pottery works are storage vessels collecting memories of meals and conversations, loves and heartaches, ceremonies and celebrations. Each earns its spot on the shelf through relationships developed and relationships ended. The Pueblo home is a sacred space full of cultural practices, ceremony, and spirituality, and through these collections you find generations of teachings and traditions.

In the exhibition, works from the museum's collection by Pueblo potters and Wabanaki basketmakers filled a shelf, positioned high within the gallery to evoke a traditional place of honor in a Pueblo home.

—Juan Lucero

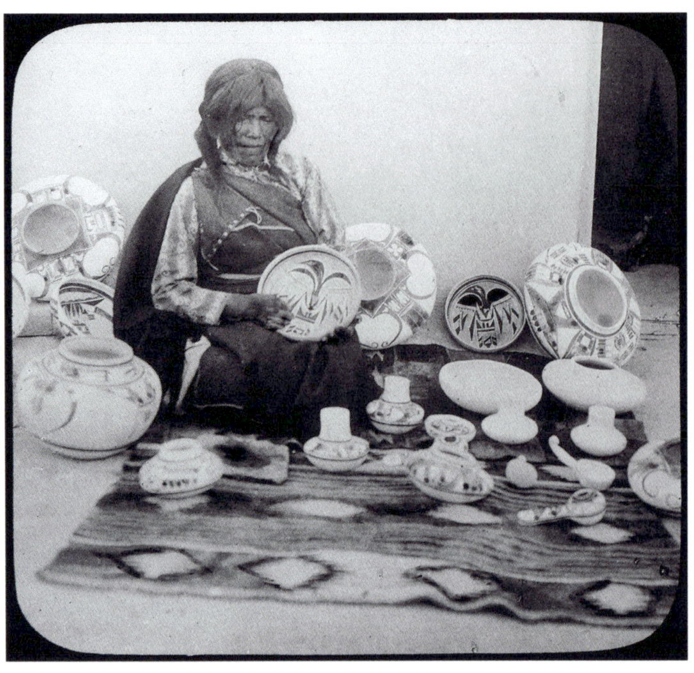

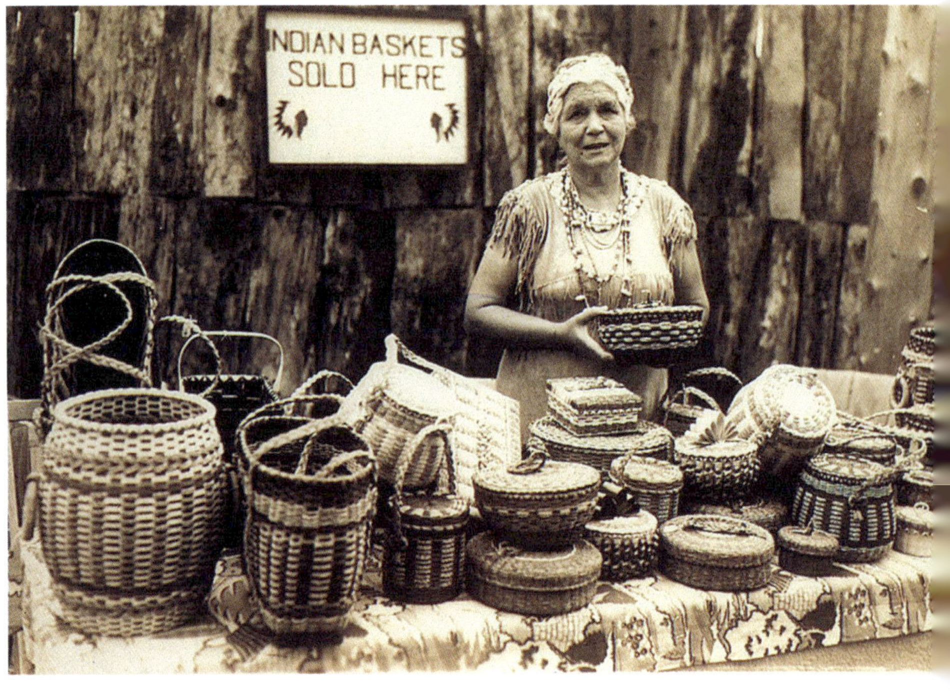

Top: Nampeyo (Hopi/Tewa) selling pottery, n.d.

Bottom: Philomene Saulis Nelson (Penobscot/Maliseet) selling baskets on Indian Island, 1953

After a discussion at an advisory council meeting about shared experiences between Pueblo and Wabanaki peoples, I thought of a way to display similarities between our cultures in this presentation. Historically and today, our people practice sovereignty through economic self-sufficiency. This side-by-side comparison of my great-grandmother, Philomene Saulis Nelson (Penobscot/Maliseet), and Nampeyo (Hopi/Tewa) shows two women who practiced their cultural art-making traditions—basketry and pottery, respectively. These photos evoke many thoughts. First, I'm struck by the similarity to other Indigenous artists selling their art and the two-hundred-year tradition of marketing baskets in our own tribes in Maine. Also how similar my own basket business looks today, with the table and wares. Yet how many more baskets are on her table on Indian Island in 1953, when weaving was still a family and community affair! Then, basket makers did not weave in isolation in their homes as we do today. The highest-priced basket on her table by the time she passed in 1977 would have been $25. Phrases of cultural pride, economic self-sufficiency, self-determination, and traditional ecological knowledge (TEK) come to mind.

—Theresa Secord (Penobscot), artist, *Painted* advisory council member, cofounder of the Maine Indian Basketmakers Alliance, and Colby Museum governor

Madeline Naranjo
Santa Clara Pueblo, born 1971
Human connections, sometimes all we need is a hug, 2022
Blackware
5 ⅛ × 4 ½ × 4 ½ in. (13 × 11.4 × 11.4 cm)
Museum purchase from the Jere Abbott Acquisitions Fund, 2022.066

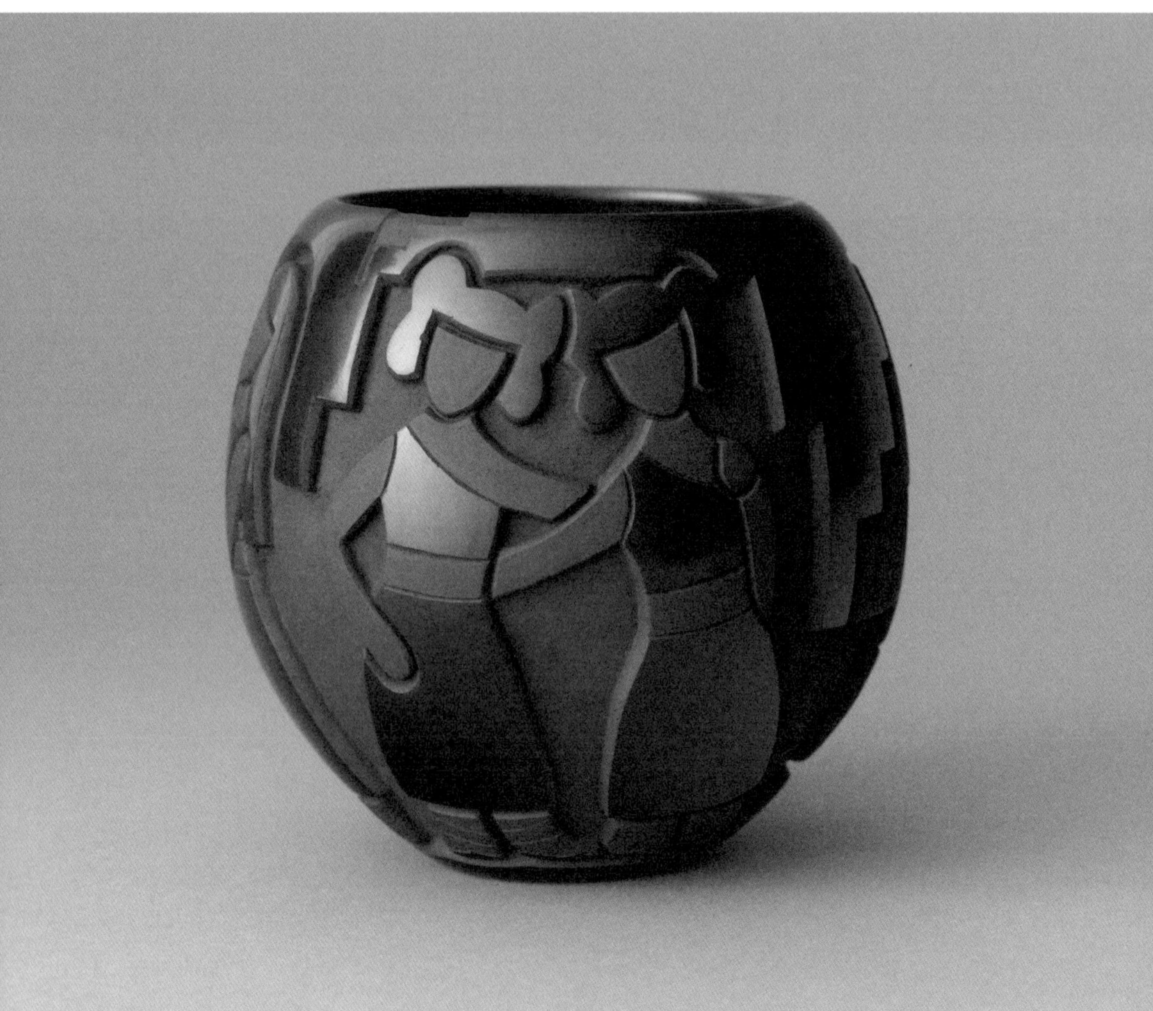

Created as a response to the COVID-19 pandemic, this piece serves as a testament to the importance of Pueblo community interaction. The hardships brought on by the pandemic were intensified in Pueblo villages. Pueblo villages are structured in multigenerational housing arrangements, with neighbors only feet away. Feast days, dance ceremonies, and life events that once brought the community together in positivity suddenly became life-threatening during the pandemic, and ceased indefinitely. This caused tribal members to live in fear, grief, and longing. Our communities aren't meant to function in an individualistic manner; we have been operating as one large family from the time of emergence. This piece serves as a reminder of the connections we lost *and* a celebration of our resilience.

Madeline Naranjo is from Kah'p'oo Owinge. Her journey with clay began at a very young age and continues today. She uses traditional methods while creating works that exemplify a contemporary flair, all the while continuing the legacy of her family.

—Juan Lucero

Following spread:
Virgil Ortiz (Cochiti Pueblo), *The Blind Archers*, 2013, from the series *Revolt 1680/2180*

This image by Virgil Ortiz comes from the artist's *Revolt 1680/2180* project, a futuristic retelling of the Pueblo Revolt, a pivotal event in the history of Pueblo resistance. Led by Tahu (the central figure), the warriors seen here are members of the Blind Archers, a group of women and girls who ensure the survival of Pueblo culture despite the threat of colonization. Of the archers, Ortiz says: "Cochiti Pueblo is a matriarchal society, with clans passed through the women. It is also the women who, when raising their children, share their stories of the past to help guide our future. One lesson has stuck with me, and lately, it resonates with growing importance. It is about how the grandmothers would inspire us with positive instructions—'do it this way'—instead of negative critiques—'don't do it that way.' The mind has difficulty coping with the multitude of negatives, yet responds quickly to the positives. I have used the character of Tahu to convey this advice of the grandmothers and their positive outlook even in the face of adversity. This attitude of the grandmothers has endured despite nearly three hundred years of fear and intimidation imposed on the Pueblo people."

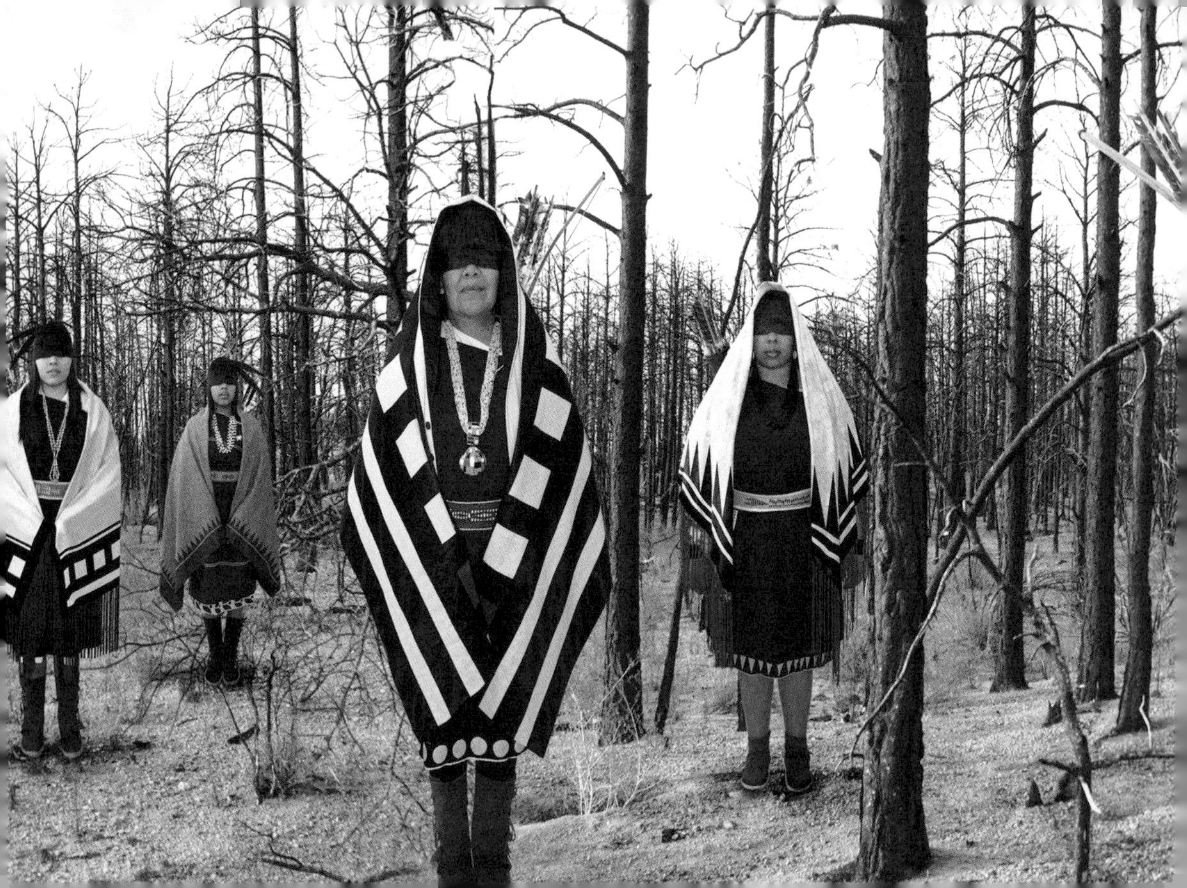

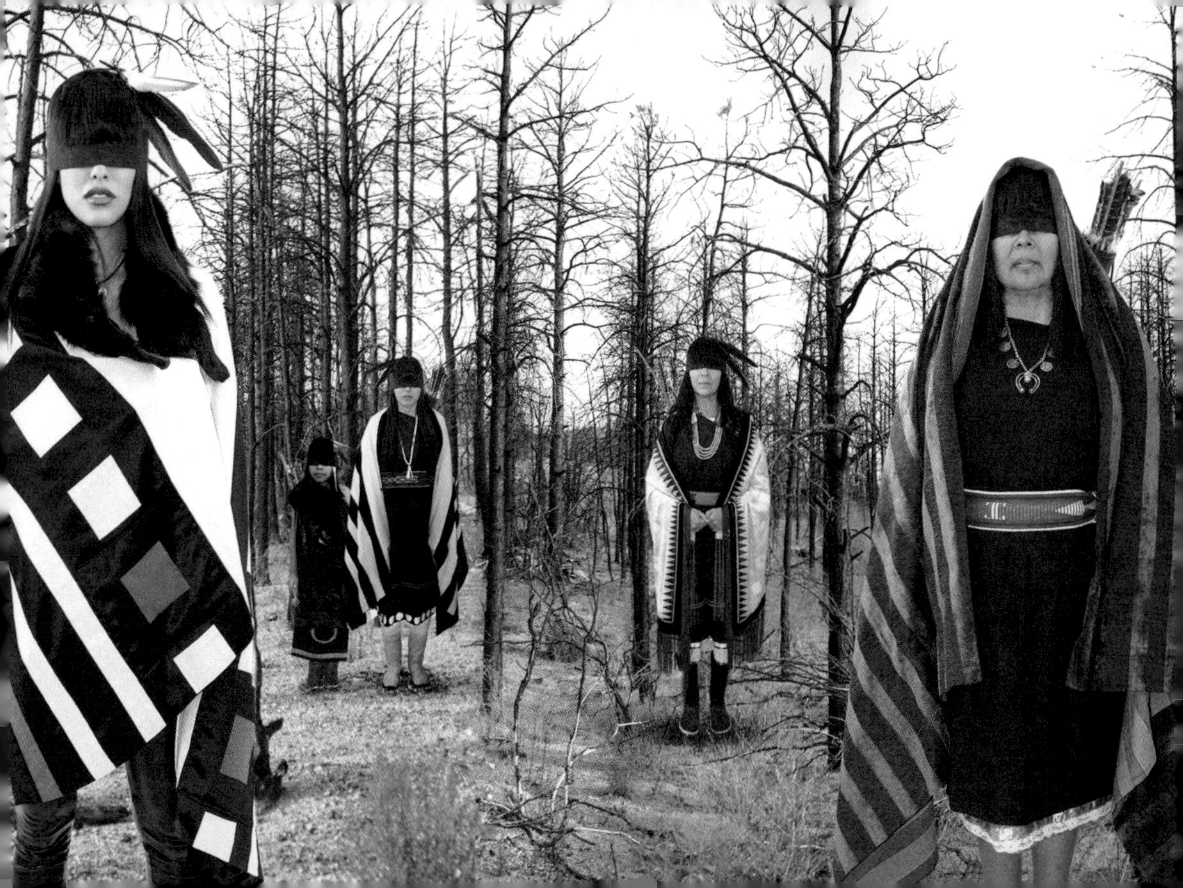

Tony Abeyta
Oscar E. Berninghaus
Ernest L. Blumenschein
Berdina Charley
Jason Garcia
Patricia Michaels
Virgil Ortiz
John Yellowbird Samora

Pueblo Survivance and Futurism

Throughout this installation of works from the Colby Museum collection, narratives focused on the Native perspective. Many of the gallery texts were written by Pueblo artists or community members, or were based on conversations with Pueblo tribal members, thereby facilitating accurate and authentic interpretation. The Native perspective owned the narrative.

White US and European art historians have consistently treated Pueblo art as craft and/or cultural practice rather than fine art, and interpreted it from an anthropological, ethnographic point of view. This museum-standard act of racist categorization has had the effect of systematically suppressing Native art and artists. But these interpretive practices are finally being supplanted by proper community interaction—by sincere efforts to support, develop, and include Native knowledge with the same degree of seriousness as institutional knowledge.

In *Painted*, the future of Pueblo art was in the hands of Pueblo community members. Each tribal member was responsible for creating, curating, and interpreting their work, emphasizing the decolonization* of museum practice.
Native presence was established by focusing on the interpretation and perspective of Pueblo community members. In the exhibition's final gallery, viewers were treated to the future of Native presence in traditionally non-Native spaces. Native art was emphasized through the power of space. Here, Native artists highlighted their identities and experiences.

At the time the TSA was painting in Taos, there was a movement afoot for museums to collect, photograph, and document the remnants of a vanishing race. Native people survived, but many museums didn't evolve beyond that era. It especially wasn't expected for Native people to work in museums, much less to curate. Today, Native people are thriving and have cemented their future beyond tomorrow, as with artists like Virgil Ortiz, who provides a vision of our people in the year 2180. The future of Native art is further establishing our presence and ensuring that Native practice continues.

Pueblo Survivance** = Futurism

—Juan Lucero

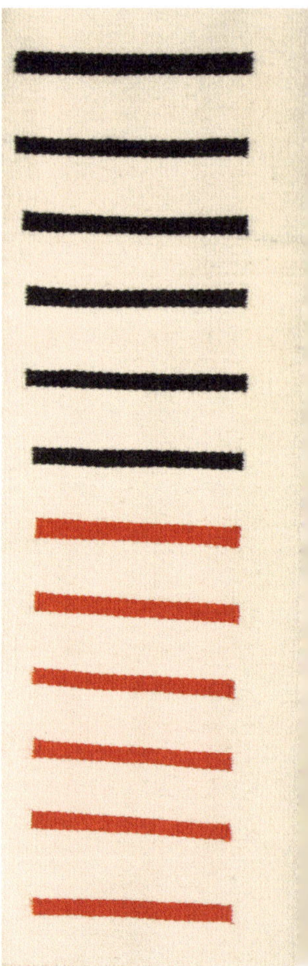

* Decolonize: to free (an institution, a sphere of activity, etc.) from the cultural or social effects of colonization; to eliminate colonial influences or attitudes

** Survivance: a narrative incorporating themes of survival and resistance that insists on the inclusion of the Native presence (per the Anishinaabe writer Gerald Vizenor)

Berdina Charley
Diné, born 1968
Shapes and Lines, 2021
Hand-dyed and natural churro wool
26 × 47 in. (66 × 119.4 cm)
Museum purchase from the Jere Abbott Acquisitions Fund, 2022.062

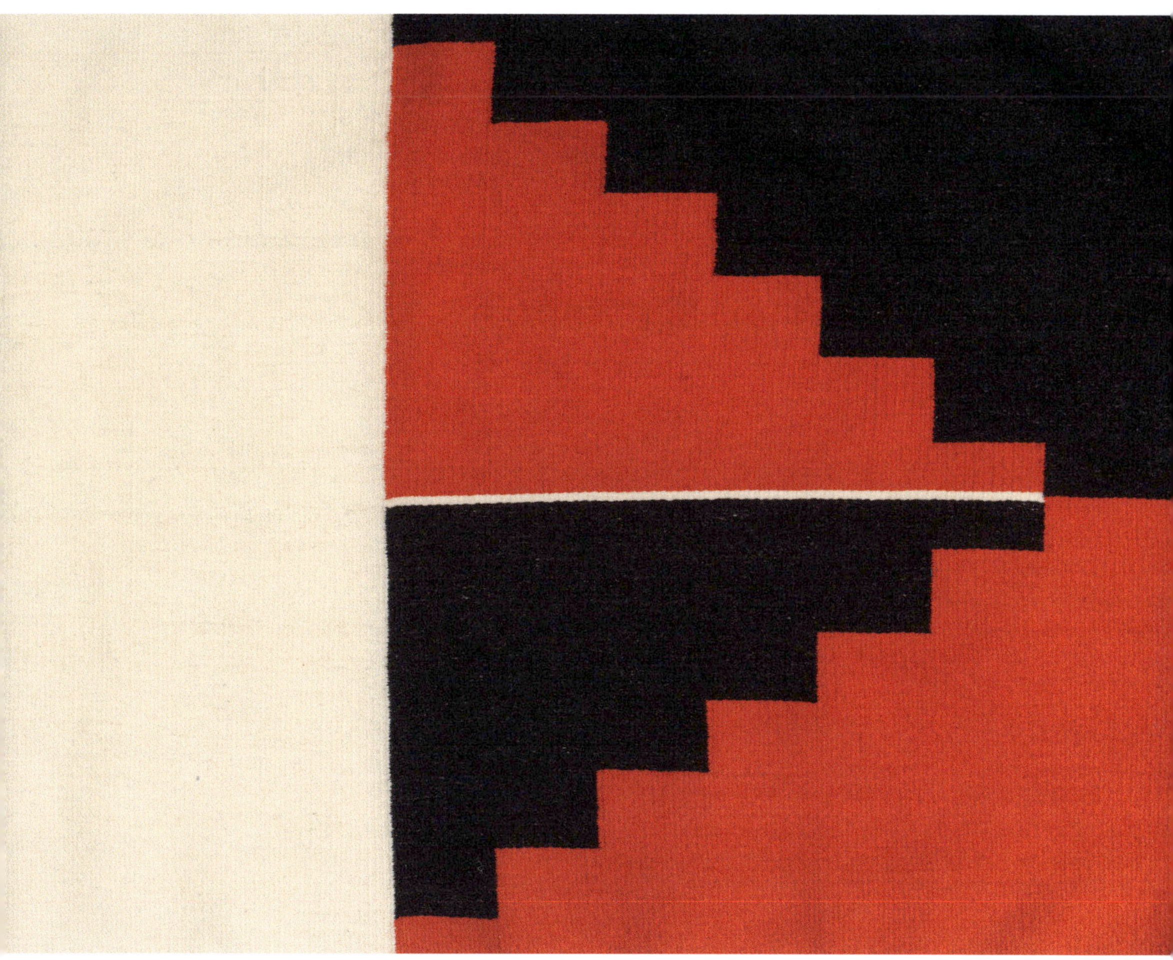

Recently I have been creating non-regional-style patterns using the traditional Navajo style of weaving—here, a weft-face weaving technique and turned/interlock join methods on a Navajo loom with a continuous warp. I love experimenting with diverse types of weaving techniques and incorporating beads, *soumak* twining, and embroidery. The wool is homegrown churro wool. The white color is natural, and the red is dyed with cochineal.

—Berdina Charley

Virgil Ortiz
Cochiti Pueblo, born 1969
Omtua, 2023
Ceramic
33 × 25 × 12 in. (83.8 × 63.5 × 30.5 cm)
Museum purchase from the William A. Oates, Jr. Fund for American Western Art, 2023.045

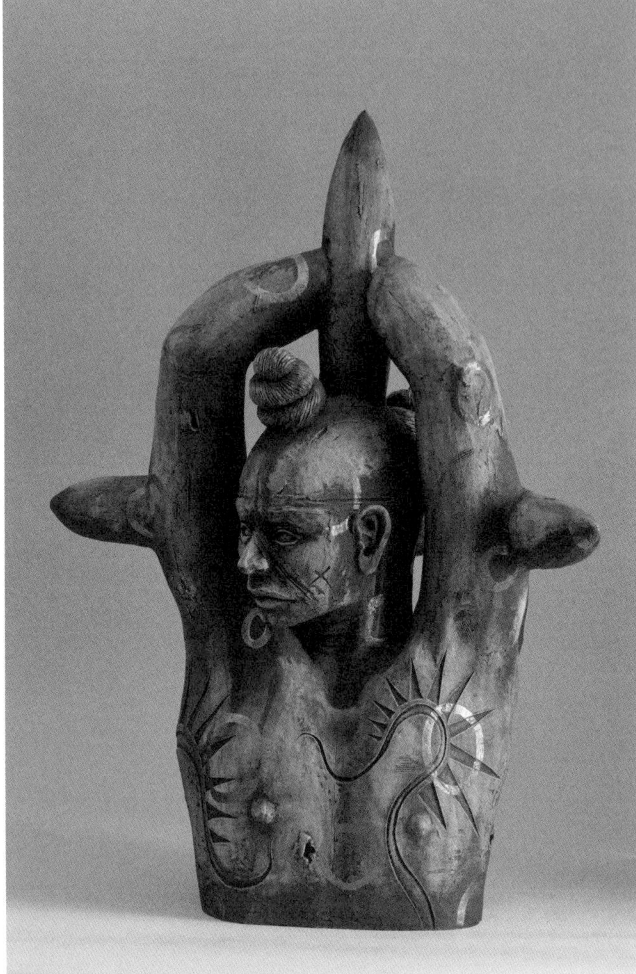

All my work is rooted in educating globally about the 1680 Pueblo Revolt. I've incorporated this subject matter into my work for more than two decades. It is an awakening of the truth. Omtua and Catua—young runners from Tesuque Pueblo, among several other messengers, carried knotted deerhide strips more than fifty miles to surrounding villages just before the rebellion. The number of knots signaled the days remaining before the well-orchestrated uprising. But this ingenious plan was cut short, and the revolt began early. Omtua and Catua were captured, tortured, and hanged, becoming the first to give their lives to the cause.

—Virgil Ortiz

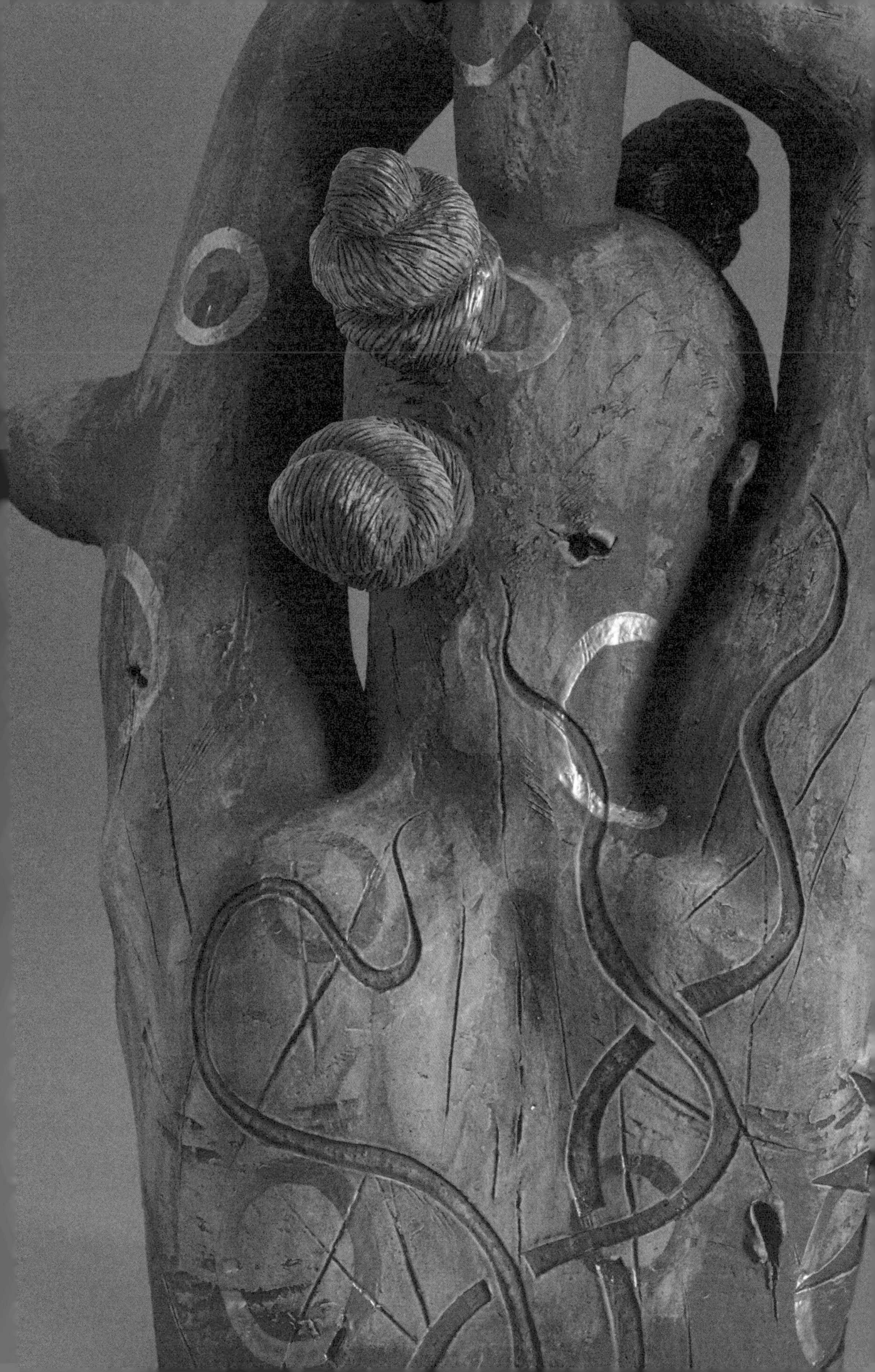

Jason Garcia
Santa Clara Pueblo, born 1973
I live off the land…and Sonics, 2023
Ceramic
14 × 10 in. (35.6 × 25.4 cm)
Museum purchase from the Jere Abbott Acquisitions Fund, 2023.011

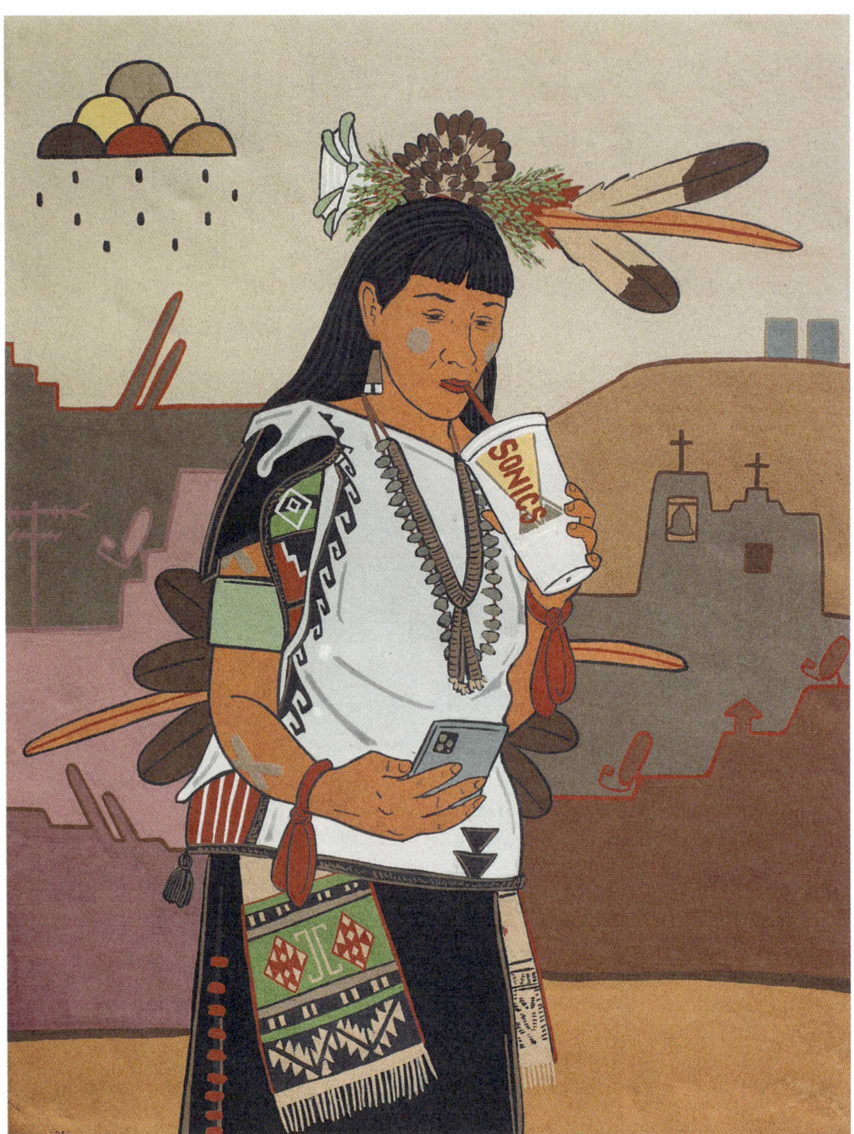

Jason Garcia
From the artist's talk at the Painted *symposium, November 2023*

I created three clay tile pieces for the exhibition. Two are individual works, and the other is a diptych titled *Back in Time*. When making them, I was thinking of the Taos Society painters and their daily life scenes of Taos Pueblo and surrounding Pueblos, and how they would use various Pueblo models. I also do work like that. I usually say that my work documents the ever-changing cultural landscape of Kah'p'oo Owinge, or Santa Clara Pueblo.

I use traditional techniques and materials in all of my work, for example mineral pigments gathered from different areas of New Mexico, Arizona, and Colorado, and traditional clays gathered near Santa Clara Pueblo. I fire the pieces outdoors in the traditional manner, too. There's a TSA painting in the exhibition by Gerald Cassidy titled *Pueblo Priestesses*, where two women are walking together. It somewhat mimics the two ladies of Santa Clara in my work *The Water Carriers*. They're walking by the Avanyu Travel Center, the local "watering hole" in the border town of Española.

Back in Time features the DeLorean, the time machine from *Back to the Future*. On the left, the lady is shown in the past. On the right, we see her in the present day with telephone antennas, power lines, and satellite dishes in the background. She also represents Saint Clare of Assisi, who is the patron saint of the blind as well as of television.

I live off the land...and Sonics, with the Buffalo dancer holding the Sonic cup in her hand and taking a selfie, reflects what I see in daily life. Such depictions are maybe not as romanticized or stereotypical as the images the Taos Society painters created, showing something that's mostly untouched or actively removed from the contemporary.

Jason Garcia
Santa Clara Pueblo, born 1973
The Water Carriers, 2023
Ceramic
8 ½ × 13 in. (21.6 × 33 cm)
Museum purchase from the Jere Abbott
Acquisitions Fund, 2023.010

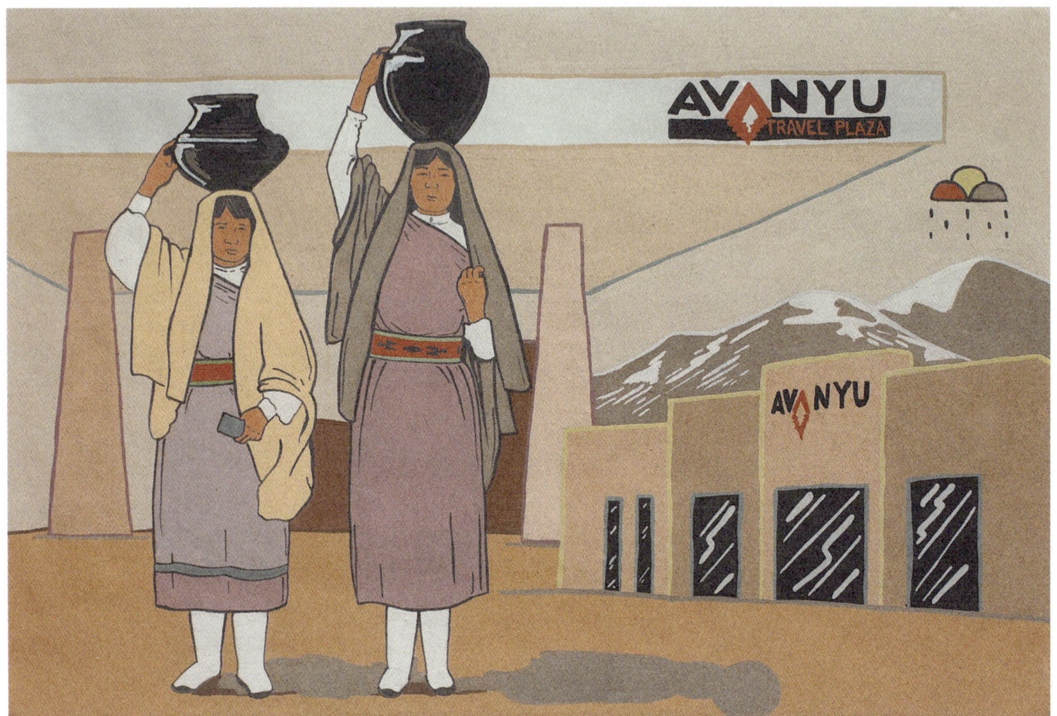

Jason Garcia
Santa Clara Pueblo, born 1973
Back in Time, 2023
Ceramic
13 × 8 ½ in. (33 × 21.6 cm) each
Museum purchase from the Jere Abbott Acquisitions Fund, 2023.012.1, 2023.012.2

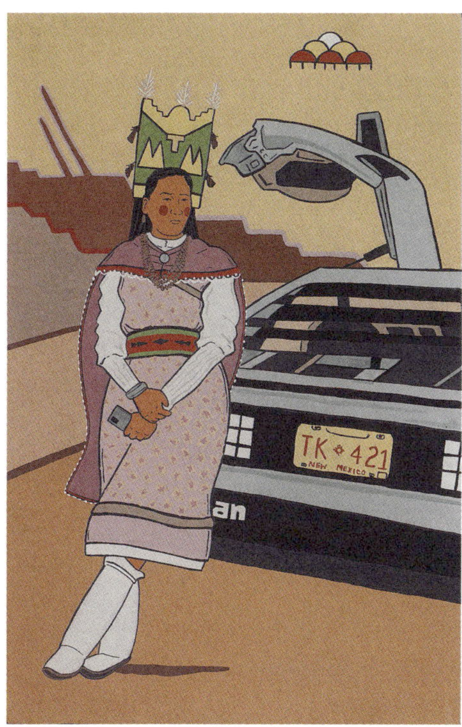

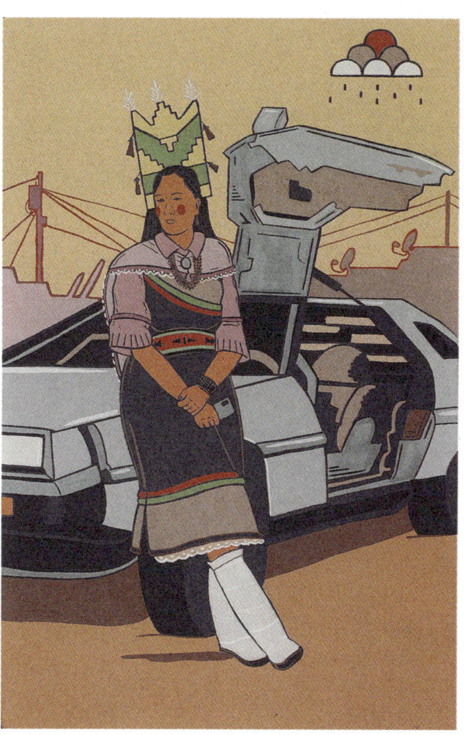

John Yellowbird Samora
Taos Pueblo, born 1973
Untitled, 2013
Micaceous clay
17 × 12 × 7 in. (43.2 × 30.5 × 17.8 cm)
Museum purchase from the Jere Abbott
Acquisitions Fund, 2023.048

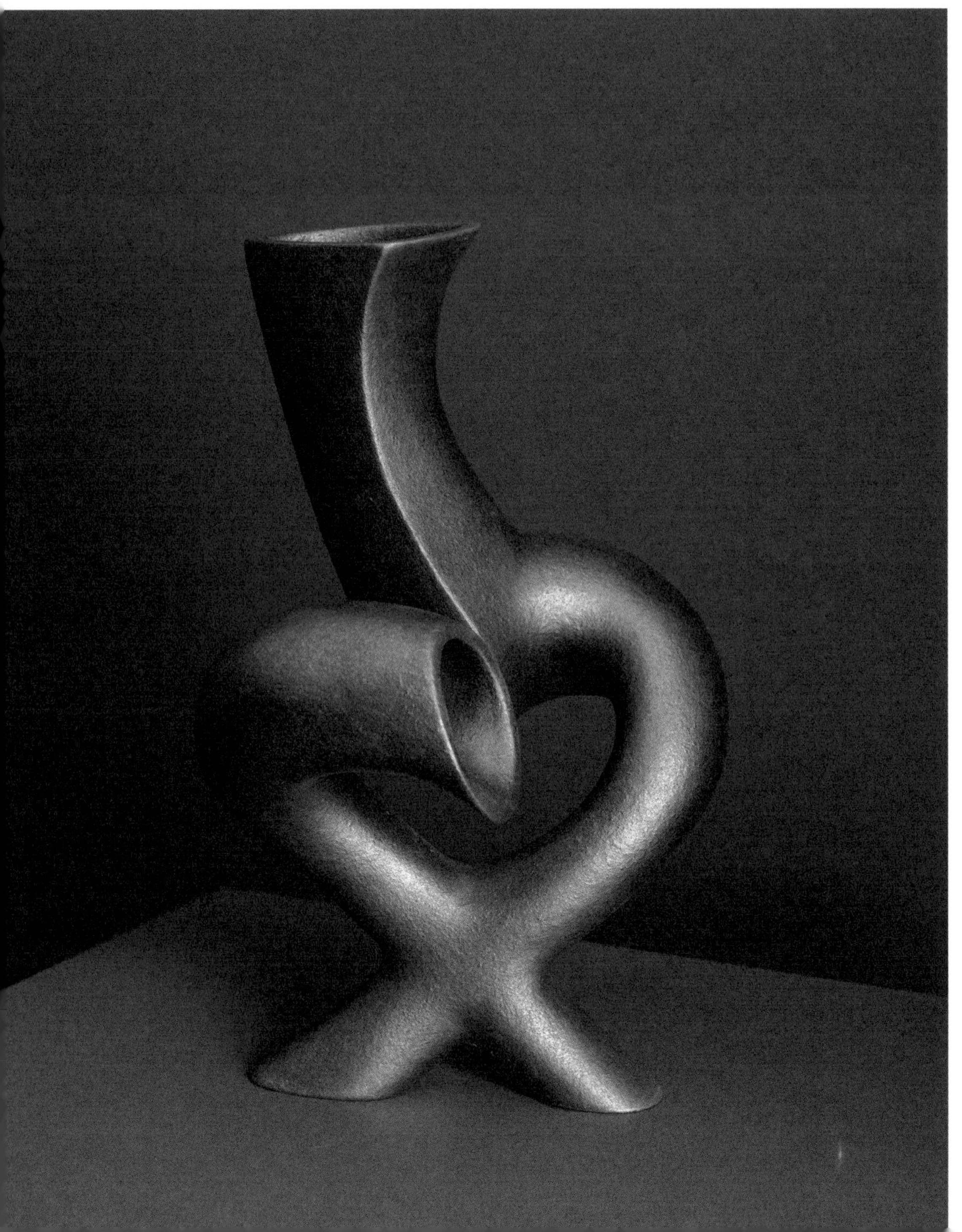

Artists Sarah Sockbeson (Penobscot) and John Yellowbird Samora spoke in Taos, New Mexico, in May 2022 during a convening of Lunder Institute for American Art fellows, Colby Museum staff, and Pueblo artists and community members. Their conversation was recorded for Sockbeson's podcast; it has been edited for this volume.

Sarah Sockbeson: Welcome, John! How would you like to introduce yourself?

John Yellowbird Samora: Hi, my name is John Yellowbird Samora, and I was born and raised here in Taos, New Mexico. I am a potter mainly working with micaceous clay, a clay body that is indigenous to the Taos area. I work in a primarily contemporary style, but I do utilize a lot of traditional techniques.

SS: What inspired you to become an artist?

JYS: Growing up here in Taos, there's lots of art and art galleries, and you can't help but be inspired around it all. Throughout grade school and junior high, I was always doing art projects and soaking up the art here in town. I dabbled in a few ceramics classes in high school, and I found that I deeply liked working with my hands. Although a lot of those classes used regular store-bought clay and glazes, and throwing on the wheel as opposed to sculpting.

SS: Getting the feel for it, experimenting. There's so much to playing with materials and different elements, especially with sculpture, and even more so with ceramics. At what point did you decide that this would be your profession?

JYS: Growing up, I was fortunate enough to be able to ski. I learned here at the ski area. But right out of high school, I had a major accident while skiing and broke my back. I had a vision of myself in a wheelchair, never able to walk again—then imagined having a sketch pad on my lap, and that somehow got me through. After that vision—and six months of rehab—I enrolled in the Institute of American Indian Arts (IAIA) down in Santa Fe and started to take classes. Soon enough, I decided ceramics was something I wanted to pursue.

SS: Were your courses more on the contemporary side, or more traditional?

JYS: Fortunately, IAIA has a really good program that teaches the contemporary techniques—using store-bought clays, glazes, kilns—but also traditional pottery, involving clay gathered in the landscape and traditional firing techniques. That gave me an all-around exposure to clay.

SS: That's what's cool about IAIA: they are passing on knowledge that other schools don't have offerings for, or don't have the same type of respect for or acknowledgment of. They understand how we do things in the Native arts world, which can be totally different from the contemporary arts world. When did you decide to embrace micaceous clay?

JYS: Once I finished all my coursework. This clay is indigenous to the Taos Pueblo here. A lot of it is treated as more of a utilitarian-type clay, and made into the minimalistic cookware you've certainly seen, which has its own traditions and prestige. I wanted to use that medium but put a more contemporary spin on it. I began trying to find my own unique look and style.

SS: There's indeed such a long history of making with clay here. You can look back at all the designs and the techniques that were used in the past alongside the people continuing the art form today. What were some makers or works that influenced you? Or maybe intimidated you!

JYS: I definitely appreciated the pottery that was out there and admired how much time and energy goes into it, but I also didn't want to just copy things. In my growing-up years, of all the art I was exposed to, the artist I enjoyed the most was R. C. Gorman. There was a simplicity to his work, yet he could create such beauty with simplicity. In my work, I try to have complex ideas, themes, lines, but still keep it very simple.

SS: How does micaceous clay differ from commercial clay?

JYS: Micaceous clay has the mineral mica already mixed in with the clay body, and so it is a complete clay body, meaning that it does not need to be processed with another additive mineral before firing. You just dig it out of the earth and refine the impurities out of it.

SS: Do you harvest your own clay?

JYS: Yes. It takes a while to make, so usually it's a big process—you want to make a bunch of clay so it'll last you a long time.

SS: Do you have specific places you always go to collect the clay?

JYS: There are a few different spots in the area. I keep going back to a few places in the Ojo Caliente area.

SS: Are those traditional harvesting spots?

JYS: They are, but not so much for the Taos Pueblo Indians. The Apaches would go to the Ojo Caliente area. There's a lot of trade, too, meaning that people would trade knowledge of different gathering places for clay.

SS: A lot of people don't realize how much chemistry is involved in making pottery.

JYS: In a clay body, you need what is called a temper, a heating agent, to help distribute the heat throughout the piece of pottery. It can be anything from sand to volcanic ash. Even old pot shards can be crushed up and refined and put back in there. In the case of micaceous clay, it's the mica that becomes that heating agent, the temper. I do know the traditional firing techniques, but I use a kiln. More recently, I've been playing around with using the micaceous clay in a raku firing scenario, which is a lower-temperature setting, and experimenting with different techniques during firing to achieve different finishes on the pots.

SS: What kind of feedback do you get from the community when people see your more contemporary style?

JYS: I haven't come across anyone who discouraged it. People seem to accept it for what it is. I do feel like people from the Taos Pueblo see that I have a gift for pottery making and want to commission pieces, but more in a traditional mode because they want to use them and see the beauty in that. So those pieces are simpler, and less contemporary. Usually people are buying my work more for the aesthetic value than for utility, but I do tell them that the material is very strong, and yes, you could cook with it if you wanted to.

SS: Do the natural surroundings of Taos influence your work?

JYS: Definitely. After I finished school I did go back to skiing again, and I love to ski and also kayak a lot. I like to be in nature. I love the water. So I try to infuse some of that into my work, for instance evoking water flowing down a mountain, or a river, and making it look smooth and effortless.

SS: What would you say are some common misperceptions about pottery, or about Native artists working in the art form today?

JYS: From my perspective, the toughest thing is when people want to know more about it, want me to explain it, but there's so much to it, you have to have a passion and a yearning for knowledge to even start to understand. There are all these little subtleties. People want to educate themselves, but it takes a long time.

SS: Right, they have to have that interest—that's why I think art is so important, because it draws people in and maybe sparks an interest in someone who otherwise wouldn't go and educate themselves. How do you initially conceptualize a piece, and where do your designs come from?

JYS: Works made with micaceous clay don't usually have a whole lot of painted designs on the outside, so I like to create my pieces more from an architectural standpoint. It's more about the form, the shape.

SS: I've seen some of your work where you played with the sense of balance, almost like an optical illusion.

JYS: Well, I think it's a metaphor for life. You need balance, whatever you decide that balance is. One thing about being a potter—as opposed to a typical person—is that you cannot be afraid of a piece breaking. You've got to accept that pottery breaks. I like to play around with balance such that sometimes a piece looks like it might fall over or break.

SS: How do you philosophize firing something and risking breakage when you've put so much time into it? Taking that risk?

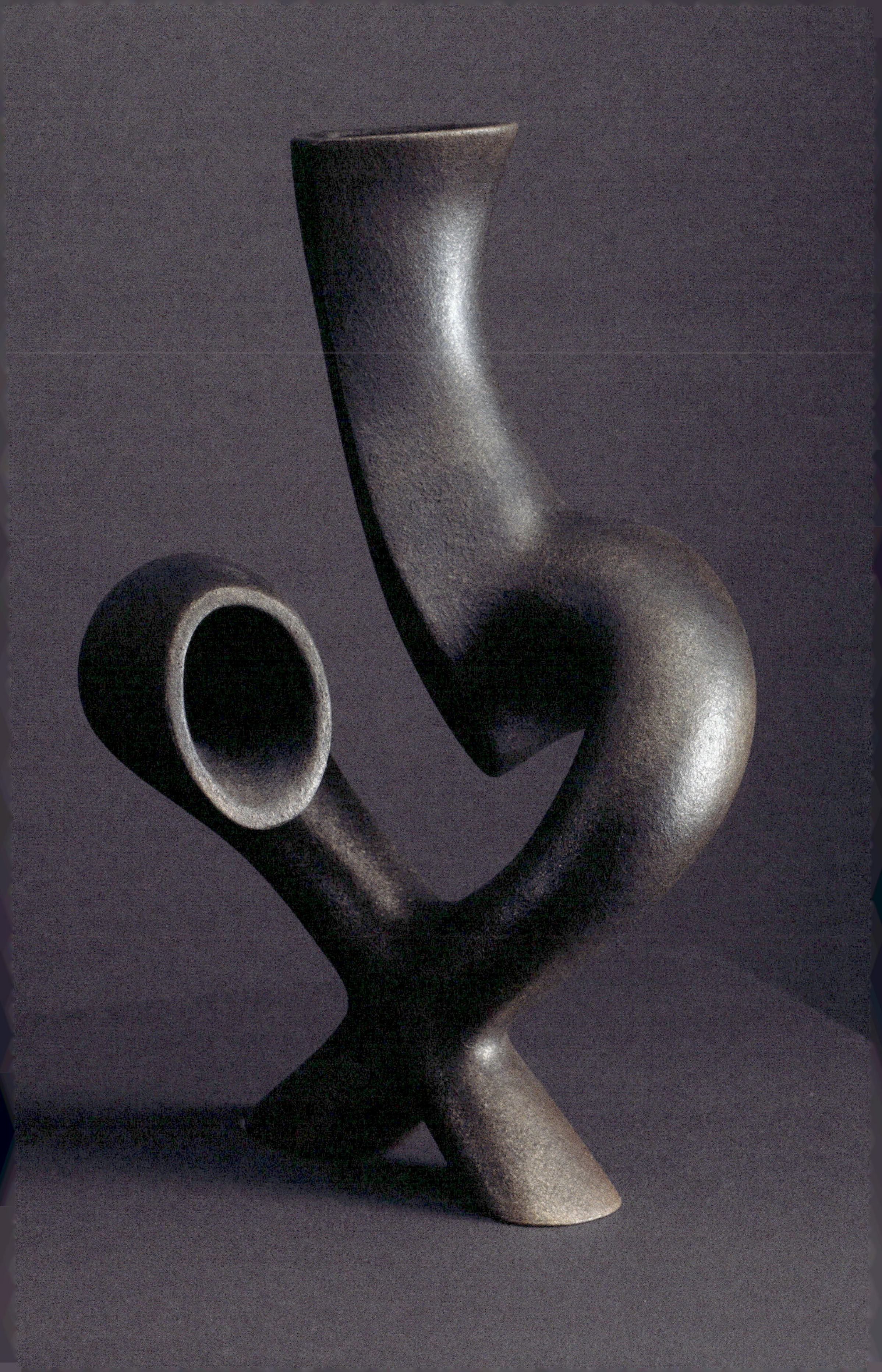

JYS: It's absolutely a risk, but as they say: no risk, no reward. Especially in clay. Part of the learning process is messing up, then thinking about it, mixing it up, figuring it out, and trying again. It's the hardest when you first start out because you just don't know, and there's so many steps along the way that you can mess up so easily. You have to have perseverance to get through that. I still vividly remember some of my first pottery classes down at IAIA. I don't think I had one piece come out my whole first semester.

But I still got an A, because my teacher saw that I was engaged and willing to just keep going. That's such a major part of it.

SS: And firing is an art unto itself, right?

JYS: Yes, it's as much of an art form as the shaping of the piece. It can take a long, long time to master it.

SS: What can you say about the different firing methods in terms of coloration?

JYS: The main two types of firing are oxidation firing and reduction firing. An oxidation fire is very clean-burning, meaning there's very little smoke involved. In that firing, you can achieve the natural color of the clay body. With reduction firing, you are infusing smoke into the pot and turning the pot black. You can also have a combination of the two. It's always fun.

SS: There must be a lot that goes into working with smoke. It can have such a major effect on how the piece comes out. If you have an intention to make it black, does it always work like that? Or is there a technical aspect you have to master in order to achieve those colors?

JYS: Each firing technique takes a lot of time, and you're going to learn different things about how the smoke responds to the pot, and even about the clay you're using. I mentioned I've embraced a raku style of firing. Raku is a Japanese style of reduction firing using smoke—reducing the amount of oxygen to create a smoky atmosphere—and I've been able to achieve different black colors on the pots. And it is much, much faster—meaning, a matter of minutes—than traditional reduction firing.

SS: What would you say is the most fulfilling part of what you do?

JYS: Taking a piece of the earth, applying yourself to it, making something, seeing how it comes out. Seeing an idea that manifested itself and actually made it through the firing, and now it's here, it's with us. Like it was birthed.

SS: It represents the culture out there in the world. What else would you like people to walk away with?

JYS: If you like art and you like pottery, check it out, immerse yourself, and try and learn as much as you can. It's so diverse. Just within pottery, you could spend a lifetime looking at and learning about all the different types, just as one could with jewelry or the many different types of basketry and weaving. There's so much out there to learn and engage in. It's fun to learn things and meet new people. You can see where they come from and how different art forms evolve.

SS: It's great having the culture be alive, not just in practice, but out there in the world, with people enthusiastically collecting it. And every piece has a life of its own.

Oscar E. Berninghaus
American, 1874–1952
Desert Nocturne (Indian Nocturne), 1919
Oil on canvas
24 × 30 in. (61 × 76.2 cm)
The Lunder Collection, 008.2011

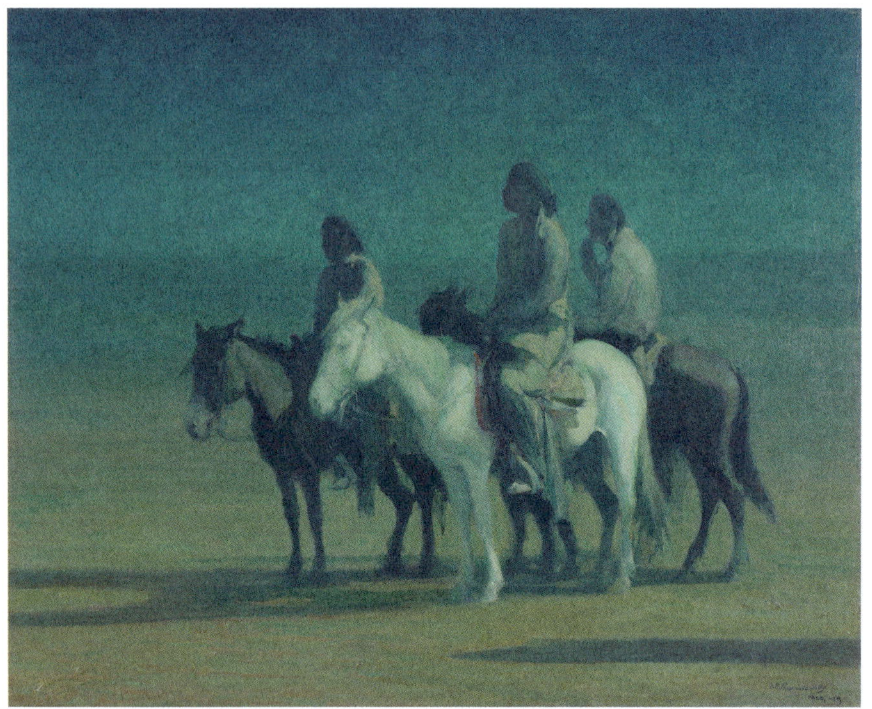

Ernest L. Blumenschein
American, 1874–1960
Untitled (Mountain Wood Gatherers),
c. 1926
Oil on canvas
23 × 50 in. (58.4 × 127 cm)
The Lunder Collection, 040.2009

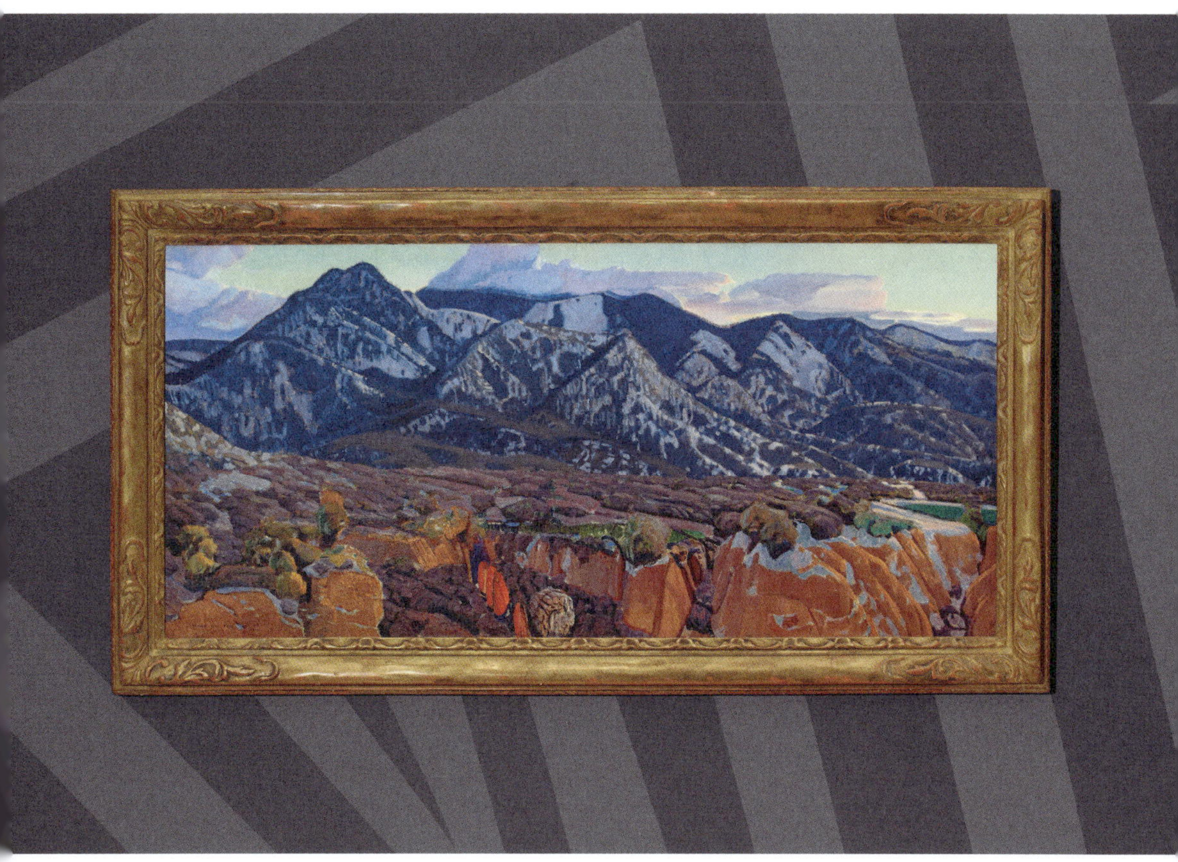

Tony Abeyta
Diné, born 1965
Citadel, 2021
Oil on linen
40 × 60 in. (101.6 × 152.4 cm)
The Lunder Collection, 2021.246

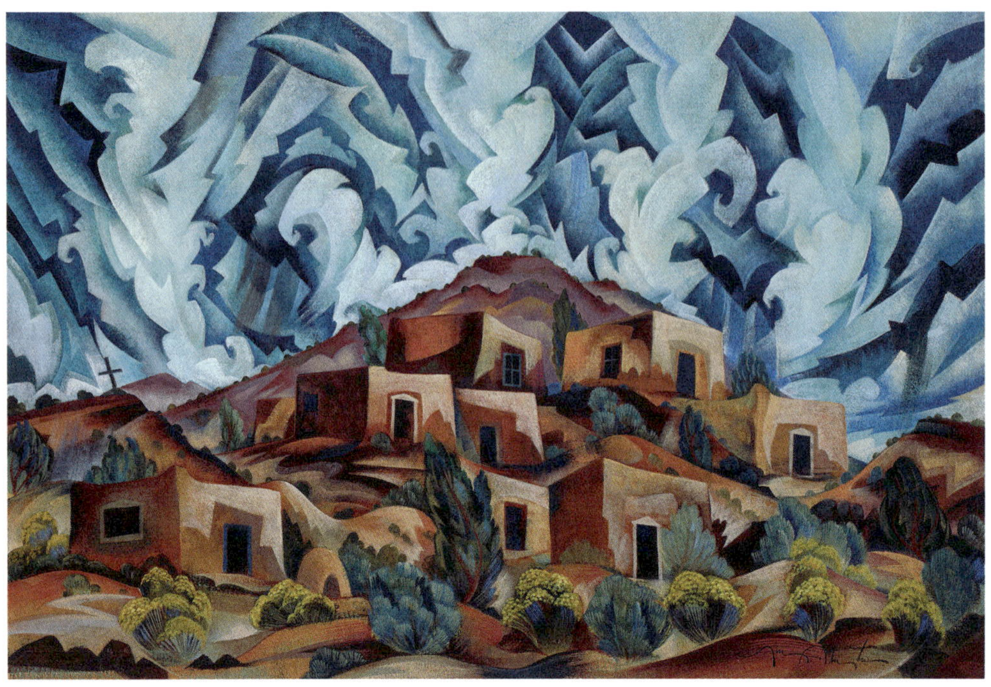

I can't count the times my father and I would take the long drive from Santa Fe to Gallup just for a mutton sandwich. Those long red planes, countless mesas, and stones in the shape of moccasins as landmarks. Every now and then we'd come across a perfect sky—a deep cobalt blue with rays of cerulean and clouds growing ever toward us as we drove under their large cast shadows. They moved with one another in an effort to graze the land. Months later, I would recall our drive, lined on the canvas walls of his messy studio. He had documented that very day, an immortalized memory. Looking across the room at half-finished canvases filled with an underbrush of color, I saw the manifestation of a life lived. In this way, it became his own, his way to have a discourse with the world. Tracing back each part of himself, conversations and feelings embedded into each stroke, his very world as he dreamed it.

—Margeaux Abeyta (Taos Pueblo/Diné), illustrator and designer

Right: Illustration by Margeaux Abeyta, commissioned for *Painted*, 2023

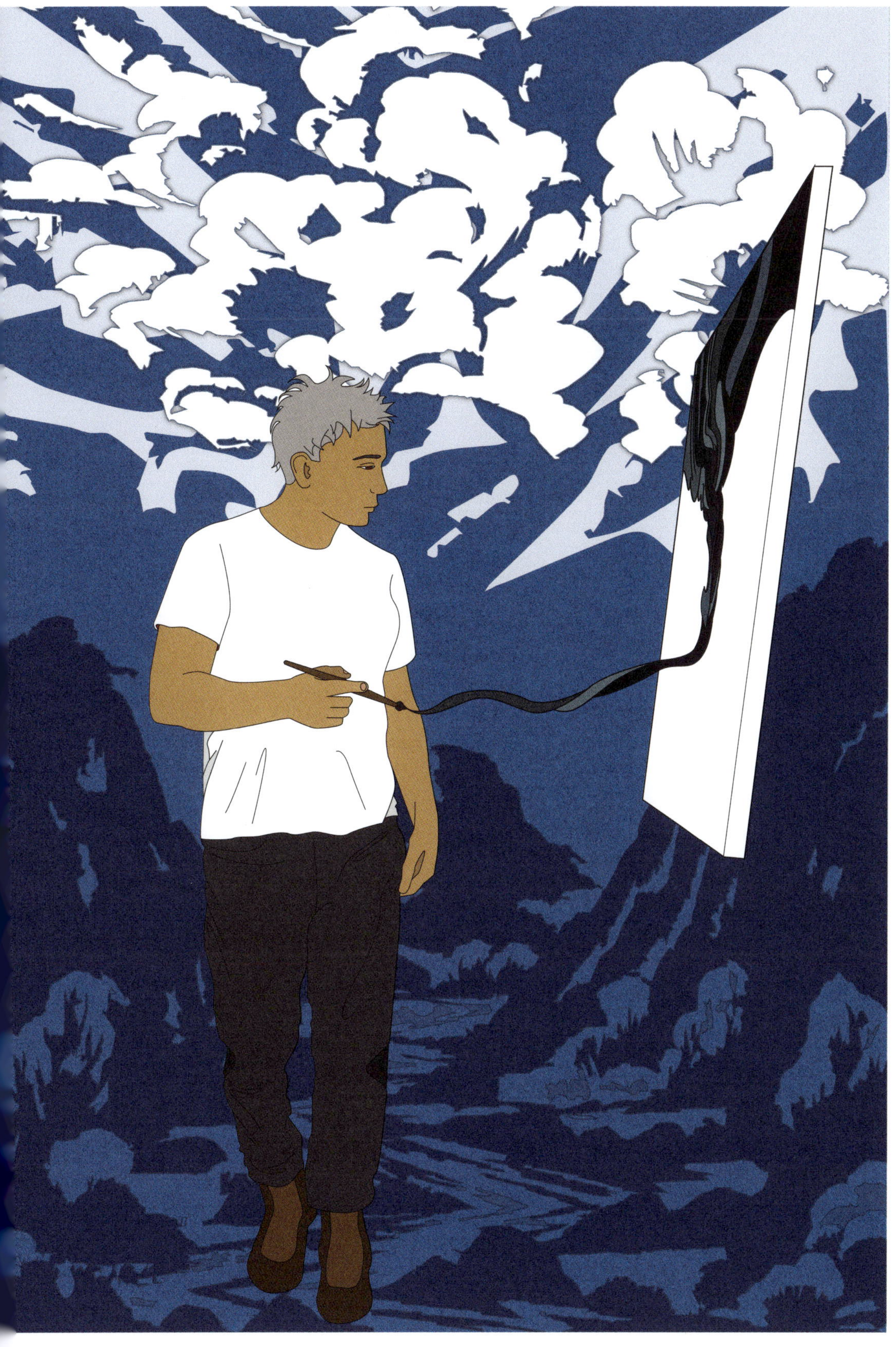

Patricia Michaels
Taos Pueblo, born 1966
Pottery Shards in the Foothills, 2023
Silk, tulle, washed leather, leather lasting, dye, acrylic, mica shards, mica dust, turquoise, shell, coral, jet stones, soil from Taos Pueblo
Dimensions variable
Courtesy the artist

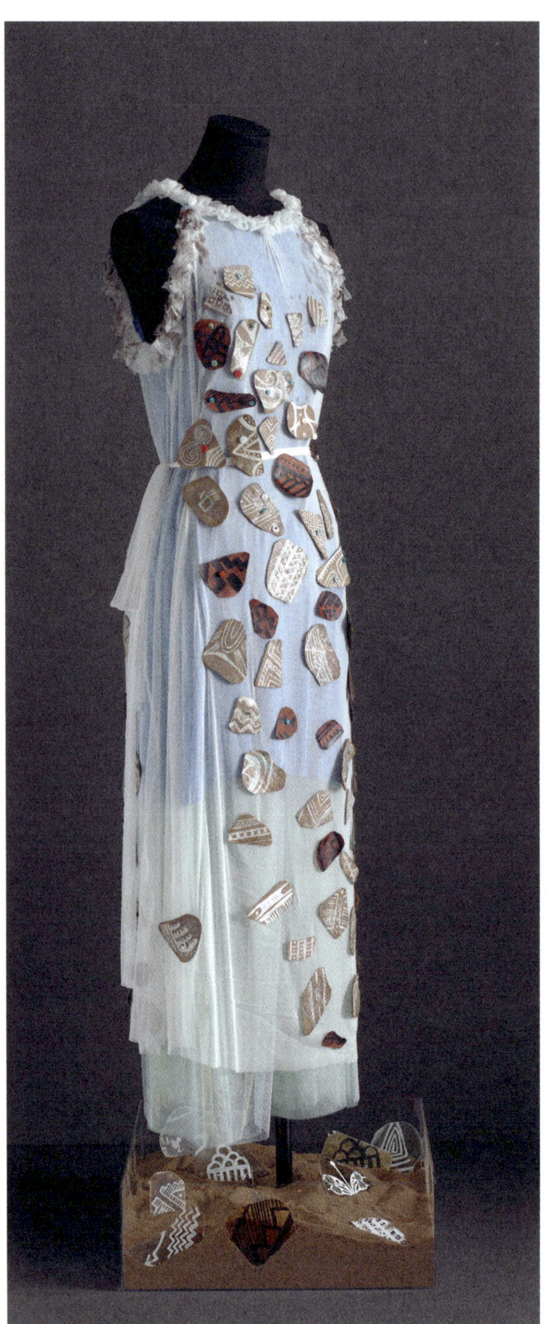

Patricia Michaels served as a member of the Painted *advisory council. This letter, written by Michaels as a reflection on the council meetings, combines her perspective on the legacy of the Taos Society of Artists with family photos from her personal archive.*

Dear Colby Museum Team,

I want to shed light on who and what the Taos Society of Artists and other painters who came to Taos Pueblo were and are to my people and me. I appreciate your time and attention to this insight into arts, artists, regalia, scenery, and models.

First, I want to set the stage for my first observations:

I grew up in a traditional family in my grandparents' Pueblo home, and in Santa Fe on Canyon Road in the Arts District. Our village house belonged to my grandfather, who was the head Water Clan leader. This meant he was in charge of our village's traditions. With these responsibilities, our household was raised to respect all tribal members and our ceremonies. Outside of this, our survival was rooted in the understanding of our relations with the other pueblos, tribes, and newcomers. My grandfather spoke some Spanish, and my grandmother spoke some English. Together they were able to create working relations with the townspeople, as well as with people from all over the world.

I was raised with stories, dances, and songs that my people held during trade and commerce with other tribes and Pueblos since the beginning of our existence in our beautiful Taos Pueblo. When a culture and its people are being killed, part of the genocide is to cut off trade routes and resources. This is what happened to Native America. Thankfully, our sacred mountain, ceremonies, and elders' wisdom survived this trade severance. Part of this survival was to learn new ways to continue trade and commerce with the European groups of people who came to our Pueblo. I say this, as parts of the old trade routes never died. People from all over the world came and continue to come. It is literally an ancient trade route.

In all of this, the one thing about Taos Pueblo that remains consistent is that we wouldn't expose our ceremonial ways of life, but we could always share what we did with our fellow relatives from other tribes and Pueblos. There was always subject matter that wasn't taboo. Yes, there is beadwork inside our Taos Pueblo that is depicted in the paintings of the Taos Artists Society and other artists because our people continued trading with friends and relations of the Plains and Woodland Natives.

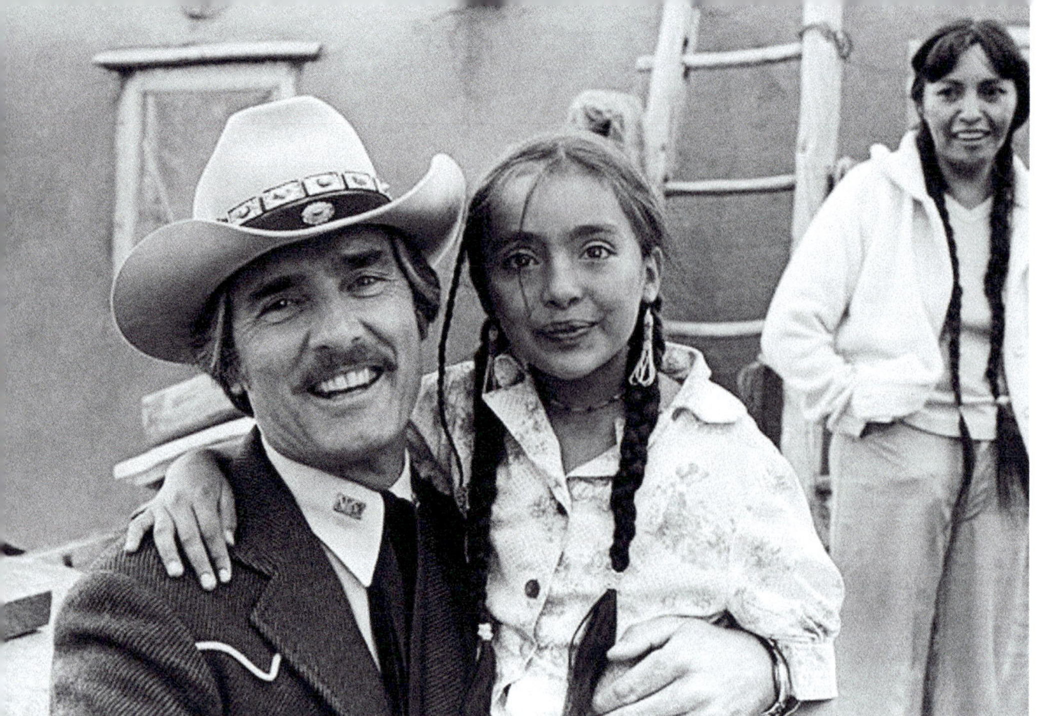

A photo shoot with actor Dennis Weaver from the TV show *McCloud*. This image of him and me was on the cover of *TV Guide*. My beautiful mother is in the background. This is upstairs at my grandparents' house.

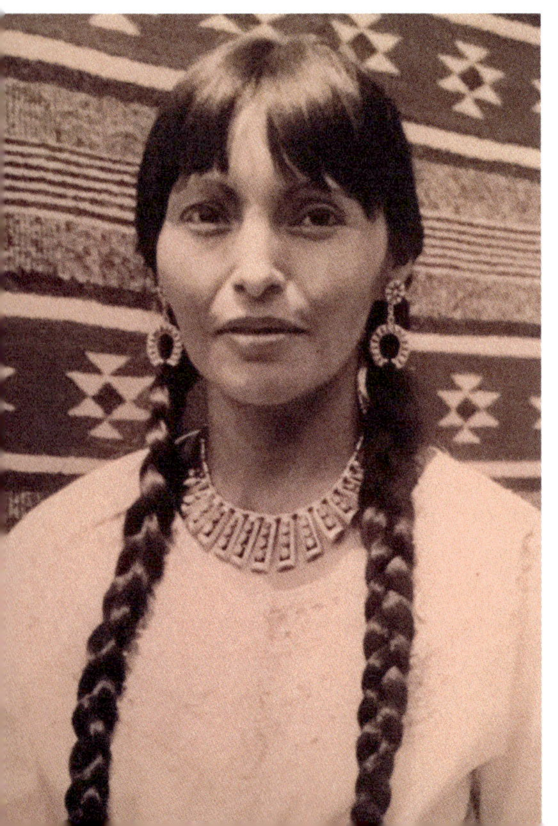

A photo of my mother, who opened the first Native-owned gallery in downtown Santa Fe. I remember her talking about arguing with my father to buy TSA paintings out of the trunk of Gerald Peters's car to sell at the gallery, but my Anglo father wanted to buy and sell only Native art, jewelry, pottery, textiles, and baskets. Point being—from the very beginning, I was raised to understand that both were important and should be appreciated. Unfortunately, my mother never was allowed to buy any of the TSA paintings.

My grandparents' home was full of beadwork, pottery, baskets, headdresses, songs, dances, and food from other tribes and Pueblos. These things were passed on through the years to honor and treasure the continued alliances with other tribes. They were so abundant that we had storage rooms at the Pueblo filled with these items. I remember when I was being advised before leaving our Pueblo home to be conscious of what I shared with the outside world.

You see, before these international talented artisans came to Taos Pueblo to paint us, other tribes visited us. In order to keep our knowledge and ceremonial responsibilities, we separated these from everything else, and never presented them to the public. In turn, we have a respectful understanding of the other tribes outside our village that we work with.

Our working relationships with artists like Nicolai Fechin, Georgia O'Keeffe, Kenneth Adams, Oscar E. Berninghaus, E. Irving Couse, Gene Kloss, Julius Rolshoven, William Dunton, Catharine Carter Critcher, and many others grew. The artists paid their models and we are still paid today. I myself have sat for many artists in Taos, including Barbara Harmon and the international Russian treasure Nikolai Blokhin, to name just two.

There were also great writers and philosophers who sat in my grandparents' home to talk, including Carl Jung, the psychologist and philosopher, and John Mankin, a writer for the TV series *Kung Fu*. My grandfather and my uncles made films, too. Recently, when my son saw E. Irving Couse's photos of Taos Pueblo at the Lunder Research Center, he told Davison Koenig, the director, "Wow, this is still us today."

These relationships with people in the arts and my Pueblo grew into families for some. Many named their children after one another's family members. Ben, one of Couse's models, took Couse's last name because they were so close. People in my village called him Ben Couse.

The truth is, we were lucky to have talented artisans visit and capture a day—or, for some, decades—in our lives. It brought recognition of the beautiful Southwest and what my village and my relatives from other Pueblos and tribes were all about. The artists' interest in who we were, and are, helped to reestablish the much-needed commerce and conversation that we all continue to have today. That is the preservation of truth, and cultural understanding.

Art is the connecting bridge that so many other societies fail to recognize. Dismissing the imagery captured over the last centuries literally negates our existence. While some may see this work as cultural appropriation, take a moment to consider the reality that while *appropriation* can easily be appreciation, *ERASURE* is final and unmistakable in its malice.

As a child, honor and pride ran through every part of me when I would go into a gallery and see one of my relatives or tribal members painted. Now, as an adult, I still have this feeling when I see paintings of my people in national museums around the world.

As the Colby Museum is a venue for a deeper understanding of our relationship with the TSA and other artists, I hope that it will show the sophistication that naturally accrued to my people and the arts.

One also has to give credit to the Native artisans who studied with these master painters, like Albert Looking Elk, Juan Mirabal, and Eve Concha. Mirabal also created future problems for Native artists because he painted imagery that was taboo. Dorothy Brett's model Trinidad told her things about the meaning of ceremonies that made clear that you must be careful how much, and what, you share.

I'm not advocating taking imagery of my people lying down, or that there aren't images out there that have grown into an overall "Native look." I know that the artists who worked with my people had a plethora of subject matter to draw from because it was a long-lasting subject and landscape for the artist and model to work from. On the other hand, I'm sympathetic to all the other tribes who historically aren't present, and that some of these recordings became fodder for misrepresentations in film, illustrations, catwalks, advertisements, and so much more. Our sacred objects and regalia have been misused as sex imagery, mascots, drunks, cigar holders, and people with no home, pride, or voice.

Native America has continued to fight genocide, which includes erasing our culture and past. Taos artists were recording who we were and shedding light on a beautiful Pueblo life, people, land, and way of living. Today more than ever, it is everyone's responsibility to undertake proper research to understand the truths they are representing. Please don't categorize my beautiful people and the work they did with artists. Some of the works illustrated include my grandfather, daughter, mother, and me, and demonstrate how work continues and relationships are built. Hundreds more images exist showing other family members working around the world, in art made throughout the ages. I'm just honored to be a part of this narrative—a narrative that is not as simple as it may look, because we have limits to what we can share.

—Patricia Michaels

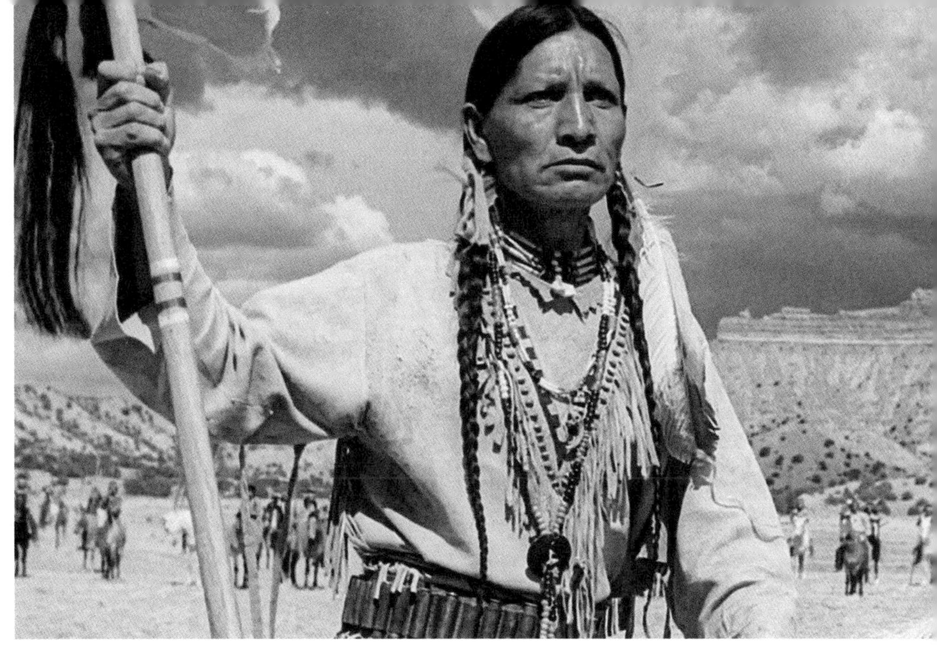

My grandfather in the 1950 film *Two Flags West*, where the US Army is against the Natives. Taos Pueblo and, I think, San Ildefonso actors filmed this scene in Abiquiu, New Mexico. My grandfather had a main part as a negotiator in the film. The truth was, they laughed about how ridiculous the script was, but they made money and my grandfather continued to get checks until the early eighties. I know this type of storytelling wasn't what they believed in, but it was a means to get to other places where their voices did count. Plus he loved riding horses and being with his fellow brothers from other Pueblos.

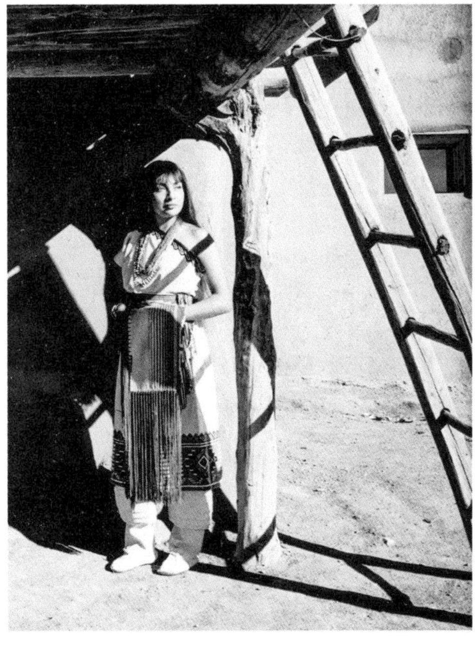

Modeling for Nancy Wood

A Dialogue between Art Histories

Sháńdíín Brown,
J. R. Henneman,
Davison Koenig,
Juan Lucero,
Ramey Mize,
Jami Powell, and
Jill Ahlberg Yohe

During the Painted symposium in November 2023, curators of Native American art and art of the American West gathered to discuss how museums can recontextualize and represent American and Native American art histories. The conversion, moderated by Painted co-curators Jill Ahlberg Yohe and Juan Lucero (Isleta Pueblo), featured Shándíín Brown (Diné), former Assistant Curator of Native American Art, RISD Museum; J. R. Henneman, Director and Curator of the Petrie Institute of Western American Art, Denver Art Museum; Davison Koenig, Executive Director and Chief Curator, Couse-Sharp Historic Site; Ramey Mize, Assistant Curator of American Art, Portland Museum of Art; and Jami Powell (Osage Nation), Associate Director for Curatorial Affairs and Curator of Indigenous Art, Hood Museum of Art.

Jill Ahlberg Yohe: Let's begin by sharing ideas regarding ways to integrate Native and non-Native art that you've found successful in your own work. And what you want to do to change or make it better. Our goal here is to understand what's happening now in curating and suggest possibilities for the future.

Jami Powell: A couple of years ago I co-curated a show with some colleagues at the Hood Museum of Art called *This Land: American Engagement with the Natural World*. It was the first time that we put our Native North American collections in conversation with a broader collection of American art, including

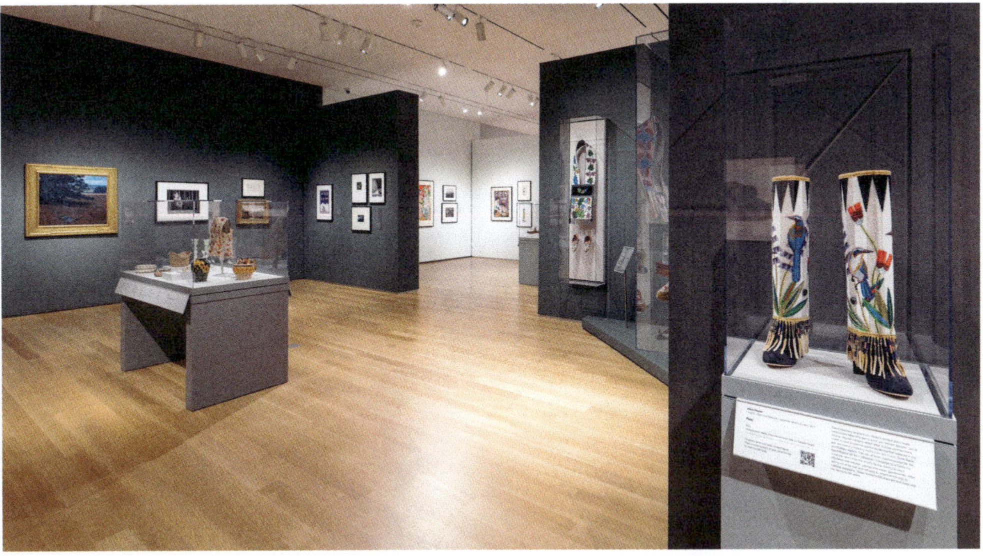

Installation view, *This Land: American Engagement with the Natural World*, Hood Museum of Art, Hanover, New Hampshire, 2022

diverse understandings of what American art can be. For us, it raised a lot of questions around who gets to decide what's included in the canon of American art and how we might tell different and more inclusive and equitable and honest stories of our history as a nation via the art in our institutions. That was a collaborative project.

I'm trained, like Jill and many of our colleagues in Native art, as a cultural anthropologist. I don't automatically assume that I have to arrange works in a gallery in a chronological timeline or a medium-specific way. I think the show at Colby is a great example of how when you place different mediums in conversation, or venture beyond a strict chronology, it gives a fuller and more realistic and holistic picture about what's happening. And so that's been one strategy I've found to be useful.

Ramey Mize: I work at the Portland Museum of Art, and we did a similar reinstallation project, a reimagining of how we were presenting and interrogating histories of American art. One core goal was to integrate work by Indigenous artists, and celebrate their ongoing presence in these lands and more broadly across the continent. One essential aspect of that integration was through consultation with Native advisors, including Chris Newell (Passamaquoddy) and endawnis Spears (Diné/Ojibwe/Chickasaw/Choctaw). *Painted* is a breathtaking example of an enactment of that methodology. It beautifully and fluidly brings that chorus of voices to bear on this space and this exhibition. For me, leaving room and

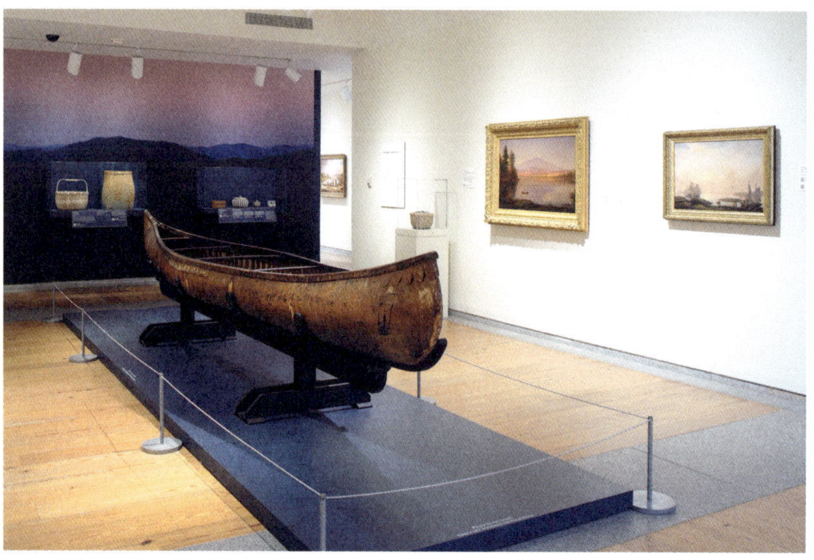

Installation view, *Passages in American Art*, Portland Museum of Art, Portland, Maine, 2022

time for fluidity and relationship building and conversation and sharing in the exhibition planning process—really leaning into the journey of it, not just the product—has been one of my big takeaways when it comes to a good path forward.

And I agree with Jami about how important it is to bring contemporary art into dialogue with historical art. I've seen some reticence in that respect on the part of a lot of American art collections. They want to stick to a chronological script that implies some kind of hermetic purity around style or form. But when we think of the grand scale of time, everything is happening everywhere, all at once, if you will. We should think more cyclically and in a more fluid way than the typical linear progress-driven narrative. So many of these amazing projects before us integrate contemporary art with historical to speak back in many ways. It's one of the more powerful aspects of the work.

And of course we can continue to improve consultation structures, compensation, and those kinds of things over time.

J. R. Henneman: I'm in a fairly unique position at the Denver Art Museum, which is the only encyclopedic museum in the world that has a department dedicated to Western American art. So, as I like to say, we tell the story of American art from a Western perspective. Now, that department is only twenty years old. In contrast, our department of Indigenous arts of North America is nearing its one hundredth anniversary. So I, as a settler scholar, have the great benefit and opportunity of working in a global institution with colleagues like John Lukavic and Dakota Hoska, whom I'm sure many of you know, who along with their predecessors and many communities have done so much hard work to tell the history of Indigenous North America at the Denver Art Museum.

The museum occupies a high-rise structure, and every floor is dedicated to a different part of the permanent collection. We do not integrate our collections, but we do borrow strategically from each other in a very collegial fashion. Note also that the Western collection spans two hundred years, which is a teeny, tiny little drop in the depth of the history of the peoples and the arts production in what we now call the American West. So when you come to the Denver Art Museum and visit the Western American galleries, you will see moments where we recognized our limitations and borrowed strategically from the other collections at the museum, for instance the Indigenous arts collection, the Latin American collection, the ancient American collections, and point to them as places to go to learn more about the deeper history. Within the Western art galleries, very carefully integrating specific materials from other collections helps our visitors understand that the history on display actually spans a much longer time. There's a much richer history of the American West there to be explored and understood.

And as my colleagues here on stage have mentioned, we have community members with whom we consult. We have an Indigenous advisory council, and it is my responsibility, again as a settler scholar, to acknowledge their expertise and ask for help to be accountable to those communities. A few examples of that include me going to council meetings every quarter and discussing what I'm up to and bringing questions or issues that might arise out of the artworks on display in the permanent galleries. And when we do temporary exhibitions or create new interpretation for a permanent gallery, we hire Indigenous readers to review the interpretive text. We've learned a lot about what we don't know and what we need to learn, and also where the boundaries are in terms of what we can and can't know.

Davison Koenig: The Couse-Sharp Historic Site is the home and studios of E. I. Couse and Joseph Henry Sharp. With the opening of the Lunder Research Center almost two years ago, our focus shifted to a larger story about the Taos Society of Artists, that includes the early artists of Taos. That's entirely dependent on the Indigenous and Hispano community largely in Taos. So our focus can't be on anything but that. In the last half-dozen years, I would say that more than half of our exhibitions and programs have been either focused on the Indigenous and Hispano communities and/or co-curated by Indigenous and Hispano communities. And our focus has entirely shifted from the preservation of a beautiful historic site to telling the story of a complex and nuanced history. But we've only scratched the surface. There's so much more to do, and it's exciting.

I must congratulate the Colby Museum, the Lunder Institute, the curatorial team, the designer—everyone who put their time and energy and heart into *Painted*, because it is groundbreaking. This is what museums need to be doing. This is moving the discourse forward. And it's happening in Maine. How cool is that? I can say that because I'm a New Englander. My family goes way back in Connecticut and Maine. I understand all you have to deal with.

I think our challenge in the museum world is how to hang paintings like these in a gallery and bring in Native voices. You have to. You need to identify who the models are and tell their stories. That's become the focus of the Lunder Research Center—to be that conduit of archives and knowledge and Taos Pueblo voices. Bringing those voices to the forefront so that we museum curators have access to that material. There's

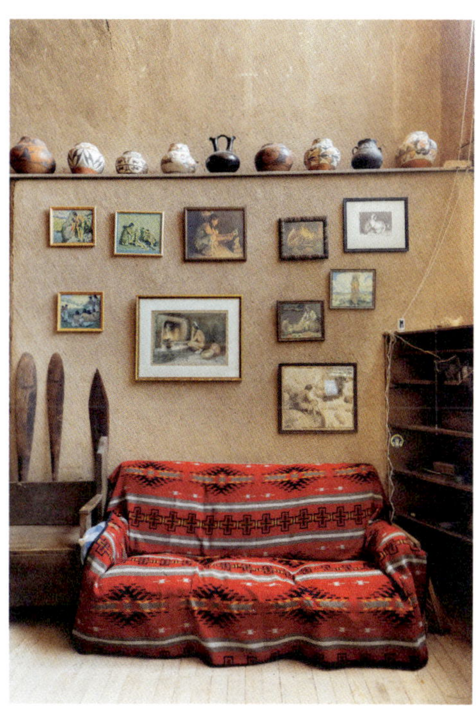
E. Irving Couse studio, Couse-Sharp Historic Site, Taos, New Mexico

no excuse to hang those paintings and not have the stories behind them, stories of the relationships of the artists and the models and why that was impactful and the context of the period and how these paintings moved the discourse forward a hundred years ago.

Shańdiín Brown: It's interesting to think about these questions, and I'm very honored to be on this panel with you all. I come from a family of artists. And in my family, people made money by selling their works. But in Diné *bizaad* (Navajo language), we don't have a word for art. So growing up and seeing the women in my family produce works to make money was an interesting perspective. And then I found my way to the RISD Museum, where I'm the first person to work full time with our Native American art collection. We've been accepting gifts since around 1900, and started acquiring them around 1944.

The first curatorial project I worked on at the RISD Museum was called *Being and Believing in the Natural World: Perspectives from the Ancient Mediterranean, Asia, and Indigenous North America*. That show put Native art in conversation with ancient art and Asian art. You might be wondering, well, how did that happen? We had a curatorial team of about eleven, several of them of color. My colleagues Dr. Wai Yee Chiong and Dr. Georgina Borromeo and I thought about the works of art outside of an ethnographic lens. We weren't labeling things—oh, this is Native, this is Asian, this is ancient. The show combined the works, seeing them as storytelling, seeing them through the lenses of materiality. I don't have an art history degree, so I don't see things through a critical, boxed-in lens. And I am fortunate as well that RISD is known for being experimental. So things that some Western art historians might cringe at, I say, let's do it.

It's also great to bring our Native students along into our processes. Some of my student workers for that show wrote object labels, especially if they were from that same home community, because I see myself more as a facilitator of knowledge than an authority. Reading past RISD curatorial files can be cringey, seeing how people thought they were authorities on things. They didn't know what they didn't know. As a facilitator, I like to get folks in from the communities to discuss our historic works. The historic pieces in the collection—most of the time, although not all the time—are tourism items, meaning they were created by folks to make money and survive. I like to think about that also in labels, in terms of what it means for someone's spirit and relationality to the work to go out into the world and find its way to, say, Providence, Rhode Island. And then bringing in contemporary artists is exciting because they're able to tell their own stories.

But to get back to the root of the question, I think Native art can be in conversation with many different categories of art. And I often question why we have to have these categories at all, when Native culture doesn't even have a word for "art." So it's about thinking with an interdisciplinary lens, and for me also

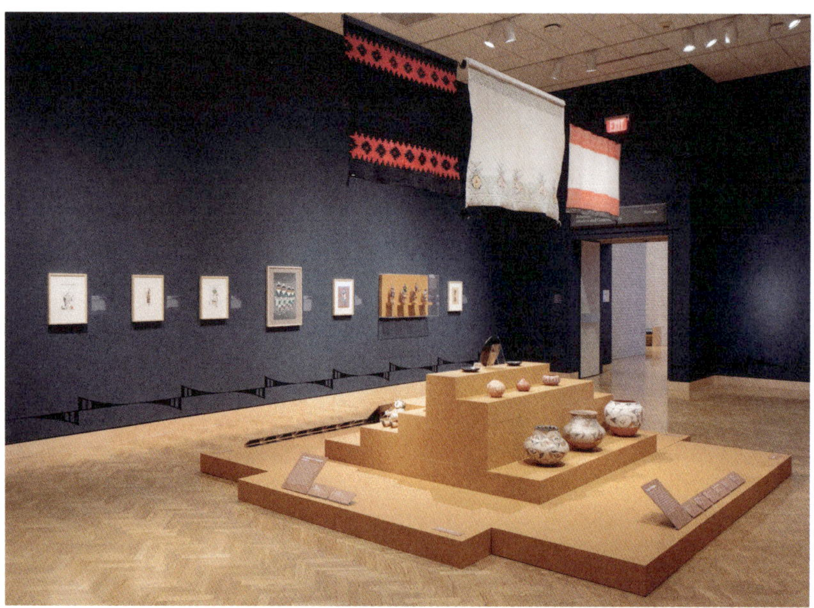

Installation view, *Parska/Shada*, Minneapolis Institute of Art, Minnesota, 2021

thinking specifically about the women who have always been making curatorial choices, even if they weren't called curatorial choices. Like my grandmother having all of our family photos on her wall. It's a curatorial project. I don't know how Western art historians would feel about me saying that, but that's what I think.

Juan Lucero: The next question is about obstacles. What are the obstacles in your efforts to put Euro-American and Native American art together? What are the barriers to elaborating on these histories, and conversely, what are the opportunities?

JP: Picking up on Sháńdíín's comment about many communities not having a word for art: when I teach with my students, one of the things I try to convey is that art as a Western concept is limiting and limited in comparison to the way we talk about things within Indigenous communities. Indigenous communities across the globe talk about things that are aesthetically beautiful, certainly, but they're also things that are used to carry knowledge and are embedded with stories that connect us to place and people and our relations.

And so thinking about how we can take that understanding and definition and apply it to things that had previously been thought of as art objects by Western makers can be an opportunity to expand into a far more generous interpretation of the things that we're placing in conversation in galleries. It becomes an opportunity. I think the danger there, and why it's so important to ground that complexity and nuance, is that there's always a danger of flattening the experience of Indigenous communities. There are more than 570 federally recognized nations that have a government-to-government relationship with the United States, and so demonstrating that diversity in gallery settings can be a challenge. Also I should say that I am an Osage person, but I speak for myself; I don't speak on behalf of my community, and certainly not for all Native or Indigenous peoples. Flattening is one of the biggest traps we face in our work.

JRH: Time is a constraint as well. Working with community, as you all know and have been doing, takes a lot of time and needs to be financially supported. So I have found that one needs the support of an institution to build in the requisite timelines for exhibition and project development to attend to the amount of listening required to do this work respectfully. It's no longer enough to be an expert. You must have expertise, sure, but now more than ever, you must listen. You must have the capacity to spend a lot of time listening. That can be a

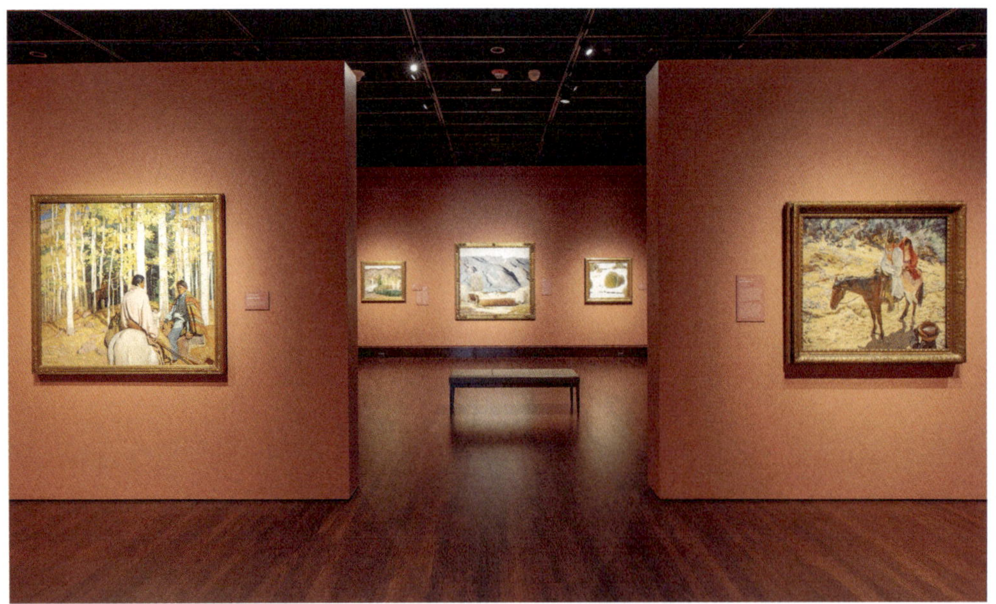

Installation view, Western American Art galleries, Denver Art Museum, Denver, Colorado, 2021

real obstacle when it comes to convincing your institution. But hopefully, that's just part of the work we continue doing.

And I do like to think of our permanent galleries, for example, as iterative. These are living spaces where the voices will change, the perspectives will change, over time. Not on a set schedule necessarily, but perpetually. That's the ideal. We don't think of the exhibits as static. We think of them as living.

DK: Building on that, time and money are huge in doing things thoughtfully, sensitively, with real relationships. That's the important part. Regarding obstacles, one of our challenges now has to do with imparting an understanding of the work, imparting value to the work, through education. Yet we're in a time and place where our information is reduced to very small bits. We talk about the myth of the "vanishing race"—well, I would argue that the Pueblo people in mainstream American consciousness are a vanished race. Most people don't know who the Pueblo people are. They don't know the connection to ancestral Puebloan peoples.

Most of our American history concerns the nineteenth century. It doesn't go back to what was happening before that and how complex and rich these cultures were, and are. So our greatest obstacle I think is getting our US educational system up to speed to incorporate this long and complex history. I often joke that our ulterior motive is to use American art history to rewrite American history because art is a great way to reach people and have important conversations. We talk about museums being safe places to conduct difficult conversations. Well, our own history is a very difficult conversation, but artists can help break that down, and they can do it through humor and sci-fi and all sorts of clever ways that engage people. And so that's an obstacle, but really also it's a fun challenge for us.

SB: Interpretation is certainly something I find challenging. I have an exhibition up at the RISD Museum now called *Diné Textiles: Nizhónígo Hadadít'eh*, which is about recontextualizing our Diné textiles as garments. At first, I was the one giving all of the tours because it's my baby. This is such a special project for me because I come from a family of Diné weavers. And then I realized that it's a crazy idea to give every single tour. There's just not enough hours in the day. So I shared with our docents how I would like the works to be interpreted. Letting your project out in the world and admitting that you can't be there for every walkthrough and hoping that audiences spend time and listen and see the vision is challenging, because we all know that museum fatigue is real. Maybe you're into your second or even third hour and you can't read every single label anymore; you're tired and you just want to look at the pieces.

I definitely think the pieces speak for themselves, because it's a combination of historic and contemporary weavings. But for certain audiences who don't know Diné history, I hope that they understand the specificities of why these particular works are so important. While I was hearing today from the Pueblo artists about the Pueblo Revolt, I was thinking about my own work with my editor at RISD, writing about the Navajo Long Walk and our forced imprisonment at Hwéeldi (or Bosque Redondo). I just briefly touched on it, and the feedback was that we needed to get into it far more deeply. Even though it's something *I'm* very aware of, the general Providence, Rhode Island, community is not. So it's a balance between retaining people's interest in a hundred-word label and also having the reader take seriously the art as a reflection of history. The event I just mentioned is why you see such a dramatic shift in Diné weavings at that moment: people had experienced such an upheaval in their lives and livelihoods. I just hope that our audiences will grasp what a life-altering, traumatic event that was for folks.

There are videos in the space, and poetry. All of these things I hope can be interpreted. To help solve that issue, I'm working with our media team on a tour that is recorded so folks at home can watch, and of course especially Diné folks. Speaking to Jami's comments about nuance, something I'm interested in talking about with other curators is how some of

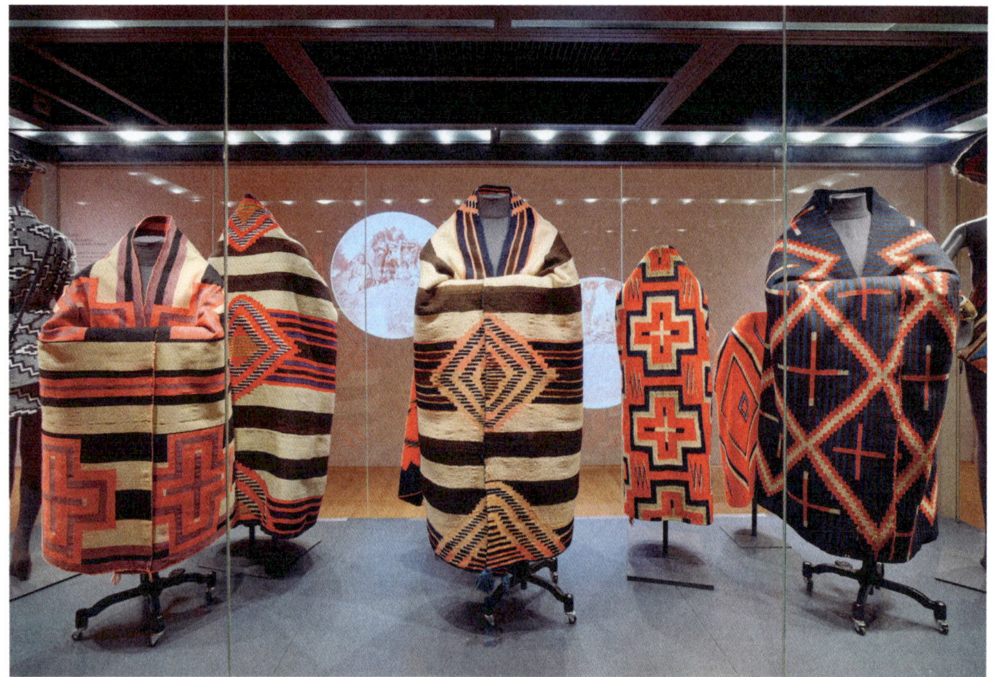

Installation view, *Diné Textiles: Nizhónígo Hadadít'eh, They Are Beautifully Dressed,* RISD Museum, Providence, Rhode Island, 2023

the textiles bear the Spider Woman cross. Diné people have very different interpretations of it. Some think about it as our four sacred mountains. Some think about it as four directions. So our audiences should know that different weavers have different interpretations. There's over four hundred thousand Diné people, which means of course that one design can't have one singular meaning. But I think that's what audiences want because it's more digestible. And so being able to communicate nuance through label texts is difficult. That's why I love being the one to give the tours. But I'm only one woman, so I cannot.

JL: Both of you bring up great points about interpretation and education. Virgil Ortiz said earlier that people ask him, "Oh, what part of Mexico are you from?" As if they forgot that New Mexico is a thing—it's no longer a territory, but one of the fifty US states. Since all the Pueblo communities have Spanish names, and were called pueblos, after all, it can be hard for people to understand their diversity. But there's enormous diversity among all the different communities in New Mexico, especially along the Rio Grande. There's old Spanish settlements, there's Pueblo villages, and there's interminglings of the two. Interpreting that in museums is a challenge. And I guess that leads into the next question of what narratives are missing in Western art, and how to present them in Western art and museum practice.

JRH: So many narratives are missing. And it's not just the more than five hundred Native nations; it's also people from the continent of Asia, people from Central America. I mean, there are so many narratives that are missing in most collections of American art, I would argue. And that is ongoing work. To your question, I don't know the solution, but I do think that in the case of the Denver Art Museum, thinking of our spaces as iterative and always more inclusive helps us not let "perfect" get in the way of "good." We do the best work we can, always striving for better.

DK: There's so many opportunities in museums, and art museums in particular, to use the works to debunk myths and convey more narratives. I mean, there's no end to the material, and so many perspectives. So the responsibility, especially in large museums with large collections, is to use those as educational opportunities. Especially talking about the West, Manifest Destiny, and westward expansion, there's so much to pull from. We must use the materials available as teaching moments that fifty years ago were perpetuating a single narrative and now make clear that there are many, many narratives out there.

We're in an exciting moment in history where we're having these conversations. At the American Alliance of Museums conference in Denver this last year, that was the entire conversation. The whole museum world is talking about how to tell a better story, how to bring to the fore voices that have been marginalized. It's not like it's just happening in pockets. We have a very long way to go in the museum world, but the conversations are happening.

JP: It's also not just about what stories haven't been told at all, but also what parts of the predominant story haven't been told. For instance, how deeply entangled art has always been with US federal policy. I hear lots of people saying, oh, art's gotten so political. But art has always been incredibly political. Thomas Moran's first trip out West was funded by the US Department of War. So many early landscape painters and photographers were being paid by the government to take images to bring back East to help craft the narrative of Manifest Destiny. And so we have to tell the complete story of that.

I tell my students that one of the most interesting questions you can ask in any museum is: Where's the money coming from? Read the credit lines on things, and dig into the history of who's paying for this, and to what end, because arts funding has always been very interestingly tangled in political projects.

It's also about not losing sight—as Shándíín mentioned regarding Bosque Redondo and women creating work and the shift in what those practices looked like—that in moments of limitation, there were still women creating incredible works of beauty and passing down traditions. We must not focus solely on the violence and trauma of these moments, even while recognizing and reckoning with that history and its impact on art production, but also amplify the incredible capacity and brilliance of the people who in those spaces of limitation were creating the great works that we're able to appreciate in our institutions today.

JAY: Does anybody have any questions for our wonderful panelists?

Sébastian Aubin: Hi, my name is Sébastian. I'm from Canada. I'm Cree. I have a question for the Indigenous people on the panel. We were a trading community back in the day before settlers came. We shared what we would maybe call art now. And we would share knowledge and trade and do different things. You could tell where somebody was from based on the beadwork, based on their hair and how they would set themselves up. Do you think now we're bringing that back, but through art in a more contemporary sense, in a place that's called an institution?

JL: Well, I think we're at a critical point where a lot of artists and a lot of people are going down the trail of discovering and rediscovering identity and what it is to be Indigenous. I think the hard part about American history is that it has homogenized us. We can say we're Indian, and people are going to think that we all look the same, or they're going to have a specific idea of what we're supposed to look like. And there's so much trauma involved, too. A lot of people are navigating the historical trauma that we have experienced in the process of reconnecting with those identities. A lot of artists are recognizing where they're from and remembering where they're from, which is valuable, but it comes with extraordinarily heavy baggage.

Art making goes back to the spirit, and is embedded within our DNA. We create what our spirit is telling us to create. And the land, wherever we're at, tells us how to create the work we're making or tell the stories we're telling.

Now that we're in a place where a lot of Native people are rediscovering their identities, it's making us stronger as people

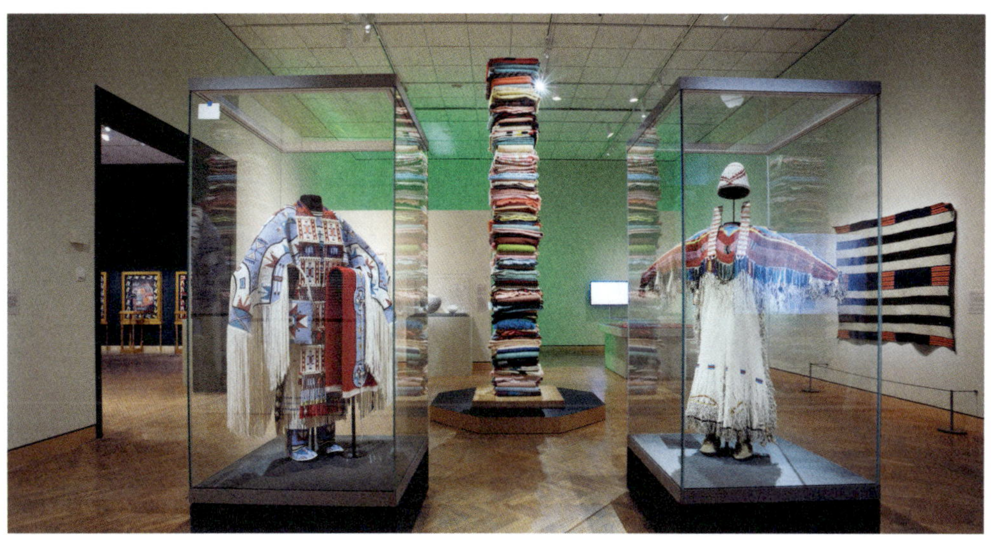

Installation view, *Hearts of Our People: Native Women Artists*, Minneapolis Institute of Art, Minnesota, 2019

across the country. Recognizing the forced assimilation. That our people were placed in these blood quantum degrees was a part of the forced assimilation, to separate our people and remove that identity from our peoples. So it's important to keep in mind that there are a lot of people who don't necessarily know where they come from, and want to explore that. And I think that can open up so many doors.

We're also at a critical point right now where museums and other institutions are listening. They are listening. A lot of the movement I've seen has happened just in the past three or four years in which museums, some of them, are willing to listen. And at the same time, we're at a critical point for people to rediscover and reinterpret their identities.

JP: I love the point about foregrounding the knowledge that international trade preceded the arrival of Europeans. That gets lost. Indigenous peoples were always incorporating materials that were traded with other communities into their artistic practices. That just ramped up when settlers arrived and those trade networks became global. But I think you're also speaking to the idea that so many people or artists try and meet expectations of what the market wants, because they need to feed their families. And thus, those outside expectations shape what the work looks like. But I see a lot of strength in artists, and I think artists are recognizing it now. Some communities never lost it. Certainly within Pueblo pottery tradition, going back to designs and patterns and practices that came from within the specific context of one's community, there's something universal about that specificity because it's so deeply personal, and I think artists and audiences are having more meaningful conversations at an interpersonal level when there's that focus on the local and specific community traditions.

SB: I'm interested in museums as places for celebration. When I was younger, my grandma would make me the cutest little Navajo velveteen outfits. And I was like, I don't really want to wear this; I want to wear Justice or overalls or Gap. But then I went to the Heard Museum on a field trip—I was maybe in the third grade—and saw these beautiful Navajo velveteen dresses in the cases. And I thought, whoa, I want to go home and put mine on too! So, especially thinking about the next generation, having Native artists who are making really cool works is a point of celebration. And I say that from a position where I don't face as much cultural oppression as my grandma, who was sent to boarding school, or my mom, who grew up in the 1970s. I try to keep my perspective as a humble person, and see also the next generations of Native people, who I hope never have to experience that type of cultural shame—that "I'm an other" or "I need to hide this." It's cool to see institutions as places where we can celebrate who we are and have such completely different experiences from our grandparents, being ashamed of who they were.

I'm likewise interested in fashion and jewelry and how we use it as cultural markers. Today I am wearing—these were all gifts—Sedna earrings and a seal cuff. My people never had sealskins, as they were desert dwellers, but even back then, you would get gifts. Gift giving is a huge aspect of our culture and fashion. Even on the body, you can curate a story to be told. I love asking other Native ladies, for instance, about the earrings they're wearing and who made them. That's the kind of work I'm interested in—seeing museums as a place to uplift who we are as people. And I think it's great to remind audiences and even Native people ourselves that we're always adapting and changing. That's how our people have survived—by adapting.

Following spread:
Installation view, *Painted: Our Bodies, Hearts, and Village*, Colby College Museum of Art, Waterville, Maine, 2023

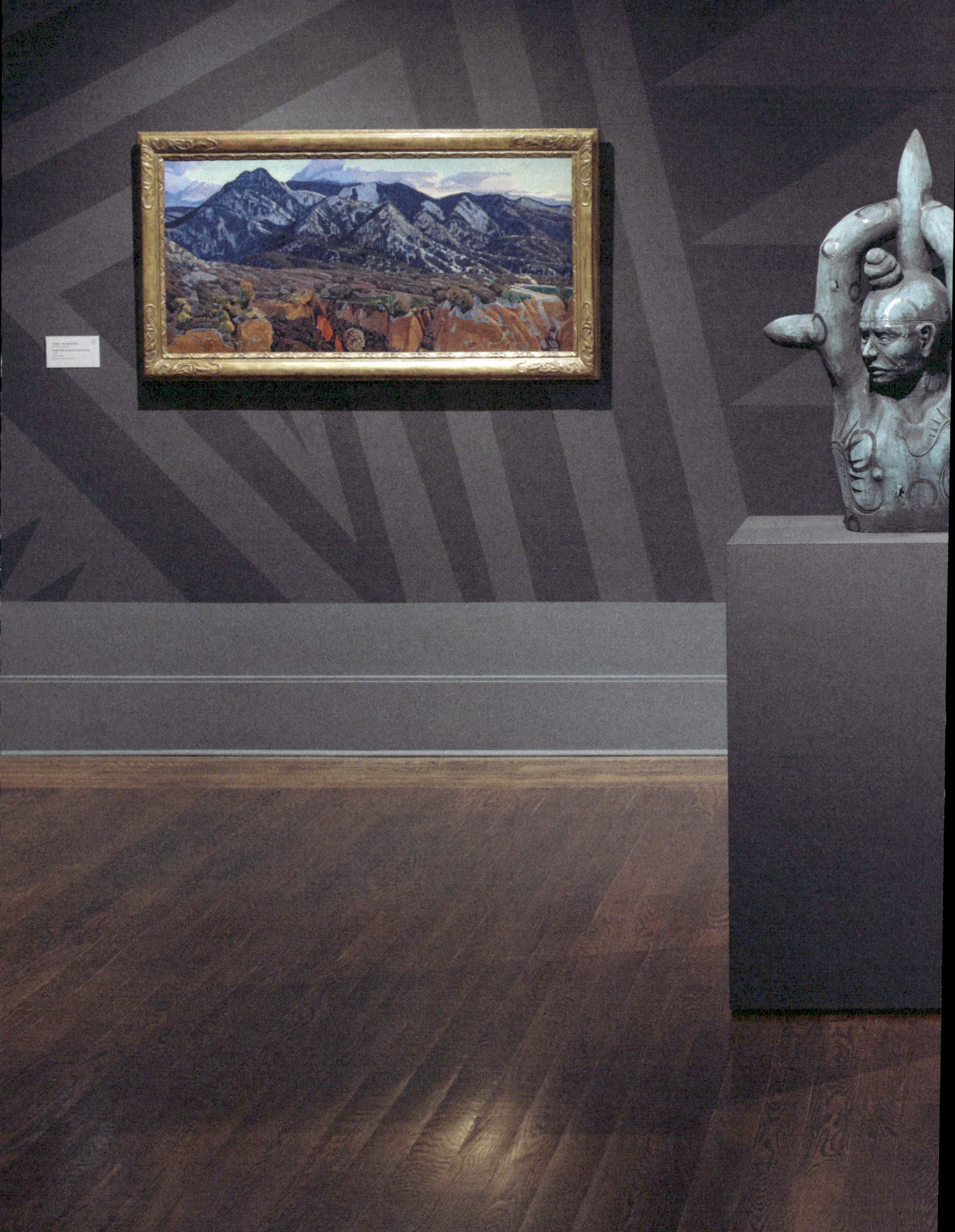

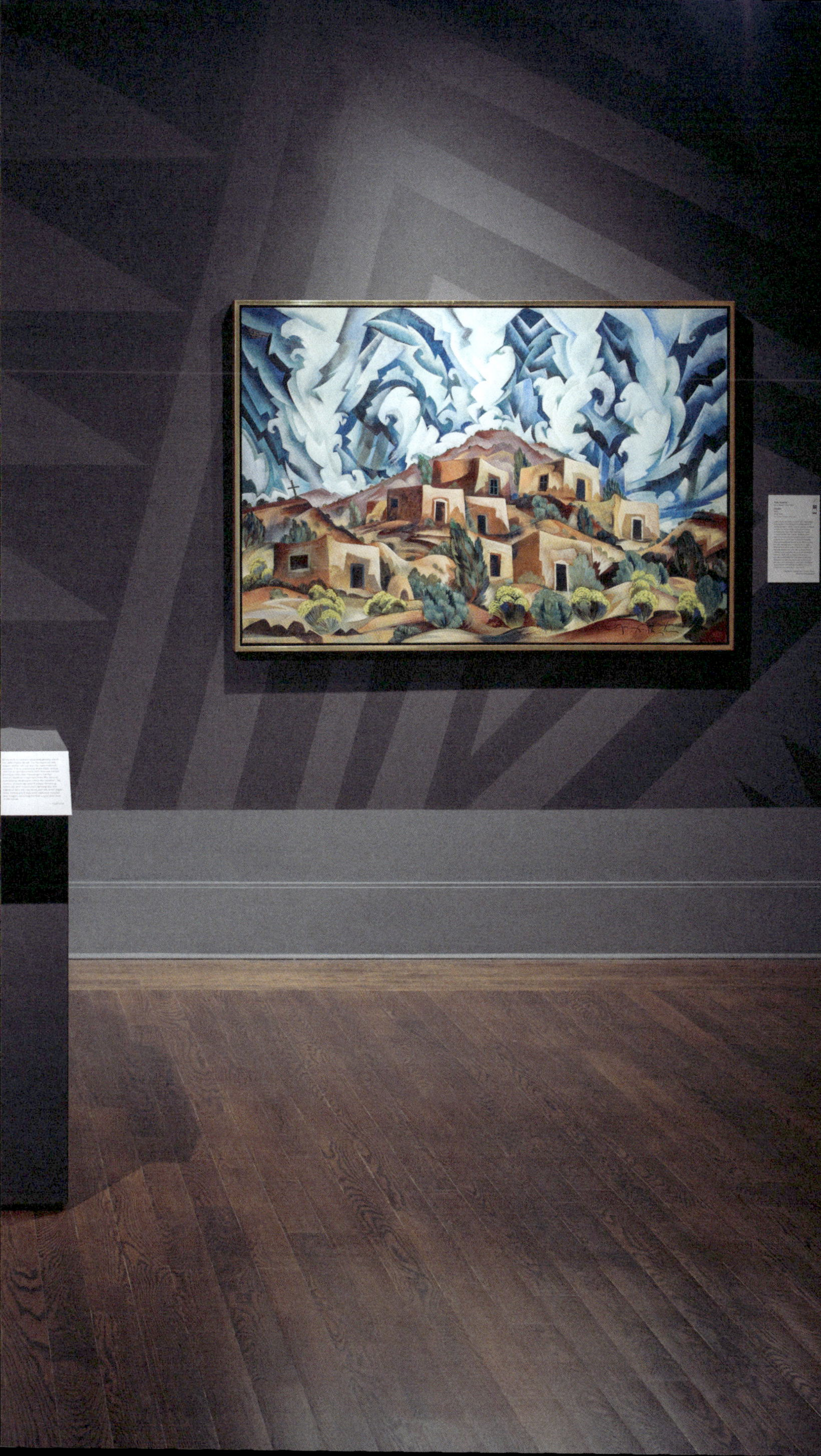

Give All You Have

Beth Finch

In 2011, fifty-two years after the Colby College Museum of Art opened to the public, it acquired its first Wabanaki artwork. Matthew Timme, a staff member in the museum's education department, wrote to Patricia King, his colleague on the collections team, to describe the piece—a contemporary Penobscot basket—for the purpose of cataloguing. "Here is the information that I have on the basket we purchased (I'm not sure if you need all this info but I'll give you everything I have)." Timme notes that the basketmaker is Sarah Sockbeson, "American, Penobscot," and the materials she used are "brown ash, sweet grass, antler." The antler is a hollowed-out slice, rough and naturally filigreed along its exterior edges and buffed to a smooth sheen within its interior curve. It resembles a lacy coronet turned on its edge, or a circular flame. Sockbeson secured this wondrous object to the weave of the basket's lid so that it serves as an ingenious pull. Timme, working from information supplied by the artist, identified the basket as a "modified acorn shape" constituted by a "curly weave," completing this observation with the parenthetical remark, "I think is what the weave is called."

Radiating from this modest document in the museum's archive is a palpable newness. Since its arrival, Sockbeson's basket has quietly but steadily informed institutional change at the Colby Museum simply by being what it is: a brilliant example of the traditional art of Penobscot basket weaving. Its colors, ranging from olive green to light brown to black, have softened with time, melding their visual and textural harmonies. These are markedly distinct from the vibrant green-blue and black basket, large in scale and with a point weave, that Sockbeson made in 2023 for the Colby Museum's collection and for inclusion in *Painted: Our Bodies, Hearts, and Village* using novel materials—aluminum house siding, found vinyl, enamel spray paint, found plastic, and faux leather. The two baskets are a powerful pair.

Founded in 1959 as a teaching museum at a liberal arts college, the Colby Museum has long focused on American art and contemporary art, but not exclusively; its collection also includes groups of artworks created by other cultures and nations. And its history of exhibitions reveals a long-standing commitment to art made locally. Yet before 2011, this museum in Waterville, Maine, lacked even a single work by an artist belonging to the Wabanaki Confederacy on whose homelands it sits. Colby presented a survey exhibition of Maine baskets in 1989 that included Wabanaki artists alongside other basketmakers, but no works were acquired for the collection. The "fine" arts have long defined art museums including the abidingly ambitious one at Colby College. Seismic change came from elsewhere and it included the founding, in 1993, of the Maine Indian Basketmakers Alliance, which established new support for elder and emerging practitioners of this ancient art form and, gradually, broader public recognition. And as art museums matured along with the fields of American art and American studies, becoming more inclusive and more aware of erasures and omissions, so, too, did the Colby Museum.

Which brings us to 2011 and a change-making acquisition. Responding to this Colby Museum collection gap, Lauren Lessing, who led the education department until 2018, advocated for that first Wabanaki basket purchase and gained the support of Sharon Corwin, then director and chief curator, who used funds at her discretion to realize it. Soon after, the museum embarked on a building expansion that resulted in the Alfond-Lunder Family Pavilion, which opened in 2013. The goal of organizing a second exhibition of baskets—this time dedicated solely to Wabanaki makers—subsequently gained momentum, and the museum's evolving understanding of what a teaching museum could be—interdisciplinary, multivocal—deepened as its facility grew. With guidance from Wabanaki community members and colleagues from the Abbe Museum, whom Diana Tuite, the Colby Museum's Katz Curator, invited to visit Colby in 2017, the nascent exhibition project expanded to encompass contemporary art in a wide variety of mediums by and about the Indigenous and First Nations people of what are now Maine and Maritime Canada.

Wíwənikan... the beauty we carry opened in 2019 and marked the first major exhibition of its kind. It was led by Jennifer Neptune, a Penobscot basketmaker and beadworker, and Kathleen Mundell, a folklorist and the director of Cultural Resources, a nonprofit working with communities on developing strategies to help sustain their local culture. The co-curators brought together, as Corwin noted in the accompanying catalogue, community advisors representing "leaders in arts and culture from the Maliseet, Mi'kmaq, Passamaquoddy, Penobscot, and Abenaki peoples." One of those advisors was the Penobscot basketmaker Theresa Secord, cofounder of the Maine Indian Basketmakers Alliance and a member of the museum's Board of Governors, who also served as an advisor to *Painted*. In the preface to the catalogue, Secord observed, "*Wíwənikan* projects a Wabanaki worldview and highlights the resilience of artists who have been practicing their own sovereignty in Maine for more than two hundred years through art." Featuring works by thirty-eight artists, including Sockbeson, the show filled the upper level of the Jetté Galleries and appeared concurrently with *Occupy Colby*, a contemporary group exhibition dedicated to environmental art. *Wíwənikan* led to the acquisition of works by Jeremy Frey (Penobscot), Alan Syliboy (Mi'kmaq), and Tim Shay (Penobscot). Barry Dana (Penobscot) built a wigwam

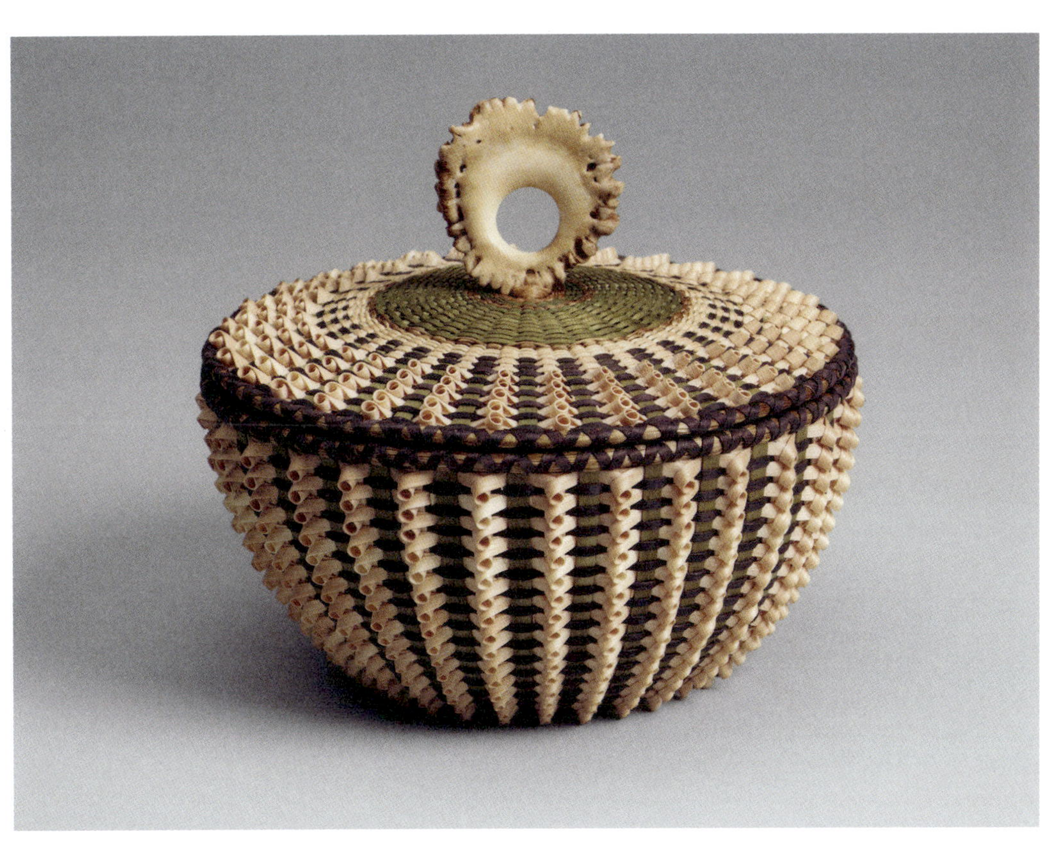

Sarah Sockbeson (Penobscot), *Penobscot Ash Basket*, 2011. Brown ash, sweetgrass, antler. 5 ¼ × 6 ⅛ × 6 ⅛ in. (13.3 × 15.6 × 15.6 cm). Museum purchase from the Director's Discretionary Fund, 2011.099

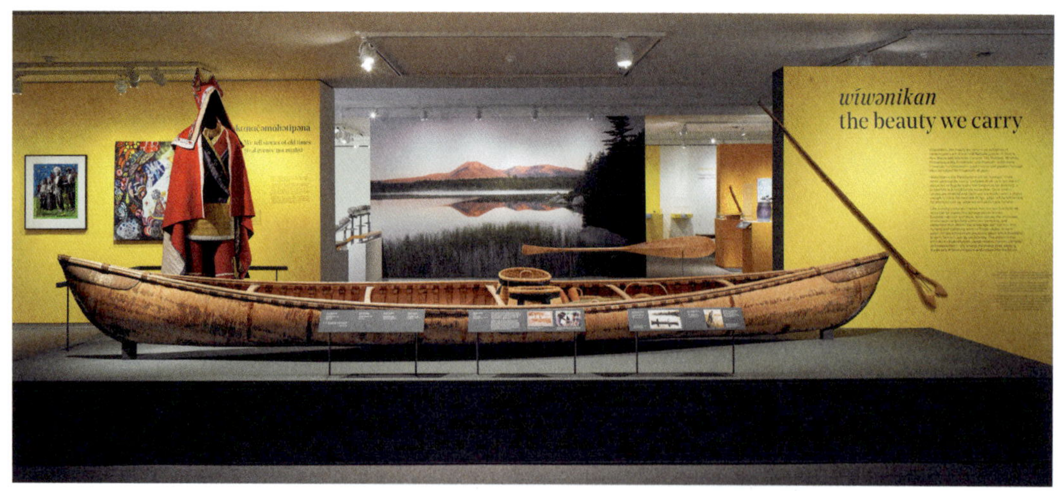

Installation view, *Wiwənikan…the beauty we carry*, Colby College Museum of Art, Waterville, Maine, 2019

on the museum's terrace. A private collector gave the museum fifty Wabanaki baskets, both historical and contemporary. And Jeremy Frey (Gabriel and Ganessa Frey also participated in the exhibition) received the Colby Museum's Cummings Award for Artistic Excellence.

While *Wíwənikan* was in development, Diana Tuite and Justin McCann, the latter the museum's curator of Whistler studies, tackled reinstalling the American West gallery of the Lunder Wing, generating content that integrated Indigenous voices responding to artworks by James Earle Fraser, George Catlin, Charles Bird King, and others. The scale of the museum's collection, facility, and programs relative to the modest size of its staff makes it challenging to sustainably develop sufficient interpretive content. This is true even when a multivocal approach allows for outside contributors. Nonetheless, not unlike the purchase of a single Penobscot basket, to do *something* in the face of an awareness of need and the systemic forces at play has seemed better than doing nothing.

There are similarities between the organizational structure of *Wíwənikan* and *Painted*, and the projects are likewise in resonance with exhibitions nationwide and internationally that have committed gallery space and exhibition and collection resources to Indigenous curatorial perspectives. *Wíwənikan* established local relationships that helped the museum see a way forward in work it understands as essential and long overdue.

Roughly concurrent with the organization of *Wíwənikan* and related work in the collection galleries, the Lunder Institute for American Art was emerging, and its inaugural staff included

Tanya Sheehan, the Ellerton M. and Edith K. Jetté Professor of Art and the institute's director of scholarly programs. Sheehan conceived a fellowship program that took a thematic approach informed by the museum's collection. The first group of fellows were experts in African American art and came to Colby in 2019 to do research on relevant works on site. The second cohort, named just prior to the pandemic, were invited to research Southwestern modernisms, a topic initiated by the Taos Society of Artists paintings in the Lunder Collection, which were prime candidates for reinterpretation from an Indigenous perspective. In tandem, the museum began developing an exhibition that would focus on the Southwest. A collection list prepared for the fellows included a group of Pueblo ceramics given to the museum by Adelaine Pearson in 1960, identifying a second and long-overlooked group of works for new research.

In October 2020, Jacqueline Terrassa became the Colby Museum's director, and, upon her arrival, prioritized this emerging Colby Museum/Lunder Institute initiative, working with the staff to successfully apply for a Terra Foundation for American Art grant to support a reinstallation that would center a Pueblo worldview. Siera Hyte (Cherokee Nation) arrived at the Colby Museum in 2021, holding a curatorial fellowship before stepping into the role of assistant curator of modern and contemporary art. She became co-curator of *Painted* with Lunder Institute research fellows Juan Lucero (Isleta Pueblo) and Jill Ahlberg Yohe. Virgil Ortiz (Cochiti Pueblo) agreed to serve as the exhibition designer. As the project we explore and study in this Lunder Institute publication took form, this team made innumerable decisions and extended invitations and requests for guidance from Pueblo and Wabanaki advisors. Lucero also catalogued the Pearson collection ceramics, a selection of which appeared in *Painted* on a high shelf, where they shared space with Wabanaki baskets.

Sockbeson, who participated in *Wíwənikan* and *Painted* (as an artist and advisory council member), was awarded the Lunder Institute's 2021–22 Ossorio Fellowship in Creative Research. This opportunity gave her time and resources to produce the basket she created for the latter exhibition. Concurrently, the research of Marisa Sánchez, who held a Mellon fellowship in the Lunder Institute, highlighted the political activism of Henry Sockbeson (Penobscot), Sarah's uncle and a Colby alumnus from the class of 1973, who had a friend photograph him that year with a forthright gaze in front of a "cigar store Indian," then a newly acquired work in the museum's collection. This Colby-educated member of the Sockbeson family became a tribal lawyer, and his act of defiance at the doorway to adulthood—a vivid representation of who he was and would be—resonates with Cara Romero's stunningly present photographic portrait of her daughter, Crickett, which was acquired for *Painted*. Works by thirteen additional artists entered the collection, including a pipe bag by Jessa Rae Growing Thunder (Sisituwan/Wahpetuwan/Hohe), who was also named the 2024 Ossorio fellow.

What has happened since Sockbeson's basket became part of the Colby Museum—all the work, all the reflecting and responding—has been iterative, encompassing myriad staff, faculty, and students past and present as well as numerous partners and advisors. What has been achieved to date has benefited from humbling assessments of where this academic museum in a small, postindustrial city on the Kennebec River has fallen short, and hopeful assessment of how it could evolve differently by joining context to purpose. The inclusion of Wabanaki community members on the advisory council for *Painted* and the presence of Wabanaki artworks in the project's galleries exemplify aspects of what this work can look like. Kennebec is a variation of *kinipek*, meaning "bay" in the Abenaki language; the Kennebec River carries the name of the bay it enters into. The Colby Museum is, of course, inseparable from this place; its work nationally and internationally begins from here and flows outward. *Painted* and the relevant developments and initiatives that preceded it have required, from all contributors, vulnerability and courage. And *Painted* will inevitably inform the Colby Museum's future work, just as *Wíwənikan* has.

Giving all we have—to return to the simple but not easy intention expressed at the outset of this institution's transformation—is a source of strength when this commitment attends to circumstances with transparency, discernment, and, to the degree we are able, foresight. In the catalogue for that project, Jennifer Neptune noted that "*Wíwənikan* is the Penobscot word for 'portage.' When we travel by canoe, portages allow us to get around obstacles, to bypass areas of water too dangerous to paddle, or to connect to a neighboring watershed. Once ashore, we empty our canoes and make decisions—about who is strong enough to carry the heaviest things, what will be left behind for others to pick up, what we will circle back for later." May this wisdom, generously shared, guide the way forward.

Beth Finch is a writer, editor, and curator. At the Colby Museum, she led the curatorial team as head curator from 2021 to 2025 and served as Lunder Curator of American Art from 2008 to 2021.

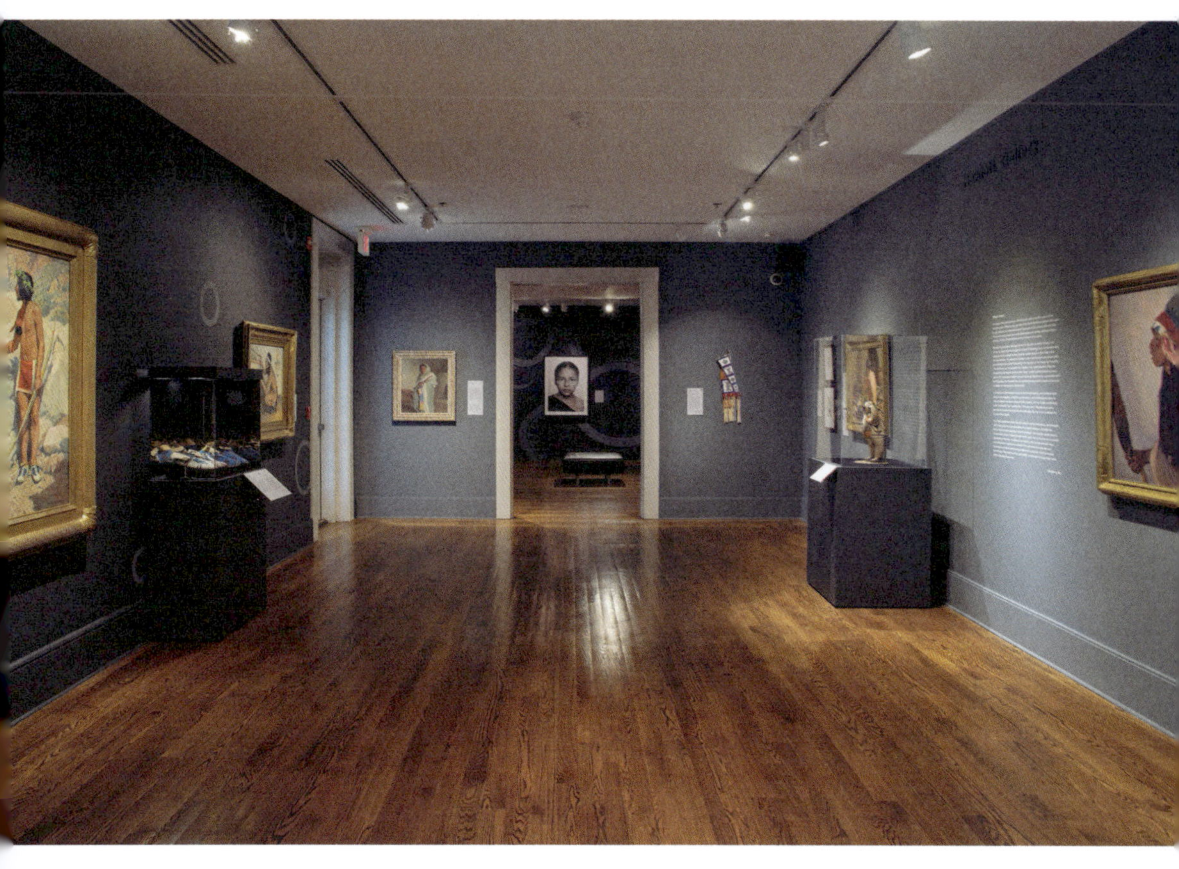

Installation view, *Painted: Our Bodies, Hearts, and Village*, Colby College Museum of Art, Waterville, Maine, 2023

Studying Science and Technology through Critical Curation and Indigenous Artistic Practices

Ashton Wesner,
Miz Insigne,
Daniel Juzych,
and Maya Wong

Since its founding in 1959, the Colby Museum has been committed to research, education, and access in the context of Colby College's liberal arts mission. Each academic year, more than 180 classes from over two dozen departments visit the galleries for transdisciplinary conversations anchored by artworks. From fall 2023 to spring 2024, students from disciplines such as art, English, history, government, and psychology engaged with *Painted: Our Bodies, Hearts, and Village*. The discussions often moved beyond analysis of specific works of art to holistic considerations about museum practice. *Painted* foregrounds a reparative and community-oriented mode of exhibition making, encouraging students not only to learn about Pueblo artistic practices, but to bring those lessons to the ways in which they engage their own communities.

To invite deep curricular engagement with the exhibition, the museum partnered with Colby's Center for Arts and Humanities to award course development grants to faculty members who incorporated *Painted* into their syllabi in significant ways. One of the recipients, Ashton Wesner, assistant professor of science, technology, and society, cowrote the following reflection essay with her students Miz Insigne '26, Daniel Juzych '26, and Maya Wong '25.

—Jessamine Batario, Linde Family Foundation Curator of Academic Engagement

Learning in the museum is a sensory immersion. For scholars of the critical study of science, technology, and society, *Painted: Our Bodies, Hearts, and Village* materializes key analytical orientations in ways that captivate, trouble, and move us—affectively, intellectually, and politically. Digital apparatuses fill the space with sonic reverberations; we are invited and carried by Robert Mirabal's musical composition *The Society* (2023). And architectural support structures are rendered beautiful vessels; as if held within a Pueblo pot, we are surrounded by Virgil Ortiz's sun, moon, and wildflower patterns painted on the gallery walls. Our attention is held rapt in myriad ways. This, we feel, is unlike reading a text.

When our Introduction to Science, Technology, and Society course visited *Painted* in spring 2023, the questions from our text-built tool kit found embodied application: How is an artifact in the world, and how is the world in an artifact?[1] How are creative and artistic practices co-constituted with scientific and technological ones? How do our institutions benefit from, maintain, and/or disrupt settler colonial investments in the supremacy of certain ways of knowing over others?[2] How do

Indigenous sciences and technologies continue to flourish through artistic practice? And how do we see, hear, and feel this survivance?[3] While being and thinking with *Painted*, our experience of answering these questions was visceral, personal, and imaginative. In this essay, written collectively by students Miz Insigne, Daniel Juzych, and Maya Wong with professor Ashton Wesner, we offer some brief reflections on how learning with *Painted* deepened our thinking about Indigenous art practices and knowledges, and expanded our approach to studying science and technology. Specifically, we found new ways to explore the politics of knowledge production and the power of cultural work to materialize Indigenous futures.

Storytelling as a Technology

We know about the "god trick"—Western science's violent attempt to establish universal truths arising from "a conquering gaze from nowhere"—from feminist and Indigenous science and technology studies.[4] Scholars like Donna Haraway and Kimberly TallBear (Sisseton-Wahpeton Oyate) have explained how Western science has disguised itself in a cloak of unquestionable authority through claims of disembodied, completely impartial, objective accounts of the world, at the expense of knowledges perceived to be subjective: racialized, gendered, affective, bodily.[5] Yet scientific and technological innovations do not happen in a vacuum. These rigorous accounts of and interventions in our world are always shaped by particular material and social contexts and routed through the desires, ambitions, predispositions, and unique life experiences of the scientists and technologists themselves. To acknowledge such situatedness is to sharpen our capacity to identify the possibilities and partialities of multiple ways of understanding ourselves, our relationships, and our natural surroundings.

The curatorial notes in *Painted* refuse to tell stories of the artworks from a disembodied position. Rather than presenting an authoritative and seemingly authorless recitation of the facts of a piece, the notes we read often included author names and tribal affiliations, were overtly inflected by the writers' own voices and perspectives, and even posed questions and critical context for interpreting the works. Hardly a hermetic container for safely preserving artworks away from the mess of their context—recalling how laboratories often masquerade as vacuums of sterile procedures, sealed off from society and subjectivity—*Painted* invited viewers to coproduce knowledge of the collection with artists, curators, and community culture bearers.

Who tells the stories of these paintings? And who defines what counts as "authentic," "invented," and "beautiful"?

Jill Ahlberg Yohe, co-curator of *Painted*, mirrors our questions about who has decided which accounts of the world are most objective and factual, and which type of person is most naturally an expert or innovator. When we encountered Joseph Henry Sharp's oil painting *Testing the Shaft* (c. 1920), we read a note written by co-curator Siera Hyte explaining the historical context of US federal land theft and economic exploitation in which this painting was made, as well as the exhibition advisory council's push for the curatorial team to "tell the whole story," including that Taos Pueblo models strategically navigated the work of sitting for artists as a source of income. Not only did this note offer us critical tools to form a situated interpretation of the work, but it also invited us to center the agency of the Native laborers we saw vividly depicted before us. We consider this personalized and politicized approach to curatorial notes as a technology for situating knowledge—knowledge about the historically specific practice of painting, about settler colonial occupation of Pueblo lands, about Pueblo people's methods of survivance, *and* about techniques of curation as forms of knowledge production and technological innovation.

Notes

1. See Joseph Dumit, "Writing the Implosion: Teaching the World One Thing at a Time," *Cultural Anthropology* 29, no. 2 (May 19, 2014): 344–62, available at https://doi.org/10.14506/ca29.2.09.
2. See Roxanne Dunbar-Ortiz, *An Indigenous Peoples' History of the United States* (Boston: Beacon Press, 2015).
3. See Gerald Vizenor, *Manifest Manners: Narratives on Postindian Survivance* (Lincoln, NE: Bison Books, 1999).
4. Donna Haraway, "Situated Knowledges: The Science Question in Feminism and the Privilege of Partial Perspective," *Feminist Studies* 14, no. 3 (1988): 581.
5. Haraway, "Situated Knowledges," 575–99; Kim TallBear, *Native American DNA: Tribal Belonging and the False Promise of Genetic Science* (Minneapolis: University of Minnesota Press, 2013).

Note on authorship and method: To write this essay collectively, each author first wrote their own reflections on learning with Painted. *We then came together in a focus group over Zoom, where we discussed our reflections for an hour. We recorded this conversation and transcribed the conversation using OtterAI, and then Ashton Wesner revised that text into its final form here.*

Afterword and Acknowledgments

Jacqueline Terrassa

Painted: Our Bodies, Hearts, and Village opened a space for Indigenous artists, curators, scholars, culture bearers, tribal leaders, and community members to claim their place in the making and telling of what had heretofore been understood as an American art history: the story of art in Taos in the first decades of the twentieth century. Its co-curators—Juan Lucero (Isleta Pueblo), Siera Hyte (Cherokee), and Jill Ahlberg Yohe—along with the project's advisory council and exhibition designer, Virgil Ortiz (Cochiti Pueblo), made protagonists and narrators out of those who had previously been relegated to mere subjects.

As this publication attests, the story of *Painted* took as its point of departure a stellar group of paintings in the Colby College Museum of Art's collection created by those who were part of the Taos Society of Artists (TSA). This collection was acquired over the years and donated to the Colby Museum as part of a much larger gift by Peter and Paula Lunder. But the TSA works had never yet been thoroughly contextualized and interpreted from a Pueblo perspective, in spite of them depicting Pueblo and Diné people and their lands. The highly collaborative process that *Painted* entailed sought, from the start, to elevate the lived experience and knowledge of Pueblo people, including specific individuals depicted in the TSA paintings and their descendants.

Through its process, presentation, and now this publication, *Painted* has contributed to a field-wide shift in research, pedagogy, public understanding, policy, and museum practice related to art made about and by Indigenous people. *Painted* also represents a shift in power unfolding at American institutions, including the Colby Museum. In these pages, former head curator Beth Finch writes, "What has been achieved to date has benefited from humbling assessments of where this academic museum in a small, postindustrial city on the Kennebec River has fallen short, and hopeful assessment of how it could evolve differently by joining context to purpose." At the Colby Museum, *Painted* has offered a framework for intentional and iterative action.

The relationships facilitated on behalf of *Painted* started with those established by Wabanaki artists, culture bearers, and expert advisors in Maine before, during, and following an earlier Colby Museum exhibition, *Wíwənikan…the beauty we carry* (2019). It was our Wabanaki partners, and especially artist and Colby Museum governor Theresa Secord D.F.A. '22 (Penobscot) and artist Sarah Sockbeson (Penobscot), who helped the Colby Museum recognize and make visible in *Painted* the connected histories of art in the US Southwest and the vibrant cultural traditions of Native artists in Maine.

Likewise, works acquired in anticipation of, during, and soon after the *Painted* exhibition now feature prominently in various Colby Museum collection galleries. The practice of commissioning and purchasing art by Indigenous artists on a regular basis continues. I thank Beth Finch, Siera Hyte, and other staff for boldly advancing more than a dozen acquisitions related to this project. I express gratitude to King Galleries and the Collections and Impact Committee of Colby's Museum Board of Governors for supporting commissions and purchases of art.

Content and pedagogical strategies developed for *Painted* are now integrated into the core lesson plans Colby Museum gallery educators use to engage primary and secondary school students during museum visits. Colby faculty members from several departments now teach with curricula they developed for *Painted*. I acknowledge the invaluable work our Learning and Engagement staff carried out to facilitate respectful teaching and learning with *Painted*.

Three artists and culture bearers who were involved in *Painted* accepted yearlong Lunder Institute for American Art fellowships in the months after the show opened, and more than forty artists, curators, scholars, community activists, and educators took part in the 2024 Lunder Institute Summer Think Tank, which built on concepts related to *Painted*, and centered Indigenous art making and art histories and the building of sovereign futures. The program was organized by Siera Hyte with Lunder Institute Director Erica Wall, and with support from Karen Platt, Manager of Administration and Strategic Initiatives at the Lunder Institute.

In November 2024, Penobscot artist and *Painted* advisor Sarah Sockbeson collaborated with the Lunder Institute again, and with Assistant Curator of Modern and Contemporary Art Kendall DeBoer, to organize a Wabanaki artist convening, which developed the core themes and principles for a fall 2025 exhibition that Sockbeson is curating for the museum. The convening and exhibition are teaching the museum how procedural tools such as contracts can and should change to reflect and support Native values.

Indigenous people who contributed to *Painted* and the subsequent initiatives I describe have been working toward the goal of cultural agency and sovereignty for a long time. We at the Colby Museum have benefited from this work. The *Painted* advisory council provided essential guidance and included Ron Martinez Looking Elk (Isleta Pueblo/Taos Pueblo), Patricia Michaels (Taos Pueblo), Theresa Secord (Penobscot), Sarah Sockbeson (Penobscot), and Joseph H. Suina (Cochiti Pueblo). Dwayne Tomah (Passamaquoddy) led a blessing in the galleries. I express heartfelt gratitude to the co-curators for their visionary work, knowledge, and humanity, which shaped *Painted*, and the living artists represented in the exhibition, including designer Virgil Ortiz, with Tish Agoyo (Ohkay Owingeh/Cochiti Pueblo).

In her role as Barbara Alfond Director of Exhibitions and Publications, Megan Carey expertly led the project from the start as its producer and editor. The *Painted* exhibition and this publication simply could not have happened without her relentless attention and skill. She benefited from the guidance of Julianne Gilland, Deputy Director for Planning and Operations, who also managed project funding, and Beth Finch. Finch shaped the early stages of the project and guided the co-curators throughout, supporting nuanced, layered curation and ongoing dialogue with stakeholders. The editorial, design, production, and curatorial processes were aided by Juliette Walker, Assistant Manager of Exhibitions and Publications, and Augusta Weiss, Anne Lunder Leland Curatorial Fellow.

The realization and activation of *Painted* involved every member of the Colby Museum's remarkable staff. Annette Fortin, Manager of Collections and Registration; Lorraine DeLaney, Senior Registrar of Exhibitions and Loans; Paige Doore, Collections Registrar; Jenna Buckingham, Collections Access Coordinator; Chris Patch, Senior Preparator; and Danae Lagoy, Preparator, were responsible for cataloging, tracking, preparing, installing, and facilitating access to artworks. They were aided by a terrific art installation team listed on page 238. Ryan Ridky, Assistant Manager of Museum Facilities and Operations, coordinated and executed the preparation of spaces and exhibition installation. Andrew Witte, former Mirken Fellow in Museum Practice, secured image rights and supported external communications. Jaime McLeod, former Communications Manager, and Louise Kerr, Director of Museum Administration and External Affairs, worked with Colby Communications to bring local and national visibility to the project. Colby College Advancement colleagues supported fundraising and donor stewardship. Karen Wickman attended to myriad payment and administrative details. From the moment of installation to closing, the museum's Security Officers shone as they capably protected the art and engaged the public.

Co-curator Siera Hyte, now Schiller Family Curator of Indigenous American Art at the Virginia Museum of Fine Arts, collaborated on programming with Jessamine Batario, Linde Family Foundation Curator of Academic Engagement; Phoebe Zipper, Lunder Family Foundation Educator for College Audiences; Kris Bergquist, former Mirken Curator of Education and Engagement; Abby Newkirk, Linde Family Foundation Senior Coordinator of School and Teacher Programs; Sheri LaVerdiere, Engagement Assistant; Jillian Impastato, Mirken Coordinator of Campus Collaborations; and Katya Schevchenko, former Coordinator of Community and Visitor Engagement. They, in turn, worked with countless faculty members, K–12 educators, artists, and community members to offer a wide range of programs.

Hyte, Lucero, and Ahlberg Yohe informed the development of this publication and planned the symposium that served as the basis for much of the content in these pages. I express appreciation to them and to the other publication contributors: Kimberly Suina Melwani and Joseph H. Suina; Nora Naranjo Morse; Brian Vallo; Beth Finch; Ashton Wesner and Colby students (Miz Insigne '26, Daniel Juzych '26, Maya Wong '25); Dominic Bellido '24 and Virgil Ortiz; and Sarah Sockbeson and Yellowbird Samora. Olivia Fountain, Andrew Witte, and Augusta Weiss provided general book assistance. We owe the stunning design of this publication to Sébastien Aubin, and its superb production to Lucas Elke of Type A Print. Lindsey Westbrook brought deft editorial attention to a wide range of texts. We thank Mary DelMonico, publisher, for her invaluable partnership.

The support of Colby President David A. Greene and the Museum Board of Governors, led by former Chair Karen Linde Packman and Chair Hilary Barnes Hoopes, was integral. The cultural, strategic, and community work they led prior to my arrival at Colby in 2020 in partnership with my predecessor, Sharon Corwin, provided me and the Colby Museum staff with the confidence to initiate what became *Painted*.

Financial resources in the form of endowment income and gifts enabled us to engage in a long-duration process of relationship building. On behalf of the museum and all of our partners, I express a deep sense of gratitude to the Lunder Foundation and Peter and Paula Lunder for their generosity and support, starting with the extraordinary gift to the Colby Museum of the Lunder Collection. Understanding what it takes to steward and activate works of art, they provided permanent resources for the care and use of the Lunder Collection as well as funding to establish and sustain the Lunder Institute for American Art, the Colby Museum's research and practice incubator.

The Terra Foundation for American Art awarded the museum one of its first collection reinstallation grants in 2021, providing essential resources to bring *Painted* to fruition. Along with Terra Foundation funding, the Mirken Family Publications Fund supported the making of this publication. Other important sources included the Pearson Art Collection Fund, which allowed Juan Lucero to research an early gift of Indigenous vessels; the Barbara Alfond Exhibitions and Publications Fund; and annual support from the Museum Board of Governors Fund and the Colby Museum Fund.

Early gifts and grants to the Lunder Institute from Alice Kang P'21, P'26 and OhSang Kwon P'21, P'26 as well as the Mellon Foundation enabled us, in 2020, to organize a cohort of research fellows to pursue original scholarship on artistic modernisms of the Southwest. The members of that cohort are listed on page 24. Jessica Horton, Associate Professor of Native American, Modern, and Contemporary Art at the University of Delaware, led the group. The program was set into motion by Tanya Sheehan, Ellerton M. and Edith K. Jetté Professor of Art at Colby College and Director of Academic and Scholarly Engagement at the Lunder Institute. The Research Fellows helped us better understand our holdings and the potential of this project. They were aided by Colby research assistants Alexis Kinney '22, Jade Ma '23, Mary Bevilacqua '23, and Katherine Zhang '24; Kinney and Bevilacqua continued their involvement as curatorial interns.

Cynthia Chavez Lamar, Director of the Smithsonian's National Museum of the American Indian, offered a catalyzing presentation to staff, students, and the Research Fellows in 2021. Several organizations and individuals generously hosted the group during two convenings in Maine and New Mexico in 2021–22. We remain grateful to Gretchen F. Faulkner, Director of the Hudson Museum at the University of Orono; Davison Koenig and his staff at the Couse-Sharp Historic Site in Taos; Elysia Poon, Director of the Indian Arts Research Center at the School for Advanced Research, and her team; and our colleagues at the Museum of Indian Arts and Culture. We also sincerely thank artist Russell Sanchez (San Ildefonso Pueblo) for hosting us at his home and studio, where we witnessed a traditional firing of pottery and enjoyed a feast of food and art. Bruce Bernstein, Tribal Historic Preservation Officer, Pueblo of Pojoaque, and museum professional, anthropologist, and curator, joined us for that visit.

Finally, though *Painted* primarily featured works in the Colby Museum's collection, loans from the Couse-Sharp Historic Site, the Indian Arts Research Center, the Millicent Rogers Museum, artists Mozart Gabriel Abeyta and Patricia Michaels, and Jay Fell '66 brought essential historical dimension to the project. We are grateful that they were willing to share with the public these rare and irreplaceable works.

Painted as a project has come to a close, yet the Colby Museum's commitment is ongoing: to create platforms for Indigenous artists and scholars to make new art and new art history from their lived experience, research, and knowledge; to mobilize our resources to uplift Native values through art; to embed what we continually learn through this collaborative and community-based process across all facets of the museum's work; and to share our practices widely. *Painted* has sought to prompt an unlearning while simultaneously offering a new way forward, one that urges a more layered and more human understanding of the complexities of art and the American experience.

Museum Staff
Christian Adame
Kiko Aebi
Jessamine Batario
Mike Benecke
Jenna Buckingham
Megan Carey
Kendall DeBoer
Lorraine DeLaney
Christina DeYoung
Paige M. Doore
Elizabeth Finch
Annette Fortin
Elisa Germán
Rae Giard
Julianne Gilland
Sae Gleba
Sarah Humphreville
Jillian Impastato
Louise Kerr
Danae Lagoy
Sheri LaVerdiere
Virginia López-Anido
Abby Newkirk
Christopher Patch
Karen Platt
Ryan Ridky
Jillian Scott
Jacqueline Terrassa
Juliette Walker
Erica Wall
Augusta Weiss
Karen Wickman
Phoebe Zipper

Museum Installation
Matt Demers
Robby Neighbor
Zoe Pellegrino
Matt Russ
Travis Sehorn

Museum Security
Liz Collins
Brittany Depalma-Yahn
Jason Lindsay
Darya Pereira
Kelly Roderick
Candace Savinelli
Eric Yahn

Museum Teaching Artists and Gallery Attendants
Kathy Carey
Danikah Chartier
Tom Desjardin
Melisa Dugal
Carrie Haberstock
Lizzie Kane
Natty Lazarian
Marti McFadden
Brie Peabody
Luca Thamattoor

Credits

All works collection of Colby College Museum of Art unless otherwise noted.

Every reasonable attempt has been made to identify owners of copyright. Errors or omissions will be corrected in subsequent editions.

pp. 10 (top), 15 (top): Courtesy Joseph H. Suina

p. 10 (bottom): H. Armstrong Roberts, Alamy Stock Photo

p. 15 (bottom): T. Harmon Parkhurst, Courtesy of the Palace of the Governors Photo Archives (NMHM/DCA), 002288

p. 21 (top): Mary Dissette, Courtesy of the Palace of the Governors Photo Archives (NMHM/DCA), Negative 004454

p. 21 (bottom): Keystone View Company, Courtesy of the Palace of the Governors Photo Archives (NMHM/DCA), Negative 089338

p. 22 (top): Tyler Dingee, Courtesy of the Palace of the Governors Photo Archives (NMHM/DCA), Negative 120216

p. 22 (bottom): H. F. Robinson, Courtesy of the Palace of the Governors Photo Archives (NMHM/DCA), Negative 148548

pp. 31, 41, 42, 46, 49, 65, 68–69, 73, 74–75, 76, 80, 81, 82, 94–95, 103, 105, 111, 112, 114 (top), 115, 119, 122–23, 129, 130–31, 159, 160–61, 162, 168, 174–75, 176–77, 178, 180, 181, 182, 187, 191, 192, 194, 216–17, 222, 225: Luc Demers

pp. 38–39, 51, 52, 59, 170–71: Courtesy Virgil Ortiz

pp. 43–45: Courtesy Mozart Gabriel Abeyta

pp. 66, 67, 86, 87, 93, 96, 98–99, 102, 109, 110, 113, 120, 124, 127, 128, 163, 190, 221: Peter Siegel, Pillar Digital Imaging LLC

pp. 77, 101, 193: Courtesy Margeaux Abeyta

pp. 104, 164–65 (baskets): Pixel Acuity

p. 114 (bottom): Stephen Davis Phillips

pp. 141–49: Ashley L. Conti

p. 166: Courtesy Theresa Secord

pp. 196, 199: Courtesy Patricia Michaels

p. 201: Rob Strong. © Hood Museum of Art, Dartmouth

p. 202: Courtesy the Portland Museum of Art, Maine

p. 205: Tira Howard

pp. 206, 213: Courtesy Minneapolis Institute of Art

p. 208: © Denver Art Museum

p. 210: Courtesy the RISD Museum, Providence, RI

This book was published in association with the exhibition *Painted: Our Bodies, Hearts, and Village*, organized by the Colby College Museum of Art and curated by Siera Hyte, Juan Lucero, and Jill Ahlberg Yohe.

May 19, 2023–July 28, 2024

Published in 2025 by Colby College Museum of Art and DelMonico Books • D.A.P.

Colby College Museum of Art
5600 Mayflower Hill
Waterville, Maine 04901
museum.colby.edu

DelMonico Books
available through
ARTBOOK | D.A.P.
75 Broad Street, Suite 630
New York, NY 10004
artbook.com
delmonicobooks.com

Publication director: Megan Carey
Designer: Sébastien Aubin/Otami
Editor: Lindsey Westbrook
Proofreader: Erica Olsen
Printer: Type A Print Inc.
Printed in Belgium

The exhibition and publication are generously supported by the Terra Foundation for American Art, Alice Kang P’21, P’26 and OhSang Kwon P’21, P’26, and Colby Museum endowment funds provided by the Lunder Foundation. The Mellon Foundation supported the 2021–22 Lunder Institute Research Fellows Program.

TERRA
FOUNDATION FOR AMERICAN ART

ISBN: 978-1-63681-146-8
Library of Congress Control Number: 2025911234

Inside cover:
Albert Looking Elk
Taos Pueblo, 1888–1940
Untitled, c. 1925–35 (detail)
Oil on board
8 ¼ × 11 in. (21 × 27.9 cm)
Collection of the Millicent Rogers Museum, Taos, New Mexico, Gift of Brad and Fran Taylor

Frontispiece:
Cara Romero
Chemehuevi, born 1977
Crickett, 2014 (detail)
Archival inkjet print
40 × 27 in. (101.6 × 68.6 cm)
Museum purchase from the Jere Abbott Acquisitions Fund, 2022.067